The Textile Art
IN INTERIOR DESIGN

The
Textile Art
IN INTERIOR DESIGN

MELANIE PAINE
PHOTOGRAPHY BY BILL BATTEN

SIMON AND SCHUSTER
New York   London   Toronto   Sydney   Tokyo   Singapore

TEXTILE CLASSICS
Melanie Paine
Photography by **Bill Batten**

SIMON AND SCHUSTER
Simon & Schuster Building
Rockefeller Center
1230 Avenue of the Americas
New York, New York 10020

Copyright © 1990 by Mitchell Beazley Publishers
Photographs copyright © 1990 by Mitchell Beazley Publishers
Photography by Bill Batten

First published in Great Britain in 1990
by Mitchell Beazley International Ltd.

Edited and designed by
Mitchell Beazley International Ltd,
Artists House, 14-15 Manette Street,
London WIV 5LB

Senior Executive Art Editor **Jacqui Small**
Executive Editor **Judith More**
Art Editor **Larraine Lacey**
Editor **Susan Berry**
Editorial Assistant **Kirsty Seymour-Ure**
Editorial Secretaries **Jaspal Bhangra, Doris Wood**
Production **Ted Timberlake**
American Consultant **Mary Schoeser**

ISBN 0-671-70534-2

The publishers have made every effort to ensure that all
instructions given in this book are accurate and safe, but they
cannot accept liability for any resulting injury, damage or loss
to either person or property whether direct or consequential
and howsoever arising. The authors and publishers will be
grateful for any information which will assist them in keeping
future editions up to date.

Typeset in Caslon Old Face 12/15 pt Roman and Nuptial Script
by Litho Link Ltd, Welshpool, Powys, Wales.
Color reproduction by Scantrans Pte Ltd, Singapore
Printed in the Netherlands
by Koninklijke Smeets Offset b.v., Weert.

Identifying fabrics
Over 1000 fabrics are featured in the photographs in this
book, either in room settings, lengths or collections of
swatches. Purchasing information – name/number and
manufacturer of each fabric – is given in a key at the back of
the book (see Fabric Directory). This is followed by a list of
the manufacturer's addresses. The manufacturer will provide
the name of your nearest stockist.

Contents

Introduction

A detail showing a section of the design from a Continental period silk lampas. The detailed floral shapes form a trellis of arabesques enclosing flowers.

I began this book with the knowledge that there would be a vast and varied range of textiles to examine and many that I knew I would want to include. Some are considered on their own merit for their beauty, originality or particular historic significance. Others are part of *The Textile Art* simply and inevitably because of a strong personal desire not to leave them out.

I have begun by looking at the basics – fibers and yarns, dyes, weaves and prints. I feel that to use a fabric successfully, you must understand it on a practical as well as simply a visual level. While there are numerous guidelines and so-called "golden rules" for using furnishing fabrics in interior decoration, you can adapt or ignore many of them and get away with it. However, if you do not know what it is you are using, or why, then it is difficult to achieve results which you, and others, can be happy with.

Fibers and yarns

The term "yarn" refers to all those threads which are used in the weaving of a cloth. These are manufactured from natural – animal or vegetable – or man-made fibers. The two distinct groups can be mixed during the spinning process, and this blending provides the potential for many more fabric types. Some fabrics are referred to by their yarn content, a cotton or a silk for example, but with others their recognized name will pertain to the type of weave pattern employed, for example damask or tartan.

Most of the textiles looked at in this book contain either 100 percent, or a high proportion of natural fiber. A few are entirely produced from man-made fibers, while some have a

Flat, graphic patterns of peacocks and stylized flowers are depicted in this section of a Spanish silk damask, circa 1600.

Part of a rare and important panel in silk cut and uncut velvet from Spitalfields, London, circa 1714. The design is attributed to James Leman.

small element of man-made fiber included either for structural or economic reasons.

Cotton is the preferred fiber, and one of the more versatile ones. It grows on bushes and is produced in a variety of countries where there is plenty of sun and moisture. The cotton fibers grow from the seedcase left after the blossom falls. When ripe, the seedcase splits to reveal the fluffy white cotton, which is then gathered by hand or mechanically. The fibers and seeds are separated and the fibers then go through a process that twists them into a lightweight roving suitable for spinning. Different grades of cotton, some poorer in quality than others, will produce varying results.

Flax fibers, which are used to make linen fabrics, are obtained from the bark or bast of the flax plant. The plants are pulled from the ground before the seeds are fully ripe and the seeds are used to make linseed oil. The fibers go through a complex process to produce the finished yarn. Linen cloth is naturally strong and smooth, generally stiffer than cotton and with a more sophisticated appearance.

Wool is produced from the fleece of a sheep. Once removed, the fleece is cleaned and treated, teased and thoroughly blended. The fibers are then carded, or combed, and passed through rollers so that they are of uniform weight and quality, ready for spinning. The smoother combed yarns create worsteds.

Different breeds of sheep will produce varying grades and types of wool. For example, the wool used in the Welsh flannel trade, which is smooth and soft, comes from the Shropshire breed, while the Lincoln and Leicester breeds produce a wool that is noted for its strength and luster and is commonly used for linings, serges and broadcloths.

Another animal whose hair produces a fiber for spinning into cloth is the Angora goat, from which comes mohair. Today, mohair is rarely used in furnishing fabrics. In the past it was used in walling cloths, curtains and upholstery. It is a strong and resilient fiber and has a good affinity for dyes.

Silk yarn is produced from the filament found in the cocoon of the silkworm, formed from a combination of fluid and gum secreted by the silkworm. Several filaments, when unreeled, are twisted together to form a single thread. Silk is the finest and, surprisingly, strongest form of natural fiber and takes dye beautifully.

You will notice that a single man-made fiber crops up more often than any other man-made type in the textiles looked at in this book. It is a cellulose fiber called viscose, whose raw material is derived from wood pulp. The wood pulp mixture goes through a long manufacturing process that involves steeping and aging in chemical activators to form it into a fine, very strong thread.

A detail of an American patchwork quilt made in 1835. The fabric pieces are chintz and the style imitates that of the Indian palampores.

"Geranium", a block-printed linen from the Baker's studio, 1902, with a pattern consisting of simple floral motifs and trailing vines.

A French bizarre silk, dating from circa 1710-20. The motifs, although similar to formal patterns, are livelier in movement and juxtaposition.

Weaves

All the fabrics looked at in this book, with the exception of felt and some types of lace, are woven. In weaving, the yarns, or threads, interlace to form a cloth. In order to handle or manipulate the threads it is first necessary to spin the yarn to insert sufficient twist to bind the fibers together. The yarn is spun at some speed to make it strong enough to withstand all potential strain imposed upon it.

A spindle, a tapered stick of wood that was notched at the top and fitted with a weight at the base, was the earliest spinning tool. The revolutions of the spindle pulled out the fibers and twisted them together, they then had to be hand-wound onto the spindle itself. In the 14th century, with the invention of the spinning wheel, there was a huge increase in the amount of spun yarn produced. This enabled textiles to become a more important part of home furnishings.

All woven fabrics are produced on a loom from two sets of threads – warp and weft. The warp threads are held on the frame of the loom, running from back to front under tension, while the weft threads run crossways, interlacing over and under the warp. Selvages are formed by additional warp threads placed at the edges to give extra strength during weaving and to the finished cloth. The threads that form the cloth may interlace in any manner that the designer requires, taking into account the use to which that fabric may be put.

The number of warp threads, or "ends" used per inch/centimeter is referred to as the "set" of the warp, while the weft threads are called "picks". The spacing and number of these threads affects the type of fabric produced. For example, scrim is very loosely woven because the warp and weft threads are spaced well apart. But not all open cloth is produced in this way. Net curtaining is produced by a method – *leno* – in which the warp threads cross each other instead of being placed parallel. The spacing of the wefts also affects the weave. In a closely woven cloth the number and position of the picks must be the same for every inch or irregular horizontal striping will occur.

The weaving configuration will also affect the type of cloth produced. For example, in the simplest of weaves, known as the "plain" or "tabby" weave, the pick of the weft goes under the first end of the warp, over the second, under the third and so on until it reaches the far edge of the warp threads. On the next pick it travels back over all the ends it went under before. Plain weave fabrics include calico, cambric and gingham.

More complex than the plain weave are the twill and satin weaves. In a twill weave the interlacing of warp and weft causes diagonal lines to be formed in the cloth. This gives the fabric greater weight, substance and firmness. Twilled effects are produced by interlacing one thread outward and one upward on

A delightful Flemish feuille de choux *tapestry from the mid-19th century. Its success lies in a complex design, fine detail and evocative use of color.*

A richly detailed Indonesian woven ikat dating from World War II. The mirrored shapes of the animal images make further patterns across the cloth.

An English woven textile in silk and cotton doublecloth. It was designed by artists from the Silver Studio (see p. 149) in 1898.

The English firm of Watts and Co. reproduce many splendid old textile designs, of which this tapestry, known as "Windsor", is one.

An African kente cloth displaying strong graphic patterning in the narrow woven strips. Many of these cloths were woven in silk and were worn by chiefs.

Part of an English brocaded silk bedcover. The cloth was woven in Spitalfields, London, and dates from circa 1760.

succeeding picks. The twill lines are formed on both sides of the cloth in a diagonal line from the right or left, from one selvage to the other. The direction of the line on one side of the cloth is opposite to that on the other side. In a herringbone, the twill line is alternated in a zig-zag throughout the cloth. The diagonal line can be short or long before it reverses. With a herringbone weave the lines that make up the zig-zags are fine, whereas with a chevron weave the lines, and therefore the patterns, are larger. Satin weave is an extension of the twill weave in which the interlacing of warp and weft gives a definite face and back to the fabric. For satin cloth, the warp is much finer and more closely set than the weft.

An even more complex weave is "doublecloth". This is produced as if weaving two fabrics of the same weight in a single operation. The result is a very strong, reversible material in which parts of the front fabric may show on the back and vice versa. If different yarns are used for each fabric this builds up areas of texture, while different colors will build up areas of color. A further variation on doublecloth is matelassé. This hard-wearing cloth has an embossed appearance, formed by adding an extra weft in coarser yarn. This causes the finer yarns on the surface to pucker, giving a quilted or blistered effect.

Other weave variations are produced by the use of floating wefts. These are weft threads, usually of a different color from the majority of the wefts, which float on the back of the cloth and are brought up to the surface when required. In a fabric that uses floating wefts the background is usually in satin weave, with the figure produced by the floating wefts in another weave such as twill. The fabric thus produced has the effect of a hand brocade.

A further factor that differentiates one cloth from another is the type of loom used to weave it on. A plain weave loom can be adapted to produce more complex weaves with the addition of a dobby attachment that produces small, simple patterns. For more complex weave patterns a Jacquard loom is employed. This loom can use up to eight different-colored wefts and one or more warps. Originally, the pattern was plotted on paper and then transferred to punched cards. The cards were then laced together and held so that they rotated to present each new card to the machine to trigger the selection of the appropriate warp or weft thread. There are sometimes many thousands of cards in an elaborate design and production of the cards was time-consuming and labor-intensive. Although many of these looms are still in use, today they are being replaced by the direct Jacquard system in which computer software translates the design and instructs the loom. This new technology has revitalized the production of complex Jacquard weaves such as damask and double-cloths.

Part of a French Lyon silk brocaded lampas, which is, unusually, figurative in pattern. This silk dates from the late 18th century.

A detail from a Javanese cotton, dating from circa 1900. Produced by the batik method, it features a stylized representation of a bird.

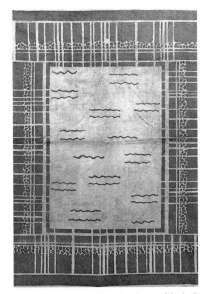

A 20th century printed velvet tablecloth from Belgium. The design is in the Art Deco style and the colors are typical of the period.

A richly detailed and brightly colored cotton quilt from Pakistan. The design combines both patchwork and appliqué skills.

Dyes

Substances which will color a fiber in such a way that the tint is an integral part of the cloth are termed dyes. Each dyestuff will vary and some will work on certain fibers and not so successfully on others. A mordant – a metallic salt – can be applied to strengthen this reduced affinity and produce superior color fastness. Yarns may be dyed before weaving, or the whole cloth colored after weaving. Piece-dyed cloth refers to all fabric which is woven in its natural condition and then dyed. This system is more economical for mass-production because it is possible to produce a long run of the same cloth and then dye lengths of it in a variety of colorways.

Before chemical dyes were invented, all cloth was colored using dyes based on natural substances such as plants or vegetables. Madder produced the familiar red of the *toile de Jouy* (see page 128) for example. The first synthetic dyes were made from coal tar products and were produced in the mid-19th century. Today, most mass-produced textiles are dyed with synthetic colors, but many ethnic and hand-crafted fabrics still use natural dyes.

Printing methods

If pattern isn't introduced in the weave (see page 8), it will be produced by one of the following methods.

Block printing is the oldest form of "offset" printing, and was first developed in the Far East. It makes use of small, carved blocks of wood on which the pattern to be printed stands out in relief. If an ink roller is run over the raised surface, and the inked block impressed on the fabric, the image prints onto it. The wood blocks themselves are usually made from pieces of hardwood and have small pins at the corners so that each block can be readily aligned with the next ones in order to print a repeating pattern.

The number of blocks required to print a design corresponds to the number of colors in the design, many blocks representing one color. Many Victorian fabrics – such as the popular Paisley patterns – and the later Arts and Crafts Movement textiles were hand-blocked using traditional wood blocks. In the 19th century, metal strips were hammered into the blocks to give a more distinctive pattern.

Stenciling and screen-printing share broadly similar basic methods. In stenciling, the design is cut into a card or acetate, which is laid over the fabric. The paint is brushed or sprayed over the card, which is then removed, leaving only the cut design to appear on the fabric. Because the cutting out of the stencils prohibits any very elaborate detailing, the results tend to have a simplified charm, and an attractive, uniform appearance.

Screen-printing follows the same principle of masking areas of cloth from pigment, but it employs a different system.

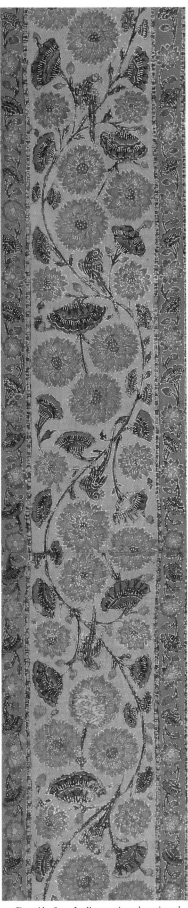

Detail of an Indian painted, printed and dyed cotton with applied gold, dating from circa 1800. The smaller flowers are confined by solid lines.

Hand-screen printing was carried out on a wooden frame with silk stretched over it. The design is marked out and the area which is not required to print on the fabric is either covered with ink-resisting wax or masked with card or paper. The hand screen-printing process can be repeated to produce designs with more than one color. Modern screen printing uses a photographically induced barrier, which gives greater design flexibility.

Resist printing is an age-old method commonly used to pattern fabrics. It is used, for example, in most traditional textile manufacture in Africa. This method employs a substance – a resist – which is applied to the cloth to prevent the fixation of color afterwards. The resist is either a starchy substance such as a resin, fat or wax, or it can be string or thread which is tied around the cloth before it is immersed in dye. Probably the most common "tie-dyed" patterns are large and small circles in various combinations, formed by binding thread around a small stone or pebble wrapped in the cloth. Such designs are found in Senegal, Gambia, among the Yoruba people of Nigeria, and more generally throughout Western Africa. These patterns are more pleasing than the scrunched-up effects achieved by irregularly bunching up cloth.

Batik is the oldest form of resist printing. Hot wax is applied directly to the cloth, on one or both sides, which then resists the dye applied to the remaining surface of the cloth. Once the paint or ink has dried, the wax is removed by heating it, either in hot water or with a hot iron. Commercial methods of resist printing are similar to the traditional ones in that a substance is applied to the cloth to prevent the color fixing when the cloth is dyed.

A similar system to resist printing is known as discharge printing. Here, the cloth is dyed to the color required and then treated with a reducing agent which removes the dye in the areas it is applied to, leaving a white pattern on the fabric and an overall even color on the background.

Authentic fabrics

Increasingly, decorators, designers and householders are seeking to reproduce authentic interiors for period houses. Fabrics used for curtains, upholstery, cushions and bed drapes, as well as for incidental decorative soft furnishings, are a fundamental part of the impact of a room and play a large part in any restoration project.

Choosing the right fabric is an easier task, you might think, than selecting a replacement window or cornice molding. However, with the enormous and very tantalizing array of furnishing fabrics available it is necessary to arm yourself with as much information as possible before making a choice between one fabric and many others.

If you want to use an authentic fabric and create what amounts to a period style, you need not slavishly adhere to

The center panel of the Indian quilt, the border of which is shown on the opposite page. The gold paint highlights the flat pattern.

An English 19th century cotton furnishing fabric that is block-printed with a stylized tree pattern in the Arts and Crafts style.

Swirling trees and peacocks form a trellis pattern in this English design for a printed textile. It was produced by artists from the Silver Studio in 1903.

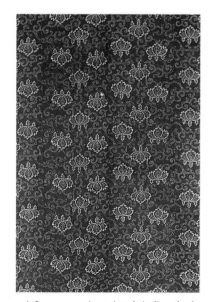

A Japanese resist-printed, indigo-dyed cotton fabric, dating from circa 1920. It was originally produced for use as a futon cover.

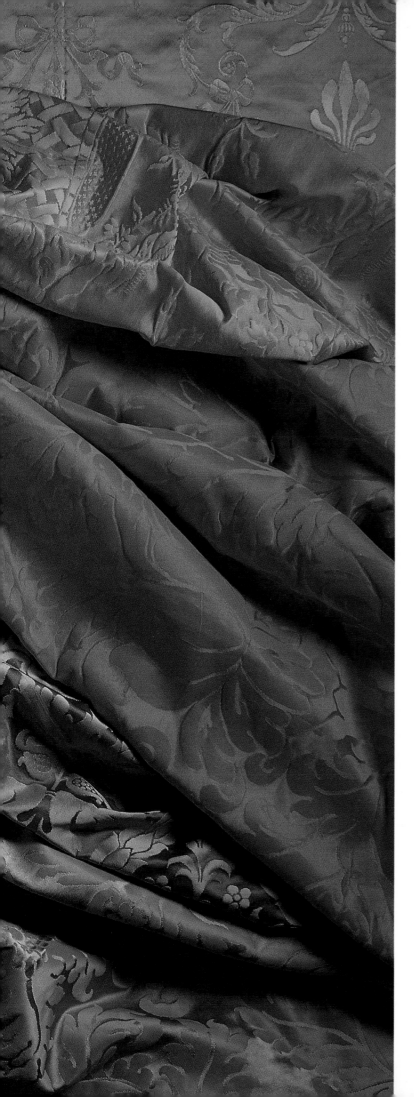

history. A general feel for the past can be achieved by putting together elements that mix well and sympathize with the overall style of the house. In all cases, you won't be covering chairs or curtaining windows in isolation, devoid of any other pointers that may indicate certain patterns or styles. The architectural details, if any – the shape of the window and the amount of light it may let in, the proportions of the room and its use – all come into play.

Some fabrics sold commercially by manufacturers today as "reproduction" fabrics, based perhaps on original archival documentation, do not necessarily reflect an equivalent popularity or prolific use in their original period. Accurately patterned chintz collections or *toiles de Jouy*, for example, are continually coming onto the market, but they are more an indication of their *present* popularity. A few original patterns that are reproduced now, perhaps initially for a specific restoration project, gain a popularity which far exceeds the exposure they had at the time that they were first designed.

The position with furnishing fabrics was, and is, continually changing, and although a fabric design may have originated at a certain time and been popular in some interiors of the period, it would not have been the only fabric available for consideration. In the same way that certain contemporary fabrics – for example, Timney Fowler's strong black and white prints (see page 18) or the many newly-colored ginghams – are popular and pertinent to *this* period of decoration, they are, of course, only part of what is available.

Charting tastes and trends *is* difficult and this makes restoration or authentic decoration confusing. There is always movement back and forward. Some of the silk damasks, for example, produced by such companies as Watts and Co. or

These splendid silk damasks are from Warners' archives. Their designs are taken from old patterns, many of which date from several hundred years ago and are of French and Italian origin. The highly stylized but intricately patterned motifs and floral shapes stand out, even in the self-colored pieces, due to the damask weave (see p 46).

Overleaf:
The richness of these damasks, brocatelles, lampas and doublecloths lies in the splendor of their designs. The beautiful patterns, copied from English and European woven fabrics that ranged in period from Byzantine to the 19th century, include hissing medieval swans, wide-eyed dragons and owls, leaping heraldic beasts and rampant lions. They are woven from wool or a combination of wool and another fiber, such as cotton or linen.
In medieval and Elizabethan times, these textiles were intended as wall-hangings, either hung singly from a simple iron pole or used to cover the walls of entire rooms. Today, they look most authentic when set against period furniture. Their warm reds and ochers and rich blues and greens look wonderful with heavy, dark oak furniture and stone-tiled floors. Or, in more contemporary style, they work as single curtains in a room where there is little pattern or texture save for, perhaps, a jute flooring. Curtains in these cloths need simple poles in dark wood or iron, and are best lined in a dark cloth rather than the standard cream fabric linings.

Warner's, are based on original 14th or 15th century patterns. Others are based on much later designs which have themselves been adapted from older ones.

Careful historical research through original documents is always a good idea. A combination of the results of your research and the establishment of the purpose of restoration, tempered by the present-day requirements, should provide you with a choice of appropriate furnishings.

Textile classics today

I have divided *The Textile Art* into fabric types rather than a historical sequence, since the intended emphasis of this book is the individual appeal of classic fabrics, rather than a century-by-century charting of textile history. Broadly, and these form the main headings, the book looks at woven cloth, printed textiles and those fabrics with an applied element.

This division, I hope, will present exciting and pleasant surprises – as you move from tartans to tickings, for example. Of course, you are bound to mix fabrics from one major group with those from another; that in itself is one of the many pleasures to be had from working with textiles. But underlying each division are, I believe, parallels in the fundamental approach to, and therefore application of, the textiles included in that chapter.

The range of textiles available is huge, stunning and very diverse. However, there are often strong links between seemingly disparate fabrics which become apparent as you begin to research. Common historical patterns emerge, in addition to geographical links, some of which can be quite unexpected. There are also connections between fabric groups which are more instantly apparent – what the cloth is made from (see page 6), its design and color. It is difficult to separate the last two factors. I have thought about this a great deal in my own work and have concluded that the impact of the fabric lies in both the style or pattern and its color, and that these are inextricably linked. In addition, you should consider the feel of the cloth – whether it is heavy, matte, smooth, shiny – and match form to function, taking into account your own preferences and consideration along the way.

The successful interior decorator, professional or not, will develop an intuitive style, enhanced by design trends and new commercial products. The skill of successfully matching different fabrics, surfaces and colors takes time to acquire and to some people it may remain elusive. Much of it will obviously hinge on personal taste, but aside from this I believe that it develops from an instinctive response to what you see and feel. It should always be remembered that fabric is essentially fluid and tactile and not simply a pattern. It should, therefore, be enjoyed and used as such.

Always bear in mind that fabrics of similar weights and surfaces work best together. But color, of course, can be a great leveller – rich fabrics such as damasks and brocades (see page 46) could mix well with simple cotton checks (see page 87) from further down the "hierarchical" scale, providing that the colors work together. For example, a deep red damask curtain could be lined with a small red and navy blue checked pattern. A mass of floral patterns, if closely linked by color, would, similarly, be effective. Monochromatic patterns mix well and in such a case the variety of designs and styles does not seem to matter so much (see page 18).

Of course, there will be occasions when violently clashing colors are successful together – it is then that the fiber characteristics (the content of the cloth) should be assessed; a common content will provide a stabilizing force.

The art of putting together different patterns and styles in a way that appears haphazard is a process requiring knowledge (of your subject) and careful thought (about its application). I hope that this book succeeds in inspiring you and that it fuels the processes for "putting together" textiles successfully.

This sophisticated interior has been decorated using only tickings or ticking-inspired stripes like the rough linen used to make the Roman shade. By keeping to monochrome colors, a very smart, graphic effect is created. When combined with plain white walls and floor, the individual elements are brought sharply into focus. The interplay of shadow and light on the different woven stripes, together with the overall juxtaposition of one kind of stripe against another, gives a very textured effect despite the fact that the fabrics are flat and linear.

Overleaf:
In this group of monochrome fabrics it is the pattern which immediately strikes the eye. Some of the fabrics have the design woven into the cloth (the striped silks and dotted diamond, for example). Others, most notably the background fabric, the large oval design to the right and the floral top left, have a printed pattern. These particular printed designs require to be read with the fabric almost flat, such is the layout and strength of the pattern. All of these fabrics sit comfortably together because there are so many of them, but if you plan to use just a few of them together you must take care to keep to the same strength of black or else make sure that the ground color is the same cream or white tone.

SELECTING WOVEN FABRICS

This chapter explores the history, nature and uses for the main categories of woven fabrics. A selection of classic woven designs – stripes, plaids, non-pictorial save for a hint of stylized foliage – is shown on the previous page.

Single color fabrics

Plain textiles such as calicoes and canvases (pages 27-31) provide a neutral base for any decorating scheme. Interest can be added with fancy weaves that give texture.

Rich fabrics

A wealth of textiles, from silks and brocades to African Kente cloth, falls into this section (pages 32-83). The characteristic richness they share makes them important components of a decorator's palette.

Graphic and linear fabrics

Stripes, checks and motifs (pages 84-105) are the staple "bridge" fabrics of many decorating schemes.

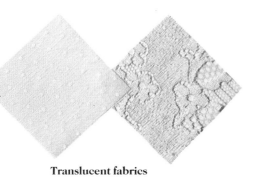

Translucent fabrics

Lace and sheers (pages 106-117) filter light and provide textural contrast to heavier, opaque fabrics.

Braids and ribbons

Flat-woven braids and ribbons (pages 118-121) are important finishing touches to many soft furnishing designs.

Woven

This chapter explores the richest strand of textile history – from grand and intricate tapestries to simple homespuns, rich tribal cloths to basic muslins. A broad range of furnishing mainstays, from undyed calico to rich silk damask, sheer and pretty lace to severe ticking stripes, is covered. It also includes braids and ribbons, those miniature textiles that often are only an afterthought, but can be an essential finishing detail. Just as over the centuries people in many different parts of the world have chosen fabrics with an emphasis on weave to decorate their living quarters, today so too can classic weaves be selected for their texture, their color, their strength.

Most furnishing fabrics are woven in some form. In fact, to be strictly accurate, the word textile should only be used to describe a woven fabric. The varying characteristics of furnishing textiles are determined by four main considerations.

The first two factors, discussed on page 7, are the kinds of raw materials used (for example, cotton bolls, sheep's fleece or silkworm's cocoons) and the quality of the yarns produced from them (cotton, wool or silk in the case of our previous examples). And the third factor, dealt with on pages 8-9, is the structure of the cloth itself, resulting from the method by which the yarn is woven. For example, a silk may be woven in a tabby weave or an intricate jacquard, producing a result that is either plain or elaborately figured.

The final factor that affects the appearance of a textile is whether or not there is any additional embellishment to the woven cloth in the form of printed pattern or stitching. Fabrics which rely on such decoration for their main appeal are dealt with in the Printed and Applied chapters.

In this chapter I have concentrated on textiles whose impact, primarily, comes from the texture and pattern given by their weave, rather than from a surface design. Such fabrics are often given a name that refers to the pattern or structure of their weave. Damask or brocade (see pages 46-51) and gingham (see page 93) are all examples of this. A few textiles are identified by the name of the raw fiber used to make them. Silks, for example, may be printed with any design, but the classic furnishing silks are patterned in the weave – they are either figured, shot or slubbed. For this reason, I have included silks here (see pages 37-45).

Some of the fabrics covered here are only produced as weaves – for example, a brocade or a shot fabric can only be woven – while others may be patterned either in the weave or by printing onto a plain woven cloth. Stripes, geometrics and motifs fall into the latter category, and are therefore examined both here and in the Printed chapter.

A woven and a printed stripe will be very different. The woven versions will have texture and depth because the pattern is integral to the fabric, while with the printed types the pattern sits on the surface. A choice between a printed or woven stripe will depend on the context you want to use the fabric in and on your budget. As a rule, a woven stripe will be heavier, more durable and more costly, while a printed one will be lighter, less long-lasting but not so expensive. The intricate patterning possibilities of a weave, and the fact that the color in a woven fabric is diffused through the yarn, give fabrics that rely on their weave to carry design and colors a depth and richness which printed varieties cannot achieve.

Single Color

The appeal of fabrics without pattern is based on two characteristics – color and texture. Although color may seem the more important, texture has a subtler, but more pervading influence.

Most of the fabrics in this section have been included primarily because of their texture. Some have a gentle overall weave pattern, like the "diamond-stitch", others have a more noticeable, definite texture.

Light has an effect on all fabrics, and in particular it plays a key role in bringing neutral self-patterned, single-color fabrics to life. Of course, natural light will have a different effect to electric sources. The textured surfaces of many of these fabrics can be exploited to greater sculptural effect by careful use of electric lighting. For example, if one of these fabrics is held vertically and with some degree of gathering, such as in a curtain, light directed from one side will highlight the top of the folds, at the same time creating deep-shadowed areas between them. Certain textured weaves are shown to their best effect under appropriate lighting. For example, ridges and

These neutral fabrics show clearly how weave structure can affect the texture of the cloth. The feel of the cloth is also characterized by the type of yarn used. Compare, for example, the heavy matte twill weave with the "ladder stripe". Both of these fabrics are woven in a cotton yarn, but the quality of the cotton and the way that it has been spun has affected the final product. The heavier one would be suitable for upholstery, the lighter one for draperies.

Herringbone weave
A strong hard-wearing weave (see page 8) in cotton yarn.

Ladder stripe
A mixture of twill and plain weaves (see pages 8-9) in cotton yarn.

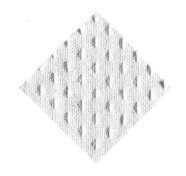

Relief weave
In heavy cotton, this textured weave is particularly suitable for upholstery use.

Twill weave
A strong weave in a heavy matte cotton produces a very robust cloth.

Floral weave
Stylized flowers stand out against a plain weave ground.

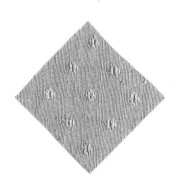

Linen union
A linen and cotton mixture produces a strong fabric that is useful for heavy drapery or upholstery.

Brocaded twill
The pattern is formed from a combination of twill and brocade weaves (see page 8).

dotted textures will be highlighted if a light source is angled across them.

The weave can influence how a color appears because different textures or weave patterns affect the density of the dye. A plain, deep blue cotton with a heavy glaze will seem brighter and more dense in tone than its unglazed counterpart, while a heavy-ribbed cotton twill will differ from a fine silk, even if they were colored with dye from the same batch. And a deeply ridged weave pattern will create shadows which in turn affect the depth of color.

In fabrics where texture is not a significant feature, colo can be considered and used on its own. Striking contrasts can b set up with vibrantly dyed flat cotton fabrics. You can almos forget that they are textiles and just play on the colors as yo would with paint. Reds, ochers and olive greens, for example will give a feeling of warmth and richness, while bright lemo yellow, emerald green and royal blue will produce a cooler sharper feel. And undyed, unbleached fabrics, with thei varying depths of off-whites and creams, give a neutral contem porary look to a room.

Basic Weaves

There are two main types of basic weave: utilitarian fabrics, like canvas or calico, and textured furnishing fabrics that are woven in neutral colors.

Fabrics like canvas and calico conjure up images of crisp, unbleached texture. These cloths were never intended to be taken seriously for furnishing; they functioned as linings, undercloths or background fabrics, useful but unseen. However, today fresh new uses have been found for them as inexpensive top-covering and curtain fabrics.

Also included are furnishing fabrics which are similar in feel to the aforementioned "undercloths" in the same group because they are also basic cloths. These fabrics are all neutral in tone: cream or off-white, bleached white or dyed very pale coffee or taupe. Many of them are matte, although a few use, for example, a mercerized yarn which gives a shinier appearance to the finished cloth. The additional interest that differentiates them from the utilitarian cloths is provided by a specific woven pattern which gives surface texture.

Basic utilitarian cloths

One of the most popular utilitarian cloths is cotton calico. Although it is coarser than, say, muslin, it can vary from a lightweight to a heavy, stiff cloth, depending on the quality of cotton used. Calico is an Indian term, and most of the calico used today is still woven there. It is often woven in cheap cotton, and in India is used for wrapping goods for export, or for clothing. Whether in its creamy, unbleached state or dyed, calico has a crisp feel. It is a matte fabric with dots of cottonseed in the yarn that give it a subtle, browned texture.

Cambric is a plain weave, woven in fine, bleached cotton, with the threads set very close. It does give a rather stiff, bright finish that is similar to the glazed plain cotton furnishing fabrics. Because of this it tears easily, so it is best used loosely, not stretched tight over a form.

Canvas, or duck, is a cotton or linen fabric which is used as sailcloth, or for awnings or tents. It is extremely strong and heavy because it is plain-woven in a quality yarn. Some canvas-type fabrics, such as buckram, are stiffened with size, a liquid solution which penetrates the fibers of the woven cloth.

Cotton drill is a similar fabric to canvas. Often used for clothing, it is worth considering for furnishing use. It is a twill weave (see page 8) which gives it a little more surface pattern than some of the other fabrics already mentioned.

The difference between canvas-type and calico-type fabrics is mainly to do with the quality and weight of yarn used and also the closeness of the weave (a closer weave will strengthen a cloth). Therefore, canvas, which is woven from a heavier density cotton, will always be stronger, stiffer and consequently more durable than calico. Although calico is produced in varying weights, it is never as heavy as canvas.

Basic furnishing cloths

Within this general group of self-patterned fabrics there is a considerable range of cloth types: from a basic plain weave, fairly roughly produced, to a quite sophisticated multi-weave which cleverly combines several different weave patterns as well as yarns.

Many of these cloths, for reasons of economy as well as durability, have a mixed fiber content. For example, it is quite common to mix man-made viscose (see page 7) with naturally

produced cotton. Fabrics which combine fibers are generally intended for heavier domestic use.

Some of these fabrics rely on a repeating motif or small geometric shape, such as a dot or square. These small patterns are set against a plainer ground, not necessarily plain-weave, but a flatter area, which further accentuates the relief created on the raised motif or shape.

Using basic cloths

Canvas-type fabrics such as buckram, duck or drill are excellent for use in decorating situations where their strength and stiffness can be exploited. Great swathes of creamy, heavy canvas can be looped across a ceiling in a large, open area. Cotton duck or sailcloth can be stretched over a wooden frame to make a screen or pulled tight across the top of a four-poster bed frame. Some of these fabrics are or can be waterproofed, so their use can be extended to outdoor furnishings like awnings, large umbrellas or seat covers for metal garden chairs.

None of the utilitarian cloths are produced as finished furnishing fabrics and so many of them are not pre-shrunk or finished in any way as to make them durable. Therefore, you will need to wash such fabric before making it up into a furnishing item. However, there is an advantage to the fact that they are unfinished: they can be easily dyed or painted. Some of them, such as cambric, have a slightly waxy finish so any dye or paint applied will adhere rather patchily, thus creating an interesting, uneven texture.

Calico looks stunning used in quantity as a curtain fabric, draped in full, sculptural folds or tailored into neat pleats. Heavy tasseled tie-backs in a single color can also look good draped against this plain cream cloth. Calico also works well fashioned into a cover to conceal an upright dining chair. A slipcover to conceal or protect fine fabric upholstery was, after all, one of this textile's original functions.

The basic furnishing cloths do not have this disadvantage as they have been designed for furnishing use and are therefore pre-shrunk and given a suitable finish. These fabrics can be very effective grouped together. Select examples which share a single neutral color and are decorated by different woven patterns. A ridged stripe, a zigzag and a dot-relief can all be placed together in the form of a collection of cushions, each

The effect of fiber content
Most of these fabrics are woven in all-cotton yarn. The use of different qualities of yarn and the fineness of the thread employed will have an effect on the final cloth produced and its subsequent use. For example, a softer cotton will drape more smoothly than a coarser one, which will form more sculpted folds. Compare the softer fine-textured cottons with the coarser Indian sort.

The addition of a man-made fiber such as viscose to cotton will strengthen a cloth and make it, generally, more hard-wearing. The thickness of the yarn used in the weave will affect the texture. A thicker yarn will give a more textured, ridged surface, although the cloth won't always be stronger than a finer one as the weave is much looser.

The effect of weave detail
A change of weave structure gives a circled motif (bottom row, near right), a diagonal dot (top row, far left) and all manner of stripes. When a cloth is stripped of the distractions of color, like these fabrics are, the ridges, twills, herringbone, zig-zag and other weave effects can be fully appreciated.

The effect of color
Neutral colors range from soft whites, produced by bleaching the yarn, creamy shades where the yarn is left in its natural state, and coffee or taupe tones produced from dyes. If the same cloth is treated in each of the three ways it will be different not just in color, but in handle as the bleaching and dyeing processes affect the feel of the yarn.

Overleaf:
Calico is one of the most marvelous fabrics to work with. It has a strength and beauty that take it far beyond its intended use as a basic, non-decorative, functional cloth. Its weight allows it to be sculpted and remain in a given shape – here, the lengths around the walls hang from drape rosettes and fall naturally into deep "swagged" folds. The chair is a clever calico sculpture, in which the basic chair frame has been manipulated into a gloriously individual shape. The fabric is plain but not dull – the soft creamy color for which calico is renowned appears deep gold when hung against natural light and almost bright-white when the same light is cast across it.

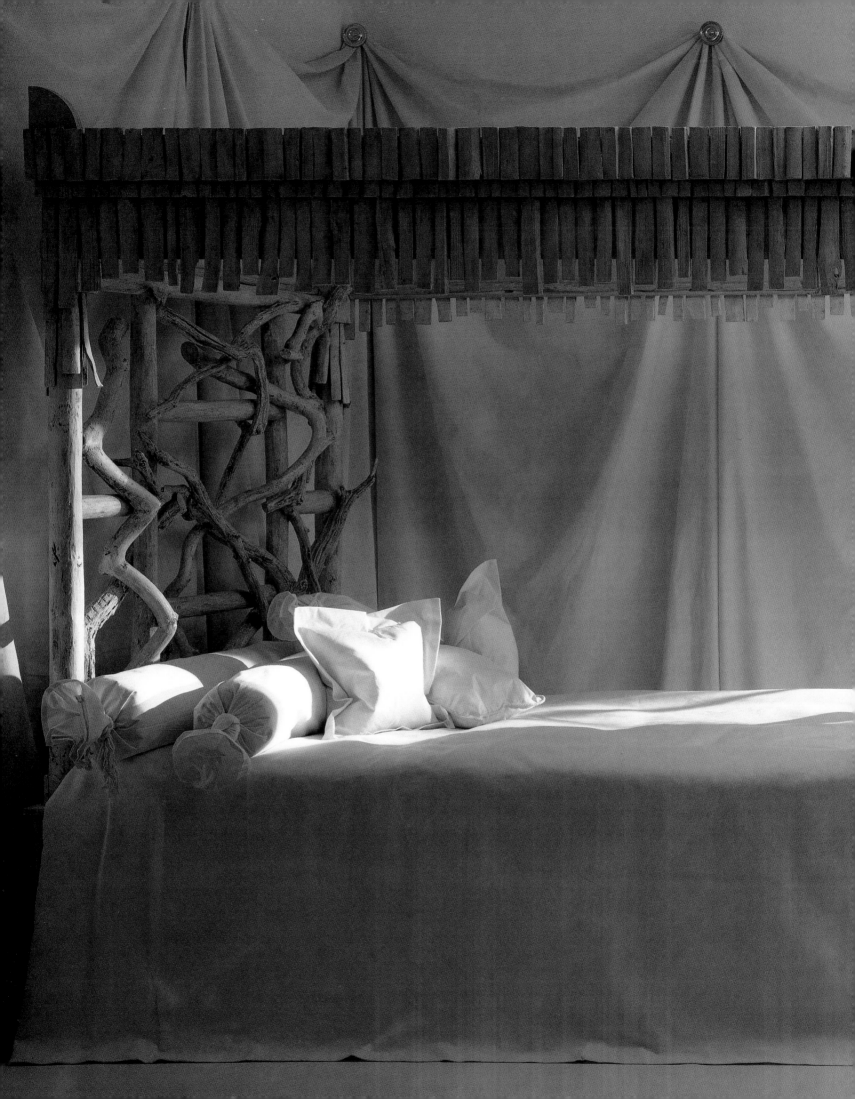

KING ST   BETWEEN JARVIS + PARLIMENT

ITALINTERIORS   359 KING

ZIGGURAT

TREDIE =   254 KING

TILE PLACE =   256 KING

SYSTEMALUX   - close by
                " lighting store   ALSO LIGHTING.
                                          AT THESE PLACES

ALSO 2 stores on Queen St near Spadina.
Japanese store on Younge St near Rosedale

L7N 1A3

PAY TO THE
ORDER OF

$

/ 100 DOLLARS

19

THE TORONTO-DOMINION BANK
463 GUELPH LINE AND NEW STREET,
BURLINGTON, ONTARIO
L7R 3X8

114

⑈110⑈ ⑈22162⑈004⑈: 031⑈5⑈0250933⑈

*A strong canvas or cotton duck has been dyed a deep rich blue for the chair cover
(above left). The chair itself has a simple metal frame, so the traditional use for a
"slip-cover" – that of protecting valuable upholstery beneath – is not relevant here.
Instead, it is a startlingly simple device for completely changing the character of the
chair. In contrast, for the tablecloth (above right) the calico has been left natural; its
smooth creaminess is given sophistication with the addition of a deep, undyed fringe
applied to the lower edge of the cloth. A casual arrangement of cushions and bolsters
(right) becomes a study of light and shadow, tucks and folds. The unbleached calico is
complemented by the textured twist of the undyed cord, used both around the cushion as
piping and to secure the bolster end.*

covered in a different weave. However, when using a variety of fabrics in a context in which they are sewn together, be careful to ensure that they have a unifying fiber. For example, joining a cloth woven entirely from man-made fibers with one woven in natural yarn may present problems. One might stretch more than the other and make joining seams difficult; one might have to be dry-cleaned and the other machine- or hand-washed.

Basic cloths should be selected carefully for specific situations. Consider the durability of a fabric – for example, a lightweight, loosely woven textile will not be suitable for heavy domestic use such as upholstery. Wear is important too; a matte, textured fabric will attract dirt and become grubby much more quickly than its shinier, smoother counterpart. Does your fabric need to be rigid or should it have give? Some fabrics will be stretchier than others; this is due to the combination of yarn used and weave structure. Weight is a factor that should also be taken into consideration. For example, a heavy linen fabric will need to be well-supported in a curtain arrangement, but conversely its weight will have practical benefits if used as a floor covering. In contrast, a very lightweight cloth can be draped from the flimsiest of poles, but will not stand up to daily use as a close cover for a chair or sofa.

All these basic weaves are often used to form the foundation of many decorating schemes – whether literally, as linings or undercloths, or in a more modern way as a neutral base against which more dominant patterned or textured fabrics are set (for example, covering a sofa that is strewn with boldly colored, richly patterned scatter-cushions).

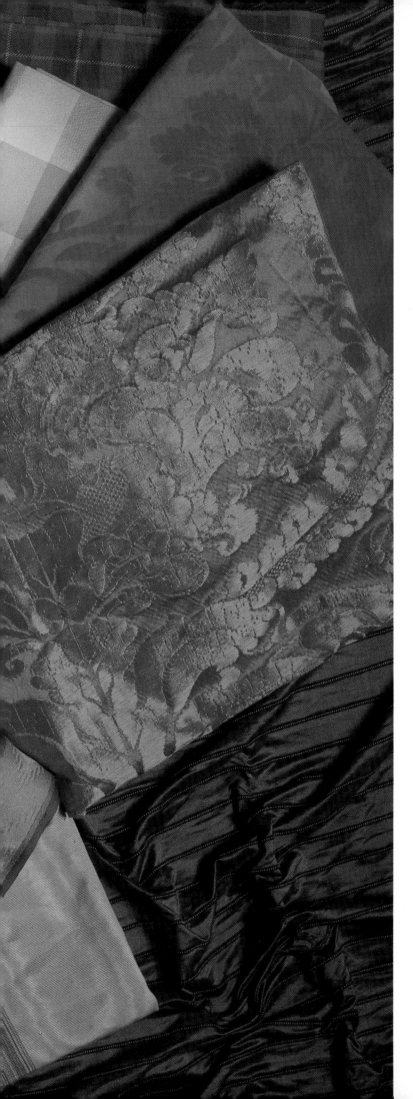

Rich

It is rare to find a printed cloth which has the depth and beauty of a textile in which weave provides the pattern. The intricacies of the weave and the combinations of different strands of fiber and color give woven textiles a potential richness. This richness can take many forms: the luxurious surface of shimmering silk and the textured patterning of a highly decorative tapestry, damask or brocade are all rich. Different fibers have their own textural richness. Linen, with its slightly coarse surface, contrasts with the shiny smoothness of most silks. Yet both, because of the nature of woven fabrics, can have an equal intensity.

Woven fabrics, in the main, tend to be heavier than their printed counterparts. It is the concentration and emphasis on the weave that is naturally going to produce a greater weight than a fabric which relies mostly on its superficial surface pattern. This weightiness also contributes to a richness and luxuriousness.

Pattern is also a factor in producing a rich fabric. Often, this means grand, elegant or traditional designs, for few woven patterns are new or contemporary. For example, the pomegranate has been used as a motif for hundreds of years and crops up on numerous silks and damasks, adding to this group's exuberance. And tartan's particular history encourages a feeling of tradition, which in turn contributes to a greater impression of richness. Dense patterns, such as floral swirls in damask or detailed figurative scenes in tapestries, give a highly decorative feel to a textile. And the number of threads and colors used to create such a pattern adds to its beauty. It is immediately obvious whether a cloth has been composed of a woven pattern or a surface-printed one. Pattern formed by printed color lacks the intrinsic quality of a pattern formed by the weave.

The vast range of textiles in this chapter – from African kente cloth to Italian figured velvets – share a depth of texture and color that make them rich.

These fabrics have a heavy, textured, rich feel to them. Their sense of history, of traditional patterns and weaves, makes their presence in room strong but not dominant. This is precisely what makes them textile classics.

Corded Silk

A shot silk (see page 38) woven in black and gold to give a green-gold shimmer, and striped in cords of black.

Tapestry

Machine-woven tapestry fabric is tough and durable – ideal for upholstery.

Damask

This rich woolen damask, woven to an original design, would work well with period oak furniture.

Tartan

A vibrant woolen cloth that is woven in a contemporary colorway.

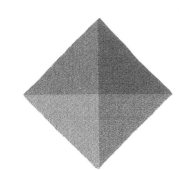

Madras

A lightweight Indian cotton fabric woven in rich, bright colors.

Figured silk

True textile classics, these fabrics have furnished houses for centuries.

Brocade

The brocade-like effect of a woven fabric is particularly rich if a metallic thread is used.

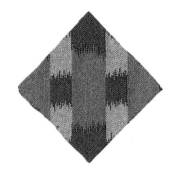

Ikat

The characteristic fuzzy edges of the ikat weave are evident in this sample.

Tribal

Rich and unusual ethnic fabrics like this Mexican weave can be bought from specialist suppliers.

Indigo ikat

This ikat is woven in the classic indigo dyes traditionally used in the Far East.

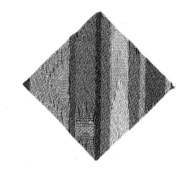

Striped ikat

This fabric is woven is imitation of ikat, but the yarns are not pre-dyed so there is no characteristic blurring.

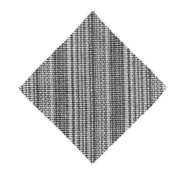

Moiré stripe

Graphic, linear stripes have been combined with a rich moiré section in this cloth.

Silks

It was the Chinese, as long as 4,500 years ago, who first discovered a silk cocoon. After careful observation and research, they managed to domesticate the silkworm and for a very long time they maintained a monopoly on silk production. There are several stories that claim to explain how the secret of silk reached the West. One of the most charming is that in AD 552 two monks on a mission to Asia came back to Byzantium with silkworm eggs hidden inside their bamboo walking sticks. It is more likely, however, that trading links between China and Persia first introduced the secret of silk weaving to Asia Minor and Greece. From there, caravans of traders brought silks to western countries along the routes that eventually became known as the Silk Roads.

In the wake of Arab ascendancy in the Middle East, North Africa and Spain, sericulture (the cultivation of the silkworm) was introduced to

A richly patterned silk damask, decorated with floral and architectural motifs, is used for walling in this English stately home.

these regions, and the west began to make its own silk. In the 10th century, Andalusia was Europe's main silk-producing center. As commercial exchanges between East and West grew, there was ever-increasing use of silk. And by the 12th century, the Italian silk industry had begun.

Figured silks

The technique used to produce the early Italian silks was often called *diasper*. A kind of lampas, it was woven in a monochrome or in two colors of silk. Typical patterns were griffins, lions or birds. Some designs had animals arranged in pairs within a geometric shape, such as a circle, with ornamental borders. At the beginning of the 14th century, with the advent of the Renaissance, the symmetrical patterns were replaced by asymmetry and movement; for example, birds in flight or running animals. Plant motifs began to be used, and often luxuriant floral scrolls would take up the whole pattern.

Further inspiration came from the Near and Far East. And some designs were influenced by the work of great artists such as Jacobi Bellini. The most favored motif of all was the pomegranate.

In order to produce these fancy woven fabrics, the weaver had to control small numbers of warp threads at will. As silk is such a fine and lustrous thread, this was difficult on a plain loom. The Chinese developed the drawloom to overcome these difficulties and allow the weaver to produce patterns many times larger than those woven on the plain loom. The use of the drawloom spread with the secret of silk production, and weavers in Florence and Lucca became renowned for weaving exquisite figured silk velvets.

Until the beginning of the 16th century most silks were large-patterned, often in a damask or brocade weave (see page 46), whatever furnishing use they were intended for. From the 16th century silks began to be designed for particular purposes; small patterns were produced for upholstery items and large, sweeping patterns for wallcoverings. By the middle of the 17th century, as Europe became increasingly wealthy, the demand for silks for interior decoration grew. And the Italian silk industry, which had dominated the European market for more than 400 years, met with competition from the newly developing French industry.

The French industry can be traced back to the 15th century, when Lyon in France became a major warehouse for foreign silks. Concerned that there was too much outflow of capital from the country, in 1450 Louis XI declared his intention to "introduce the art and craft of making gold and silk fabrics in our city of Lyon". This fledgling industry was strengthened in 1536 when François I gave Lyon the monopoly of silk imports and trade.

Many of the French weavers were Huguenots, and when they fled France late in the 17th century, as a result of religious persecution, they took their silk weaving skills to Germany, Switzerland, the Netherlands and to Great Britain, where they founded the Spitalfields silk industry. Throughout the 18th and 19th centuries the silk industry continued to prosper throughout Europe, with Lyon dominating the market.

In the mid to late 18th century there were significant developments in the mechanization of weaving looms that increased the possibilities for fancy weaves, and gave the silk industry great impetus. Foremost among these was the invention of the Jacquard loom (see page 9), which perfected the method of producing figured fabrics.

In contrast with Europe, a viable silk manufacturing industry in America was never established, in spite of several attempts, notably in the 19th century, to do so. One of the exceptions was the Shaker community, especially in Kentucky, who were highly successful in producing silk of a very good quality. There were other manufacturers, usually individual entrepreneurs attracted by the challenge, who managed to grow mulberry trees and weave quantities of silk. However, the bulk of silks used in America were imported from Europe.

Plain silks

From the middle of the 19th century, as the Industrial Revolution made mass production of silks possible, plainer silks, that were easier to weave in the new European mills, began to feature in the homes of the new middle classes. Most of these silks were not patterned but woven in such a way that the surface had a texture or shimmer that provided a very rich effect. Such fabrics are very versatile, and therefore still popular today. Shot silk, for example, appears to be one color from one position and another from a different view. In some examples, the contrast is so vivid that it is difficult to believe that it is the same fabric. This change of color is achieved by weaving the warp and weft in contrasting colors (examine the cut edges to discover which two colors have been used). The beautiful colors of shot silk create an unparalleled luxuriousness, especially if woven in a taffeta, when it is accompanied by a unique crisp, rustling sound.

Slub silk is a thicker, more textured cloth that is woven with a silk yarn that resembles an unevenly spun cotton thread. Bourette silk yarn is interspersed with tufts of fiber. While the similarly textured tussah silk is produced from cocoons spun by wild or uncultivated silkworms, which produces a rough, pale brown yarn.

Using silks

Silk takes dye superbly so that it sings with color. But paradoxically, it loses color when subject to prolonged exposure to light, and this disadvantage must be considered when planning a scheme that includes silk. If you want to use your silk unlined, bed hangings are a good choice as they are usually far enough away from the natural light source to avoid fading. For an interesting effect, mix plain silks of different colors or use a silk narrowly striped in multi-colors or banded in two contrasting shades.

Silk damasks and other figured silks were originally used in grand houses and stately homes as walling fabrics; with heavy protective curtains at the window, the walls were relatively safe from the ravages of light. Today, in the general absence of these window curtain "layers", and, more importantly, in the presence of electric light, using silk on a large expanse of wall or room is not a practical suggestion. However, in small spaces – tiny rooms, perhaps without windows, or alcoves – the hanging of silk on the walls and ceilings can be marvellously

A pale yellow brocaded silk with a floral pattern, from Lyon in France, dating from the 18th century.

A Spanish silk brocaded with corded silk and metal thread, dating from 1720-30. The tree of life symbol is depicted in a large repeat.

A hand-woven silk designed by H. Scott Morton and woven by Warners' in 1883.

A French reversible silk fabric with a pattern depicting insects, dating from the early 18th century.

A white and red Italian silk lampas, dating from the late 16th century.

effective, especially if combined with trailing swags and tails to create the illusion of a great tent.

As long as it is lined and interlined to stop the light fading the fabric, silk makes wonderful draperies. It falls into gentle folds and will stay in these softly sculpted pleats under its own weight. Silk drapery looks best overlong, so that the fabric spills onto the floor. Above window level you need not use lining, so you can take advantage of the delicious weight and feel of a fine silk by, for example, scrunching it into barleycorn twists, intertwining these with rich ropes and looping the result over a chunky pole.

A lightweight silk is ideal for covering small, elegant chairs and a length of such silk looks exquisite entwined around a chandelier chain. This weight of silk pleats well and can be used successfully as a lampshade cover as long as an inner protective lining is made.

When choosing a silk, bear in mind that its appearance may alter in different lights. Some silks have an almost metallic effect which can change according to the direction of the light. Use such fabrics in situations where the cloth is viewed from different angles so that the effects of this light change can be fully experienced. And all silks, but in particular shot silks, take on a startlingly different character in subdued artificial light or in candlelight, so you should always examine samples of the silks you are considering under all lights before you make your final choice.

Don't feel that you have to stick to either figured or plain silk. You can combine the two types effectively, using a figured type as a feature fabric with a shot silk woven in the same two colors as the figured silk's pattern as a lining material.

Silk is still a luxury fabric, but it is not necessarily expensive.

The Watts collection of fabrics, from which many of those shown here are taken, represents one of the finest ranges of 19th century decorative designs in current production. The Company was founded in 1874 by three prominent late-Victorian church architects, George Frederick Bodley, Thomas Garner and Gilbert Scott, the Younger. Watts and Co. was set up because these three architects were unable to find firms to carry out furnishings and wallpaper to their satisfaction, and the Watts' designs were primarily for use in the partners' own work.

The late-gothic art of Northern Europe and the refined style of the English Renaissance house provided much of the inspiration for new designs, which combined strength of pattern and a bold usage of large scale with elaboration of detail.

The designs feature beautifully drawn flowers and foliage and were inspired by formal 15th century patterns. They have names like Bellini, Crevelli and Van der Weyden, which indicate the source from which they are derived.

All these silks have a luxurious quality, inherent in the texture and pattern of the designs. The rich colors, some taken from original medieval sources, and the use of burnished gold make these some of the most beautiful and tactile fabrics available. As full-length draperies, cascading onto the floor (preferably a dull stone or polished wood surface), these fabrics are magnificent. The arrangement can be grand or simple and understated. You should line the curtains well to protect against fading, although these silks have a beautiful surface when faded and slightly worn.

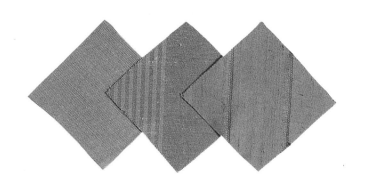

The immediate impact of these textiles is undoubtedly due to the luxurious sheen of the silk fiber. The quality of the silk used and the fineness with which it has been spun and woven are the main factors which produce this richness of surface.

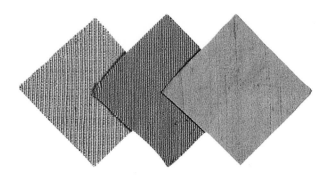

Even the heavier, slubbier silks like these textured noils and tussahs have a surface which reacts to the light in a way that no other woven fiber would.

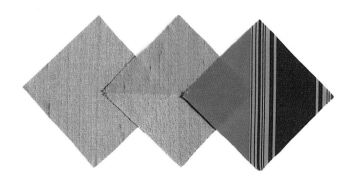

A feature of silk is the way that the fiber holds the color. The colors here are not especially vivid, but their brilliance is immediately obvious. In my opinion, one of the most beautiful fabrics in the entire book is shown here – the exquisite burnt orange shot silk with a wide stripe.

A corded weave gives silk fabric a firmer texture. Providing that any of these silk fabrics are used with care, they make elegant window or bed hangings. They will benefit from interlining, which will give them greater body and weight as well as helping to protect the silk from the effects of light.

Although some fine figured weaves are very costly, there are numerous importers of well-priced Indian and Chinese silks. Often, these are tussah twills, noils or slubbed cloths with an appealing texture. If you can't afford a large length of a fine figured fabric you could buy a small amount and use it on scatter cushions, coordinating it with an inexpensive plain imported silk for the drapery.

The neutral-colored slubby silks and noils, with their surface texture and grainy brown specks, are wonderful to use as formal curtain arrangements, with loose swags held over drape rosettes or poles with ornate finials. They can be made to look more decorative by trimming them with textured braids or deep fringes in the same neutral tones or in toning colors.

An unusual idea, in a situation where a window is not required for light or is perhaps inaccessible for pulling curtains, is to hang a piece of lined silk from a simple (concealed) rod or pole within the window recess, with sufficient surplus fabric to allow fullness at the sill. This then forms a backdrop for decorative items, such as a stone urn or terracotta pot. If taffeta is used, a sculptural effect can be achieved down the entire length, as the stiffened fabric tends to remain in its folds or shape without support.

This highly polished day bed deserves the rich flourish of shiny silk taffeta. The bed-cover and bolster fabric is deliberately chosen to clash with the intense bottle green of the inner curtain, thus adding to the dramatic effect achieved by the full swirl of the bed curtains. The bedcover is decorated with the Napoleonic bee motif (see page 157). For striped silk on the walls a more subdued color was selected so that the full impact remains with the central bed arrangement.

Damask and Brocade

Unlike silks, damasks and brocades are distinguished by their weave, rather than their fiber content. They may be produced in silk, cotton, linen, wool or man-made fibers.

Damasks

A true damask is a monochrome figured textile in which the shiny surface of the satin weave ground contrasts with the lusterless sateen weave figure. Other details may be in twills or plain weave (see pages 8-9). In its classic form it is reversible. Its name derives from the Syrian capital Damascus, which was an important center of the silk trade. Although traditionally silk or linen, damasks can be woven in wool or a mixture of fibers.

Damask is a genuinely classic fabric which has existed unchanged for many hundreds of years. The original figured designs – pomegranates and stylized florals – were first produced in Europe in the late 15th century. Today, fine silk weaving houses such as Watts and Co. still copy these originals. Damask's fluidly formal patterns have also been simulated by other means. Methods such as flocking and embossing that rely, like damask, on the contrast between matte and shade to create pattern have been widely used. Many pile fabrics copy the designs of silk damask (see page 7).

Silk was not the only yarn traditionally used for damask weaving. White linen damask cloths and napkins were fashionable at princely courts in the 16th century. Since then, these classic items have become more widely available, although they are still luxury items. They are predominantly made in Ireland, England and France.

The establishment of linen damask production was the result of two main elements – Flemish linen thread and the Italian technique of silk damask – being brought together. This happened because Flanders included the port of Bruges, the most important Northern European trading center with Italy. Initially, the local Flemish craftsmen copied the patterns of silk damask in their own thread, but by the early 16th century they had introduced their own designs. These were often figurative images, such as hunting scenes, of the type found in Flemish tapestries (see pages 52-5).

In the latter half of the 17th century the art of weaving linen damask spread to other countries, in particular Holland and France. When the Huguenots fled France at the end of the 17th century, they took these skills further afield, bringing the secret of linen damask production to Ireland and establishing the Spitalfields silk industry in London, England, as well as centers for silk production in Germany, Switzerland and Holland. From England, damasks, mostly woolen and worsted types, were exported to 19th century America.

Brocades

Brocade is a damask-based fabric that is woven in either one or two basic colors. What distinguishes it from regular damask are the additional colors that are applied to the woven surface rather than an integral part of it. The technique resembles embroidery, with the additional threads produced by floating wefts (see page 9). By their nature, brocades are heavier than damask fabrics. Looms can imitate this process today.

Brocatelle, like damask, seldom uses more than two colors. It usually has a satin or twill figure on a plain or satin ground and is distinguished from damask by raised areas of pattern that are formed by a double warp.

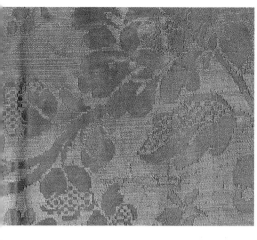

A mid-18th century silk damask furnishing fabric woven in two shades of green.

This damask is a document design, called "Gainsford", from Watts and Co.

An English hand-woven silk damasquette. Dating from circa 1880, it was produced by Warners.

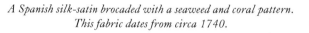

An original 17th century silk damask that was used to upholster a chair at Ham House, Surrey, England.

A Spanish silk-satin brocaded with a seaweed and coral pattern. This fabric dates from circa 1740.

A bizarre silk damask brocaded with silks. Circa 1708, it was made in Lyon, France.

An English silk brocatelle woven on a Jacquard loom. Known as "Venetian", it dates from circa 1860.

A 19th century silk and cotton brocatelle, hand-woven from a design called "Fleury" by Morris and Co.

Floral patterned damasks
Most damasks are patterned with motifs that take their inspiration from flowers and/or leaves.

Rich detail
Further richness is added with stripes, satin grounds or brocaded motifs.

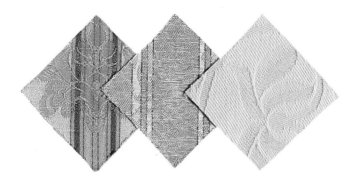

Color choice
Damasks can be complex and multi-colored (left and center) or subtle shades of one color (right).

Flowing patterns
Large, flowing patterns are good for window treatments, but may prove a problem when matching pieces on upholstery.

damask and brocade

Using damask and brocades

Rich, heavy and luxurious damasks and brocades do not drape into soft folds easily and are therefore more suited to formal drapery such as swags, full-length, sweeping curtains or tablecloths. The formality of the pattern dictates its use as a fabric. Damasks will not sit well in a cool, modern interior unless the intended effect is to startle. If this is the case, the introduction of a single antique chair in faded damask can be a deliberate and effective counterpoint to modern minimal decoration. Both damask and brocade work well with old furniture; they offset polished wood or gilt gloriously.

In fine silk, damask was used in palaces and stately homes as a wall covering because the pattern repeat, which was often as large as 80 inches (200 cm), was suited to long drops. Both damasks and brocades are good for walling because their flat, intricate patterns show well over a large surface area.

Monochrome or two-color damasks in different patterns can be mixed together in one scheme. For example, a small-patterned damask will make an effective contrast lining to an expansive floral pattern, and a cushion covered in one design can be piped in another.

Richly patterned damasks can look wonderful against dark, carved woodwork – for example, on a grand four-poster bed or a simple coronet. Or in contrast consider using off-whites, pale coffee colors and other neutral tones together in one arrangement – mixing different scales of pattern – on swags, curtains, pillows and bed-covers.

The weight of the fabric adds to its sophistication and "grandness". However, when used in quantity the heavy weight of the fabric may be detrimental unless very strong pole or track fixings can be used. The use of heavy rope tie-bands can have a practical effect, as well as being decorative – since they can help to hold much of the weight, thus reducing the stress that the walls or window frames may have to bear.

Each item here has a strong presence. The single red-on-red antique damask curtain is braided on the leading edge and base for additional texture and definition and held back with a chunky antique tasseled rope tie. It is frequently the case with period curtains that only one of a pair has survived. Single curtains or other asymmetric arrangements can be a very successful way to make decorative use of a single surviving panel. With antique fabrics, use old, or "faked" old, poles and fittings. Ornate finials or drape rosettes often work well with this sort of heavy silk damask. If applying new braid to a faded and worn fabric, "age" the trimming so that it is in keeping. The fabric thrown over the sofa is a richly patterned red and gold silk. The sofa itself, covered in a now-faded damask, is imposing, yet softened by its aged upholstery.

Tapestry

In the strict sense, tapestry should only be used to describe a hand-woven material with a ribbed surface created as a design is woven. Combinations of threads are used to form a picture in the same way that color is built up in a printed image. Today's tapestry is machine made by using three differently colored threads in the warp and two in the weft, giving eight separate color effects. Further warp threads can be used to introduce still more colors. On all types of tapestry cloth the weaves are arranged so that the better-quality yarns are brought to the surface. Traditional yarns are cotton, wool or worsted. Tapestry often looks embroidered; this is deliberate as it was originally produced on a loom in imitation of intricate needle-worked textiles.

The development of the art of tapestry

Tapestry has been called the "mirror of civilization" because so many tapestries

A fine Dutch tapestry woven in silks and wools, dating from the late 16th century.

represented scenes of everyday life. The designs often depicted a great historical exploit or an incident in the life of the lord of the house. Most tapestry production was of wall-hangings for domestic interiors – castles or stately homes. Enormous luxurious tapestries were hung on walls, as bed canopies and sometimes as screens. Sometimes they were also draped over furniture and chair-backs, thus they would virtually have covered entire rooms. Such tapestries tended to be regarded as portable wealth and accompanied their owners on their travels.

The earliest Western tapestries do not display subjects of chivalry and other profane splendor, as did most of those produced during the prolific periods of tapestry production. Instead, many early tapestries were woven in the quiet seclusion of monasteries and represented the patience and dedication of the devout religious servant.

The first tapestry to be

woven in the West is the 11th-century *Cloth of St Gereon*, fragments of which reside in a museum in Lyon in France, and in the Victoria and Albert Museum in London, as well as in other museums across Europe. The forms are of heraldic beasts, bulls and griffins, set in decorated medallions, surrounded by smaller background motifs such as scrolls and heads. A border runs along the entire length, with intertwined curves and lines, and heraldic heads (see pages 156-7). The decorative motifs – especially those of the border ornamentation – which repeat identically at regular intervals over the entire surface, are similar to motifs that appear in illustrated documents of the same period.

The next surviving tapestry is of the late 12th century, by which time the style had changed considerably, and tapestries began to depict similar themes to those that were depicted in other media of the time – for example, paintings, manuscripts and so on.

There are no surviving examples or records of tapestries produced between this period and the late 14th century.

Travel was extensive during the Middle Ages – royalty and nobility, with their entourage of merchants and strolling players, were always moving from place to place, accompanied by their tapestry weavers. However, the occasional work of these artisans was soon transformed into a major industry, backed by financial institutions, changing what had originally been simply a means of religious decoration into an important commercial enterprise.

A magnificent Louis XIV Gobelins Chancellerie tapestry. Note the use of the fleur de lys *motif (see page 157), which appears both in the background and also on the drapery.*

The origins of the technique itself are difficult to chart with certainty. Centuries before, the Copts wove narrative accounts into their panels in much the same way. It is possible that the invading Arabs took on this idea of depicting scenes and that it was acquired by the Crusaders.

From the 14th century tapestry was regarded as an important decorative art in both France and Flanders, at workshops in Brussels, Arras and, less importantly, Tournai. Output in England, Scotland and other European countries was on a minor scale in comparison.

The French hold on the tapestry industry was strengthened in the early 14th century when the king of England, wanting to put pressure on the land of Flanders, decided to stop supplying wool to them. To escape starvation, Flemish weavers emigrated to the city of Aubusson in France, where there was wool in large supply and an established tradition of weaving cloth. In 1601, the King of France, anxious to protect the French industry from foreign competition, prohibited the importation of tapestries into France, which boosted the industry at Aubusson both commercially and artistically. The variety and the quality of the subjects featured on Aubusson tapestries is considerable. From natural scenes with beasts, real and imaginary – griffins, dragons, unicorns, lions – to cities or castles.

During the Renaissance, under the influence of Paris fashion, both French and Flemish tapestry weavers began to reproduce the effect of fine paintings. Although these tapestries called for a high standard of technical skill, inevitably they looked more like a copy than an original work of art.

In 1665, Louis XIV gave Aubusson the title of "Manufacture Royale". However, despite this title, production output remained small, unlike that of the workshops at Gobelin, which were also given Royal patronage.

The Gobelin tapestry workshop in France was set up during the mid-17th century and was designated a royal manufactory in 1667. The competition between countries and courts to set up workshops became increasingly intense.

A profound change of taste took place as the 17th century gave way to the 18th, and this had such repercussions on tapestry production that it caused a complete metamorphosis. There were distinct reasons for the gradual decline of the tapestry industry that began at this time. The old narrative "mural" style was going out of fashion. Instead, wallpaper, carved paneling or other materials replaced tapestry on many walls. The imitation of the picture frame or cornice frequently found on tapestries of this era (see page 55) was an attempt to follow the new decorative tastes.

By the end of the 18th century, all tapestry workshops found themselves in difficulties. The art of tapestry was not able to free itself from the "picturesque" which had been its strength in

One of a pair of Louis XV Aubusson tapestries woven with scenes from La Fontaine's fables, after J.B. Oudry. Note the background patterning device.

An English wool and cotton machine-made tapestry woven by Warners in 1910.

A 16th century Italian tapestry, probably from Florence.

A Flemish tapestry depicting a hunting scene in an orchard, dating from the 16th century.

earlier centuries. And the French Revolution had a devastating effect on tapestry production – many beautiful tapestries were burnt in order to yield their meagre gold content. Tapestry had become identified with the decorative power, luxury and dignity of the Sovereign and the aristocracy; with their decline, the art of tapestry died too.

"An ornamental cloth, woven in wool and gold thread, telling a story" was the brief description of tapestry provided in a late 19th century Italian dictionary. At the beginning of the

19th century manufacture of tapestry was in decline and numerous workshops had closed down. Tapestry had become primarily the preserve of aesthetes and scholars. There was a proliferation of writing on the subject of tapestry, the interest stimulated perhaps by the slowing down of the craft itself. Despite the demise of the industry, the art of tapestry weaving continued to be held in very high regard and looked upon with the same degree of admiration accorded to the great paintings of the time.

An early 17th century Flemish verdure hunting tapestry. It is a complex design with compact elements.

An Aubusson tapestry of landscape and birds, early 18th century. The main scene is more central to the design than in the Flemish example (left) and the various pictorial elements can be more easily "read".

This fine, very rare Louis XV Beauvais tapestry L'Operateur, is one of fourteen, and is woven in silk and wool. The canopy is wonderfully depicted in exquisite shading and fine detail.

A Brussels tapestry woven in silk and wool. The frame-like border gives it the impression of a painting.

At the end of the 19th century, William Morris and his Arts and Crafts contemporaries attempted to revive the art of tapestry once more, and many new pieces were produced. William Morris said of tapestry: "It may be looked upon as a mosaic of pieces of color made up of dyed threads…" Today, there is a small but successful industry in contemporary hand-woven tapestry, still in a way imitating paintings.

Machine-made tapestry is also produced today. It is mainly designed for upholstery use as it is a highly durable, practical fabric that stands up well to everyday wear and tear. It retains a distinct tapestry feel and is heavy and fairly stiff in the way that a hand-woven tapestry certainly is.

Using tapestry

Tapestries, antique or modern, demand special attention. They are often heavy, and because of this treatments should be simple and straightforward. With curtains, avoid twists or swags and opt for an ornate pole to introduce a decorative element. Most antique tapestries should be viewed flat, as pictures, for that is

With such a rich heritage of hand-tapestried examples to follow, it is no wonder that these modern machine-woven fabrics are so vividly colored and patterned.

Modern motifs

Simple, graphic trellises and floral motifs abound – some are very stylized, while others are closer in feel to the traditional tapestries, being rich in detail and pattern.

Pattern scale

Large designs that incorporate bold geometric motifs resemble carpet patterns and should be used boldly, perhaps contrasting two patterns with the same colors on a single item; while the small motifs that crisscross the textured surface in delightfully contrasting colors will mix well with larger, more flowing patterns.

hat they were. The softer, modern machine-made tapestry will eat fairly well into curtain headings, either by hand or with irtain tape, but the headings will remain bulky so the usual illness allowance should be reduced. Heavier tapestries, and rtainly the stiffer antique ones, can be hung quite simply with irely any fullness, by means of a fabric slot sewn to the reverse de of the tapestry, through which a pole or rod may be run. se heavy, preferably old, rope tie-bands to pull back antique pestry curtains. With modern tapestry curtains you can either e single-color rope tie-bands or flat braids (see page 118).

Small pieces of antique tapestry can be made up into cushion vers or tablecloths, bordered with old rope or fringing. reate areas of rich, tapestried texture with piles of such shions on a plain sofa or double layers of fragments draped er a table. The subtle density of pattern in antique tapestry mands careful positioning. The pictorial and decorative detail und in most tapestry looks best offset against plain areas of bric or paint.

Modern tapestries tend to feature geometric or stylized floral tterns and are therefore more versatile than the pictorial riod types. Many of today's machine-made tapestry fabrics e softer and more flexible than the hand-woven period pestries. Modern tapestry often contains a man-made fiber ch as viscose, which reduces the fabric's cost as well as adding its versatility. However, some of these fabrics are not pecially strong or dense, and when they are stretched over an pholstered form, for example, the light-colored warp is often vealed.

Modern tapestries, which can be purchased by the meter, ill tend to imitate some of the qualities of the period ones. trength and durability, although mainly dependent on the eave structure, remains one of the required characteristics. apestry-type fabrics are therefore used extensively for pholstery, from fender stools to large, comfortable sofas.

Patterns are often geometric, resembling the style of some ilim designs (see page 66). Two complementary patterns may e used together on the same item of upholstery. For example, ie inside of an upright chair could be covered in one pattern, hile the outside back is upholstered in another, contrasting ie. The colors used should be from a coordinating or mplementary color range.

Large, antique tapestries, when not hung on walls, can be raped over tables to form a permanent display surface for ecorative objects. Partly drape one over another for textural ntrast. Subtle, somber lighting, perhaps candles, will help to nvey a moody period feel and have the added advantage of reserving the tapestry, as strong electric light and prolonged xposure to daylight will damage old textiles. Modern, heavy tapestries may also be used in this way, with edges hemmed neatly or perhaps frayed for an alternative finish.

Similarly, tapestry fabrics can be hung over chair backs. Tapestry cushions are a good way to make use of fragments of old and new tapestry. Use the fragment on the front, with a plain fabric on the back, and pile up the cushions against each other along a window seat or long sofa. Add textured braids, tassels or fringes to finish the edges of the cushions. In the right architectural setting, a concentration of heavy, dark-colored tapestry textiles used over dark oak furniture or on walls will create a strong medieval feel.

Old, pictorial tapestries and hangings can still be found at auction or in specialist shops, although in general they are expensive.

There are many contemporary tapestry designers who weave tapestries to commission. If you are looking for a tapestry to fit a particular hanging space in a room, you could commission the color combination and style of tapestry to suit the room scheme – pictorial or abstract, somber or bright.

If you are intent on hanging a tapestry, you don't have to be able to afford a large piece. A series of smaller tapestries may be hung together as long panels, against a wall. One of the advantages of this kind of woven textile, as the number of old ones still around indicates, is that they last and over time, like good paintings, they become more valuable.

Overleaf:
Machine-woven tapestry, mainly due to the softness of the yarn used to weave it, has a greater flexibility than the hand-woven sort. It can therefore be used in curtain arrangements in addition to its more traditional application, upholstery. Its weight and thickness give it valuable insulating properties which are especially effective for curtaining. Hang two curtains back to back in an archway or space dividing two rooms, but limit their fullness as the thick fabric makes soft, deep folds.

Pile

abrics in this category have a "third" dimension. When handled, their noticeably raised texture feels almost separate from the ground cloth. The texture is made up from rows of loops set on a simple ground weave. These loops may be intact, as in a terrycloth, or they can be cut, as in velvet and similar fabrics.

The pile, that is the horizontal rows of tufts, is formed by looping each warp thread over a wire which in the case of a cut pile fabric holds a cutting blade. Cut pile fabrics like velvet appear smooth, but have a fur-like texture. The direction of the pile and the way that the light hits it affects the density of color, which can change from deep and shadowed to brilliantly shimmering.

Velvet

Whether woven in cotton, wool or silk, velvet is a luxury fabric, especially if produced by one of the special processes such as Genoa, Utrecht or *gaufrage*.

Genoa velvet is patterned during the weaving process and is consequently very expensive. It has a multi-colored pile, which may be cut or uncut, set against a glossy satin ground.

Among the special velvets,

A view of the King's closet at Knole House, Kent, England. The entire room is lined with late 17th century wall-hangings which are woven in a rough mohair velvet.

are those that have a pile that is formed in a slightly different way to other velvets. With this fabric only half of the pile threads loop over each wire. As a result, the tufts are arranged alternately and therefore the foundation cloth is more uniformly covered. The fabric may be plain or it may feature an elaborate embossed design.

And *gaufrage* or Utrecht velvet has patterns branded into the surface using heated metal cylinders which have the design etched onto them.

Other pile fabrics

Corduroy, where stripes of pile alternate with stripes of ground cloth, is generally made of cotton and is mostly used for clothing rather than furnishing.

Chenille, known as poor man's velvet, is produced in two stages. It begins as a fabric woven with four or more closely set warps; this finished cloth is cut to form a new yarn. It is cut horizontally into narrow strips and the warps are twisted, leaving the severed wefts to create the pile. This tangled effect protrudes on all sides of the yarn which is then rewoven. The

An important English cut and uncut silk velvet. This fabric was woven in Spitalfields, London, circa 1714. The design features architectural and plant motifs and has been attributed to James Leman.

esult is a very sumptuous fabric often used for *portières*.

Cut pile fabrics are extremely hard-wearing, heavy cloths produced by one of two methods. With the velvet method, two fabrics, each with their own warp and weft, are woven at once, with a space between them. Warp threads interlace with picks of both fabrics and the length of pile is regulated by the distance that the fabrics are set apart. Both cloths are woven with the pile threads extending between them. A knife, traveling alongside on rollers, cuts the pile and the cut cloths are wound onto two rollers. The second method is similar to that used to make Genoa velvets, and is the method used to produce uncut moquette.

Velour is densely covered in a short, usually mercerized, cotton warp pile with a plain backing. Mercerization is a process by which fibers can be made permanently lustrous, using a mechanical process and caustic soda. Velour is used for upholstery as it is hard-wearing, yet smoother than velvet.

An Italian silk voided velvet, dating from the early 16th century.

A figured velvet used to upholster gilt chairs at Ham House, Surrey, England.

A silk and terry handwoven figured velvet, with a pattern designed by Owen Jones, dating from 1870.

Cut pile fabrics

This group of fabrics illustrates the rich variety that can be achieved with a pile surface; pile need not mean simply flat velvets.

Patterned pile

It is interesting to note how the traditional designs featured on some of these fabrics, particularly the floral and lattice ones, are interpreted when woven in pile.

Single and two-color velvets

Spotted or shaded patterns, or a plain surface, are the most versatile cloths to choose for upholstery that has to blend with patterned curtains.

Thick pile fabric

Due to the nature of a pile weave, fabrics are often quite unyielding. Their use is best confined to upholstery or drapery where the stiff bulk of the cloth is not a hindrance.

Pile floorcoverings

Until the mid-18th century, like Eastern kilims (see page 66), all Western woven floorcoverings were flat. In France Aubusson carpets were made by a tapestry process (see page 52), while in England fote-cloth was made on broadlooms with rough wools. During the 18th century a loop-pile carpet industry developed in Brussels. In 1740 the Earl of Pembroke came across this production on a tour of Europe and returned to England to set up a carpet-weaving factory at his country house at Wilton in Wiltshire.

Traditional carpets are still woven in Brussels and Wilton, with a linen ground warp and a colored pile warp. Only one row of loops appear on the surface at any one time, the others being hidden in the body of the carpet. Wilton use oval rather than round wires to give a longer pile than the Brussels weave. When cut, it produces a velvet-type carpet.

Using velvet

Velvet is not as versatile a fabric as, say, a damask. Because of the pile, it is best used flat or smoothly draped. Although velvet is traditionally used as an upholstery cloth because it is strong and fairly hard-wearing, it does have disadvantages when used on furniture. A plain velvet can look shabby in a relatively short time because the pile will flatten in areas where contact is greatest under the weight of people sitting on it. Darker colors are best for minimizing this effect; lighter ones do tend to develop a dusty appearance where the pile flattens. Figured velvets are generally less susceptible to this because the pattern disguises any crushing.

Heavy velvet has long been popular for curtaining because its densely woven structure makes it a good light-excluding material. Velvet was also extensively used as *portières* to keep out drafts. Velvets are best used in a period context as they don't mix well with modern prints or lightweight woven fabrics. However, in a period house furnished with antiques, heavy draperies spilling onto polished floorboards and set against richly colored walls look very effective.

Using other pile fabrics

Moquette is very suitable for upholstery use as it is so hard-wearing. However, because it is quite bulky it is difficult to use on small or intricately shaped items and is generally restricted to items like large seat squabs.

Like velvet, chenille is best used in a period context; keep to its original use as a *portière* or table covering.

Terrycloth and corduroy have limited furnishing use. Apart from towels, terry can be used at bathroom windows. Corduroy can be used for cushions and seat covers. Its economical nature and simple self-colored stripe give it a practical appeal for family or children's rooms.

For those who thought pile simply meant plain velvet, look again! These marvellously varied fabrics are all linked by their characteristic surface – the "raised" weave or pile.

Stamped velvets
The deep red velvet here has been gaufraged, which means that its pattern has been branded onto the surface of the velvet using heated metal cylinders. Traditionally used for upholstery, such fabrics are splendidly rich.

Strié velvets
The blue striped patterned fabric has a strié effect in the pile, which is achieved by additional colors woven together. This gives added textural quality as well as making the fabric appear slightly faded.

Kilims

What distinguishes kilims from other carpets and rugs is their flatness – they have no pile. Kilims are woven by a technique known as "slit tapestry", which is the most universal method of producing rugs. Small areas are woven with a weft thread that is not continuous, but instead turns back on itself. Blocks of color produced in this way build up to make the pattern, with small, narrow slits forming between each area. The threads meet at the edge of each woven area, but do not join. If you hold a kilim up to the light you will see these slits. Occasionally the yarns are looped and interlocked, thus losing the slits, but in most kilims this is not the case.

Kilims are usually made from cotton, sometimes from wool, and occasionally goat's hair is added to make them waterproof. They are produced in the East, by nomadic tribes in Persia (Iran), Turkey and Greece. Kilims are also produced in India; these are known as "dhurries". The narrow slits in kilims make them potentially weak and therefore they were not used as a floor-covering in the East; their original uses include wall-hangings, tent-coverings and curtains. Because kilims are double-sided and almost perfectly reversible, they make very effective curtains or bed-hangings. Narrow kilims originally made to hang on either side of a tent entrance are wonderful to use as show panels that you don't intend to draw.

Using kilims

A continuing love of everything ethnic makes the kilim a popular element in interior decoration. These versatile flat woven textiles can be hung on walls or at windows, draped over tables or used in upholstery to close-cover chairs.

The nature of the weave means that most patterns are geometric – squares, diamonds and checks. This non-figurative patterning means that kilims can be placed in many different interiors. For example, a cool, uncluttered room decorated in neutral tones will benefit from a splash of color in the form of a large floor kilim, while faded antique kilims are sympathetic to many period settings.

If a kilim is to be used underfoot, then it must be sufficiently robust for this purpose. If there are loose threads the rug is not going to last and its fragility might prove dangerous. Kilims that are too fragile to use on the floor can be hung on the wall.

The effects of prolonged exposure to bright light – whether the source is sunshine or electricity – will fade the colors of a kilim. To some, this fading will be beneficial to the appearance of the rug. Indeed, it has been said that some manufacturers deliberately leave kilims to lie on sun-soaked hillsides in order to give the effect of an older piece. But others will see it as destructive and will want to site kilims away from direct light.

Overleaf
The juxtaposition of so many kilims, from hanging panel and table throws to upholstery and floor coverings, provides a rich mixture of patterns unified by common color and tonal range. The geometric shapes in the designs are softened by the use of rich red-oranges, ochers, grays, moss greens and black. Because they are double-sided and look almost identical on each side, kilims make good room dividers across an internal archway or perhaps as a screen for a bed.

An antique Sennak kilim from North-West Persia (Iran).

A contemporary Polish kilim, with a pattern taken from an old design.

A Belouch kilim from Russia.

An antique Bessarabian kilim from Russia.

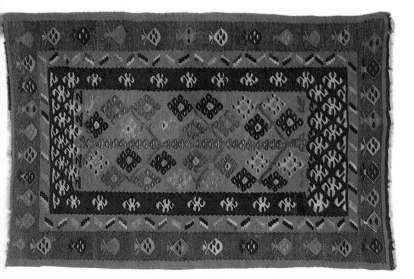

An antique kilim from the Yugoslav-Bulgarian border.

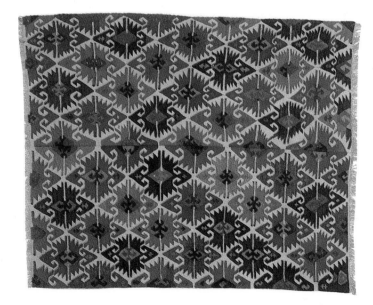

A fragment of a Turkish kilim, dating from the early 19th century.

Tribal Weaves

Woven tribal or ethnic textiles are a world apart from the other furnishing fabrics examined in this book. While there are a few textile designers whose work is influenced by ethnic fabrics, the majority of mainstream manufacturers, past and present, show little, if any, ethnic influence in their textile collections. The exchange to have a long-term impact on the development of Western textiles was the importation of painted and printed calicoes from India in the 18th century (see page 138). And this had as much to do with established trading companies as it did with inquisitive textile manufacturers.

What is a woven tribal textile?

These woven textiles are produced by peoples of the "primitive world"; tribespeople living in small communities and using traditional methods which have survived for many hundreds, even thousands, of years. Their tools and equipment are simple, like the basic back-strap loom. Sometimes weaving equipment is made by a carpenter; elsewhere, a loom may be a makeshift construction slung between a nearby tree and the weaver's body. In areas where weavers are itinerant, traveling between villages for work, lightweight, portable looms have a mechanism that enables the weaver to utilize whatever is at hand to secure the yarns. For example, large stones or dragweights are used by Yoruba weavers in Nigeria to hold the very long warp threads used to make their textiles.

The range of tribal textiles is vast – from the bold geometrics of a Navaho blanket to the fine detailing and complex weave of an African kente cloth. This section deals specifically with woven textiles; printed or applied types are dealt with on pages 180-3 and 197. However, it would be impossible to cover all the world's rich collection of tribal textiles in a few pages. What is presented here is intended to whet the appetite and stimulate personal research. Numerous sources where contemporary and antique tribal textiles can be bought are given in the suppliers directory (see pages 218-236).

Using tribal textiles

Enthusiasts tend to use these textiles *en masse* for a splendidly rich effect, but those who prefer a quieter approach display single items in special places such as above a mantelpiece, thrown over a bed or upholstering a favorite chair. If the item is valuable, you should seek expert advice on suitable mounting and lighting in order to conserve the textile safely. And if you want to clean it, consult a specialist too.

Small scraps of tribal textile can be made up into rich cushions; either cover both sides, the front alone, or, if the piece is very small, frame it with a border of plain fabric. These look especially effective if a selection of patterns, colors and styles are piled up together on a plain-covered sofa or chair.

Although tribal textiles work well with ethnic artifacts or furniture, they can also be mixed successfully with certain styles of modern or antique furniture. Bold, simple lines work best – a Shaker bed or a Le Corbusier *chaise* for example.

If you want to mix tribal textiles with other fabrics you should do so with care because although they sit happily with some designs, they won't work with many Western textiles. A geometrically patterned tribal cloth made up into a curtain could be mixed successfully with an overdrape made up in a modern black and white stripe, but would clash violently with a floral patterned chintz.

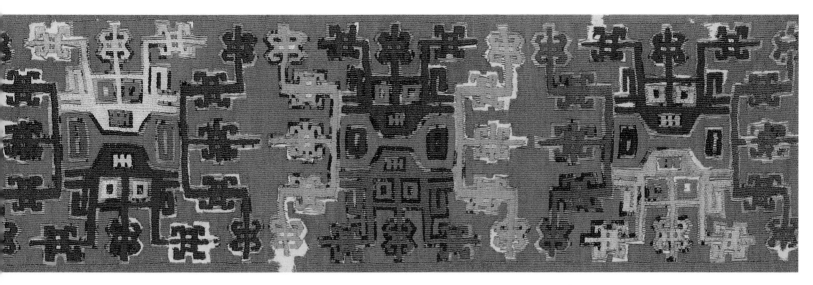

*A slit-tapestry from the Nazca culture of Peru. It dates from AD 200-600 and is
decorated with an iconograph depicting stylized trophy heads.*

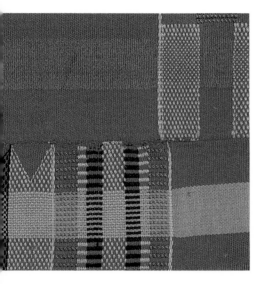

*An African kente cloth woven in silk and cotton from
the 20th century.*

*A richly colored 20th-century narrow strip silk kente
cloth originating from Ghana, West Africa.*

*A brightly colored 20th-century narrow strip silk
African kente cloth from Ghana, West Africa.*

*An Inca warp-faced abstract pattern with zoomorphic and anthropomorphic motifs,
dating from AD 1400-1500.*

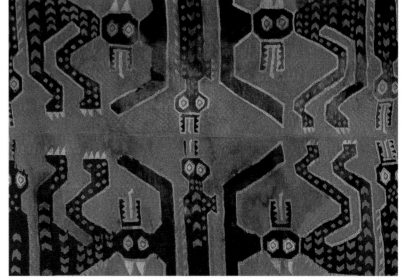

*A textile fragment from the south coast of Peru dating from the 8th-12th century. It is
part of a slit-tapestry depicting stylized felines.*

Ikat

The word ikat comes from the stem of an Indonesian word *mengikat*, which means to bind. The ikat technique is used all over the world, notably in Central America, the Ivory Coast and Indonesia. Also known as yarn-resist dyeing, ikat involves the deliberate, selective binding (or tying) of sections of the bundled yarn to a pre-determined pattern. When the yarn is subsequently dyed, the dye won't penetrate the sections where the threads are bound. The yarn preparation before dyeing, the way that the threads are bound and how the specially dyed threads are then positioned during the weaving process combine to make a beautiful and sophisticated textile, instantly recognizable by the characteristic fuzzy edges of its patterns (an appearance caused by the dye bleeding into the tied area).

Patterns are often geometric – blocks, circles and stripes – but each element is softened by the feathering of

A woven cotton "kasuri" (ikat) futon cover from Japan, 1920. There are Japanese "heraldic" motifs printed between the main ikat sections.

colors into each other, which gives a kaleidoscopic effect.

The binding and dyeing process is extremely labor-intensive and time-consuming, adding to the expense of producing the cloth and making it a luxury item.

The ikat process

Most ikats are warp ikats in which only the warp threads are dyed with designs. The textile itself is a warp-faced plain weave, where the warp ends are set so closely together that they entirely cover the weft threads. The design is then shown off to full effect. The warp threads are tied in groups following a pre-designed pattern and then dyed in bundles. Next, the threads are unbound to reveal stripes or horizontal bands where the colored dye has not taken. The threads are then re-tied in different places and the whole process repeated in a different dye bath, darker than the first. And so the process continues until all the dyeing and patterning has een achieved. Finally, the warp threads are untangled and wound onto the loom, laid in such a way as to "shift" the bands of color. This, together with the unevenness of dye strength, produces the characteristic fuzzing of the pattern.

The history of ikat

Traditionally, throughout the Far East, ikats were woven in narrow strips (because of the size of the looms available), about 18 inches (45 cm) wide, in silk or cotton yarn. The strips were sewn together and used for wall- or bed-hangings or clothing. In Indonesia, ceremonial coats, known as *chalats*, were lined with silk ikat. These *chalats* were often bestowed as gifts and worn as status symbols, draped as many as six at a time over the recipient's shoulders.

Some of the traditional ikat patterns are symbolic representations of aspects of everyday life. The tree of life, cypress trees and the pomegranate are recurring symbols. Until the advent of synthetic dyes in the late 19th century, colors were produced from plants – madder, saffron and indigo.

Ikats first came to the West over one hundred years ago, when the Dutch settled in Indonesia and were captivated by the wonderful ikats which were widely produced there. Many were exported, through established trade routes, to Holland and were used to make richly patterned bedcovers, curtains and other light furnishing items.

Using ikat

There are many contemporary ikats produced in Asia to

Left:
A 19th-century silk woven ikat "parda" (hanging) from central Asia. This textile is gloriously patterned and colored.

Right:
A 19th-century woven silk weft ikat "selandang" (shoulder wrap) from Sumatra.

*A selection of contemporary ikats in silk and cotton.
A silk yarn gives an ikat pattern a closer, flatter
appearance than a cotton. The heavy cotton cloths more
closely resemble the traditional ethnic fabrics.
However, the patterns of the cloths shown here are less
detailed than the Central Asian originals (see page 73),
although they are produced by the same dyeing method.
The silk versions are suitable for curtains, bed-hangings
and upholstery in situations where there would be only
light use. The cotton ones, although thick, tend to stretch
and therefore are not suitable for use on close covers.*

Overleaf:
*With some fabric types it would not be successful to mix
old with new – the play of one against the other would
be unsettling. But these modern versions of traditional
woven patterns mingle happily with older, original
cloths. By starting with a blue-and-white theme, it is
possible to introduce concentrated areas of vivid,
contrasting color such as the embroidered cushions on
the bed or the decorative wall-hangings.*

*An Indonesian woven ikat with mirror images of birds and animals – a traditional
patterning device in many ikat cloths, especially those with a figurative, rather than a
geometric pattern.*

European designs, all of which can be used in the most elegant of settings. The cheaper Indian cotton ikats, if selected in colorways like indigo and cream, will mix well with more sophisticated furnishing fabrics.

Narrow ikats can be hung like banners at windows. They should be almost flat, with few gathers, and suspended from wide arrowed "tabs" that loop over a curtain pole. Paint the pole and finials in one of the ikat's colors for a rich, dramatic effect.

Ikats make beautiful bed-hangings and covers because the pattern can be displayed flat, and so won't lose any of its effect.

Antique ikats can be used as soft furnishings if they are lined with a supportive backing cloth.

Of the fine antique ikats available, many are woven in silk or fine cotton yarn. This makes ikat textiles extremely light and perfectly suited to use for flowing curtains or draperies.

However, the brilliance of the dyestuffs is not always long lasting. Therefore these cloths must be lined well if they are t be hung at windows or in a position where light may adversel affect them. Many of the patterns demand to be seen flat and s using them as "panel" curtains or simple pull-down shades no only suits the design, but is also an effective way to display highly decorative textile. Woven ikats also make wonderful ric bedspreads, and because they are flat the pattern is displayed t full advantage.

Traditional woven ikats may be hung on walls as decorativ panels. Bear in mind that their coloring is often very brigh and can be rather dominant, so consider the positioning of thes cloths with care, maybe making your ikat textile a centr feature with other decorative elements in the room taking thei lead from its pattern or color.

Madras

Originating in Madras, India, the term "madras" was first used to describe a black-and-red check cotton fabric woven for clothing. Today, the term is used loosely to cover a wide range of inexpensive, lightweight plain and sateen weave cottons made in India.

Like the African kente cloths (see page 71), madras cottons are sometimes woven with rayon or other synthetic fiber, mixed with cotton. Some of the checked cloths that are loosely referred to as "madras" contain silk, again woven with cotton.

The coloring of these cloths ranges from pale pastel to vibrant and unusual strong colors. Neither are particularly light-fast, and are therefore prone to fading. The vegetable colors also have a tendency to lose dye if washed in a machine. It is therefore best to send them to a dry-cleaner or hand-wash them in cool water with a mild detergent.

Using madras

Madras cotton checked fabric is inexpensive and cheerful, and although there are disadvantages that must be borne in mind, it has some worthwhile furnishing uses.

Madras cottons are very thin. This has advantages and disadvantages when making soft furnishings. It is best to use interlining for most items, especially draperies, unless a fine,

flimsy effect is desired. If it is, the fabric can be hung unlined but bear in mind that the light will adversely affect the dye, and possibly the fabric itself, eventually. The thinness of the fabric does mean that it can be easily gathered up into fine little pleats or bunched (see opposite). The checked patterning looks as effective bunched or pleated as it does flat, draped over a table as a cloth for example.

Madras checks are very difficult to pattern-match. Because they are woven without much adherence to strict pattern repeat you may find that there are "extra" stripes in a row that should only have three, or that the dimension of the check varies as the pattern repeats, making it difficult to match the pattern at seams. You should therefore avoid using it in situations where a perfect match would be important.

Different-colored madras checks can be mixed together pile lots of colorful cushions onto a sofa that is either covered in an undyed, neutral canvas fabric or one of the main colors taken from the checks. Quantities of fabric can be swagged up over a pole, looped and held in place with bright, wide ribbon in a toning color. For small curtains, trim the leading edge with a multi-colored fringe or braid that mixes well with the colors of the cloth.

The thinness of the cotton used to weave madras-checked cloth permits a profusion of folds and swags – for example, entwined around a brightly painted pole. Drape more rather than less, and add heavy rope ties for textural interest and definition. Madras cottons are not especially color-fast, so a setting that is well away from strong light, such as this bed arrangement, is ideal.
This inexpensive cloth takes on a rich exuberance when used in abundance. In a pile of small cushions, contrasted patterns and clashing colors are exciting. Using a different madras fabric for piping or bands of edging highlights this contrast.

Tartan

Although tartan is firmly interwoven with Scottish history, the word itself is not Gaelic in origin, and may have come from the conquering Romans. Despite the fact that tartan cloth is now frequently used as a furnishing fabric, its origins were as an apparel textile. Tartan's alternative name, plaid, refers to a kilt-length piece of cloth. The clan tartan system was a type of uniform that allowed people's origin and status to be identified from their clothes. Most of the clans had four tartans, the chief tartan for the clan chief and close family, the clan tartan for other clan members, the dress tartan for formal wear, and the hunting tartan.

To be authentic, tartan must be woven on a twill threading. The set – the number and order of the colors used that together make up the pattern – must follow closely that considered correct by the clan, and there must be the same number of threads per inch/centimeter in both warp and weft. Apparently, the early sets were not recorded, but were memorized by generations of the men and women who dyed, spun and wove the material. Practically all tartan sets can be broken into two blocks: one showing a large area of single color, banded on both sides by a second color, and the second showing more colors, fine lines and squares. Outside Scotland, few commercial firms are careful about the set of tartans, which explains why there can be such a wide variety in the patterning of one tartan.

Until the advent of synthetic dyes, all yarns used for tartan were dyed with vegetable dyes indigenous to the locality – alder bark, rock lichens and blueberries, for example. The advent of aniline dyes coincided with the Victorian passion for tartan, and the first in a long line of riotously colored tartans were produced. Red, azure, dark blue, deep bottle green, black and white are traditional colors, but today cerise, mustard, orange and other violent hues can be found.

Tartan is a plain weave twill fabric, with the stripes of colored yarn introduced in both the warp and the weft. The effect of this is that if only two colors are used – yellow and blue for example – alternately in stripes of even and equal width, the finished cloth will be checked in three colors – yellow, blue and green in this example. The result is hard wearing, especially when woven in the traditional wool. Woolen yarn was used for water resistance as tartan kilts were unwrapped from the wearers and used as blankets at nighttime, particularly on the battlefield. The descendant of this Scottish tradition is the highly durable tartan checked woolen travel rug.

Using tartan

Whether woven in wool, as originally, or from cotton or silk, tartan is a versatile cloth that can be somber or bright, formal or fun. In a soft silk, it can b

A detail of an antique tartan fabric, woven in a woolen yarn. The set (the pattern) belongs to the Grant clan.

...gloriously rich mixture of
...aditional tartan patterns and
...ntemporary plaids inspired by them.

...he effect of fiber

...e shimmering, beautiful silk plaids
...ve an elegance and sophistication
...hich immediately adds a touch of
...xury; in a well-lit interior, the fabric
...rface will appear lustrous and jewel-
...e. In contrast, the matte woolens
...sorb light, thus darkening their
...mber greens, blues and blacks.

...e effect of pattern

...e two-color tartans have a flat
...aphic quality which makes them a
...od choice for walling. The use of a
...hite line, present in several of these
...rtans, breaks up the darker areas into
...over-laid grid which defines the
...rtan pattern.

successfully used as window draperies, while in a tough wool it is effective as an upholstery fabric. Mixing several different tartans together can create a lively effect, as shown in the photograph on this page. And tartan also harmonizes well with a range of other fabrics, especially plain weaves, simple stripes or small-motifed designs.

Tartan cloth has the advantage of being a rich fabric at the same time as displaying simple, linear patterns. This dual quality can be exploited in the application of tartan to entire wall (or floor) surfaces. The richness of the cloth lends texture, warmth and a feeling of luxury. And because the simple plaid pattern is not distracting, it can provide an excellent backdrop for other tartans or patterns.

Tartan cloth can be used for upholstery, as long as it is in a dark colorway, and it makes a wonderful backcloth to vividly patterned cushions. If you want to use one of the traditional sets in authentic colors, choose plain, squareish furniture to offset the pattern. If using a modern tartan in an unusually vibrant color, perhaps woven in silk, select the type and style of furniture carefully, and take into account the fineness of the silk.

Consider using tartan cloth as a sharp contrast to plain, light fabrics. For example, in the lining of tails (in swags and tails) or as borders on a Roman shade. For these applications it is better to use a thinner fabric, such as a cotton, rather than the thicker woolen cloths.

Tartan can be used to stunning effect in formal swags and draperies. A rich, heavy, somber cloth can be used in many period-style schemes, set against mellow wooden paneled, stone or beamed walls.

Long associated with warmth and comfort, tartan cloth will lend these characteristics to any room setting. A whole room furnished with tartan, from walling cloth through curtains to scatter cushions, looks splendidly rich. Mix traditional woolen cloths with shiny tartans woven in silk; the contrast between matte and luster surfaces is intriguing. Different tartan patterns, too, mix well.

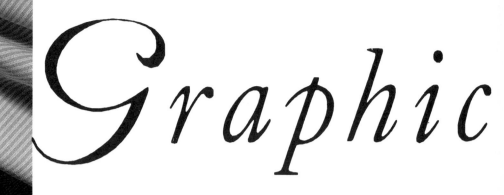

Graphic and Linear

*T*hese woven textiles are linked by an easily recognizable pattern set on a plain background. The pattern may be simple or sophisticated, striped or checked. Motifs – small patterns placed geometrically or haphazardly on a background devoid of any other pattern – also fall into this category. The repetition of small motifs, whether dots, squares, or lines, over a large woven area creates an overall geometric pattern that is a striking contrast to figurative patterns like the damask scrolls shown in the previous chapter.

Although the fibers used in these fabrics range from cotton through to silk, with some of them, such as ticking, the characteristics of one fiber, cotton, is essential to the cloth's clean, crisp appearance. The straightforward way that cotton is spun and woven gives a clear definition to the pattern which is

Traditionally, these are the basic cloths: the "in-fills" used in interior situations to break up larger areas of pattern or color. Practical, strong fabrics, their surface texture and pattern is often confined to subtle changes in weave structure (lower left corner) or combinations of two or three colors in close tones (middle bottom and all stripes across top). All the fabrics shown here are woven in cotton yarn and are best suited to upholstery use, being a little too heavy for curtains (although they would make excellent, formal draperies).

Geometric motif
A small motif woven in a tough cotton. This fabric, by the way it is woven, is reversible.

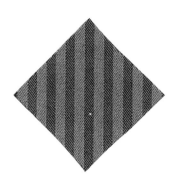

Herringbone weave
A very useful and elegant cloth, suitable for curtains or upholstery.

Large herringbone
A "magnified" version of the herringbone weave, wov in two shades.

Fine stripes
A lightweight cotton cloth is an ideal match for a fine stripe.

Formal pattern
*An tough, strong cloth that is excellent for upholstery. Its pattern can also be reversed.
(This is the reverse side.)*

Leaf motif
Small leaves set in a striped formation. The "shading around the motif gives additional texture.

Zig-zag
Strong and graphic, this zig-zag pattern is woven in a heavyweight cotton.

Jacquard pattern
A lattice work pattern in a jacquard weave. It produces a strong, closely woven cloth.

essential to the appearance of the fabric. The effect is almost like drawing with thread; the patterns created by the stripes or geometrics are easily read.

Geometric ornament has a long history, dating back to the earliest civilizations. Egyptian and Greek ornament contain many geometric forms such as the key pattern. And some of the earliest, most complex geometric designs, such as grids of triangles that form hexagons, are found in ancient Rome. Islamic geometrical forms have also had a profound influence over European design, through architecture and the decorative arts to textiles.

The appeal and magic of some textiles is revealed as soon a you see or handle a piece. The fabrics in this category howeve are only fully appreciated when seen in use in particula situations. For example, small, repeating patterns look goo enhancing modest areas, such as a chair seat. But a miniatur pattern doesn't have to be used on a small item. Large areas wall or a complete interior could be covered with one of thes geometrics without the pattern being entirely lost, nor wou the fabric dominate the room space. The patterns could b treated like a wallpaper in a furnishing situation, but with th added benefit of the special qualities of a woven textile.

Stripes and Checks

Stripes and checks are often thought of as patterns that decorate utilitarian items – mattresses, deckchairs and so on. These cloths are often woven in inexpensive cotton for economy reasons. They have a variety of traditional uses in domestic utility situations – bedding, tablecloths, loose covers over dining seats. Although those utilitarian cloths form an important part of this section, it also takes in the more sophisticated stripes and checks that would not look out of place in a smart town house.

Ginghams

In the early 1800s many of the utilitarian cottons that were imported from India, were termed ginghams, whether they were checked, plaid or striped. A true gingham, however, has equal width stripes in both directions of the weave, and is only woven from two colors, with the threads set up in such a way that a third color is formed where the two colors meet. The original vegetable-dyed colors – deep indigo blue, reds and greens – have remained the most popular today, though most are now produced with chemical dyes.

Using ginghams

Gingham's country checks are traditionally used for kitchen curtains or tablecloths or for simple bedroom furnishings. Traditional blue and white gingham was often used to make slip-covers for rather grand or formal chairs to protect their upholstery when they were not in use. This idea can be carried into a more contemporary treatment by using the slip-cover as a furnishing idea in its own right. Choose larger checks – many ginghams now are woven in all sizes of check – in bold, bright colors or the more restrained traditional ones. Use plain bands

of piping to define the chair's shape or fasten with small flat bows in a contrasting gingham.

For a dramatic and strongly graphic arrangement, use monochromatic ginghams in bold colors – mixing red and white with black and white for example. Combine the two fabrics in drapery and formal swag arrangements, with one bordering the other or used as contrast linings for tails. Surprisingly, these traditionally humble cloths can be vibrant, striking and quite sophisticated. Mix small and large checks together, in cushions or shades. Use the smaller ones as narrow borders to define a Roman shades whose main fabric is a larger gingham check. Pipe loose-covers or lightweight upholstery in a similar combination.

Gingham is a fairly thin cotton fabric – and so for most curtain use it should be lined and interlined. Plain curtains can be lined with a contrast gingham check.

Tickings

Ticking is now established as a classic furnishing fabric, and is more adaptable for interior use than gingham. Originally, it was handwoven in linen as a covering for feather mattresses. Its characteristic herringbone weave was intended to keep the feathers in and the ticks out.

Using ticking

Today, ticking is often used for curtains and upholstery. Its stripes will give texture to a neutral modern interior, while it can take on a formal look if used, for example, on a polished wood chaise. Another former use of ticking was as a lining fabric, inside suitcases or suits. Nowadays it can be used as a lining for a dramatically patterned curtain fabric or as the

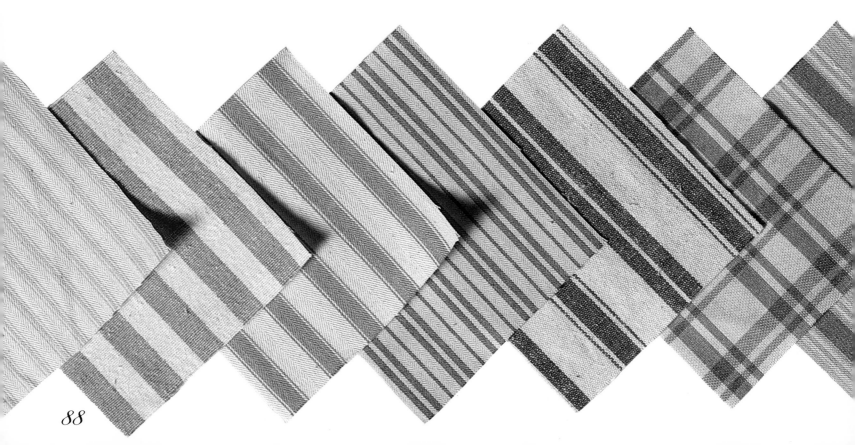

Top row; right to left:
Gingham-inspired, but not a true gingham, this check has a country freshness. A heavy cotton stripe in blue and coffee is a variation on the more usual blue and white. The classic blue-and-white ticking pattern is in a soft cotton weave. Consider the fresh look of simple green and white stripes and checks; the stripe is in a crisp cotton, while the check is in viscose. Stripes of different widths can be effective, as in these green-on-cream examples and blue-on-cream examples. Multicolor checks or stripes can still seem utilitarian if natural colors like these olives and yellows are used. The fine yellow stripe is an alternative colorway to the green stripe fourth from the left, while the broad green stripe is a variant on the blue stripe second from the left. The final fabric is a classic ticking in a fine stripe.

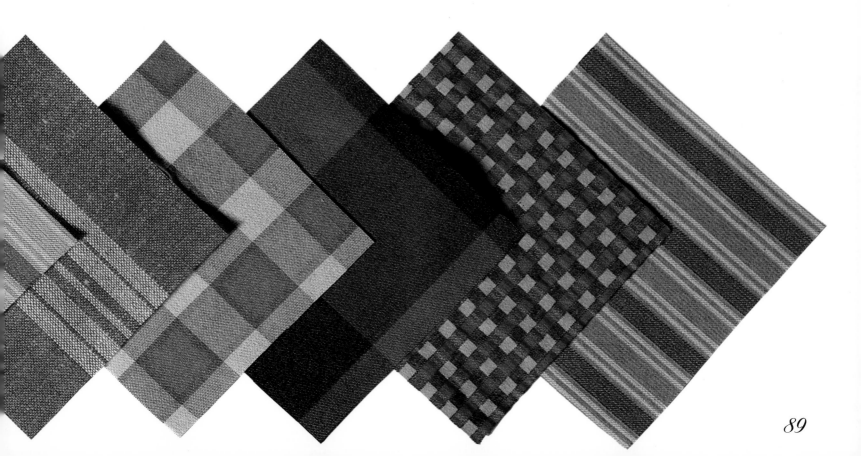

Bottom row; right to left:
This multicolor stripe is reminiscent of deckchair fabric. A tricolor variant on gingham, this cloth is woven with a slight dimpled texture. Next to it is a simple gingham check, but woven in giant squares for a different effect. Blue, cream and red checks woven in a soft viscose contrast with the texture provided by the heavy linen yarn used for the natural-colored stripes. Deckchair stripes – but in soft colors and a soft cotton rather than primaries on a canvas cloth. An overlay of checks in two sizes is kept simple by using natural cream and brown. Two widths of stripe in a heavy, rough cotton are followed by a ticking-inspired stripe in cream and claret. A plain weave stripe is sandwiched between two genuine tickings with the classic herringbone weave.

underside of elaborate draperies designed for four-poster beds.

The strong stripes of ticking cloth are well suited to the simple linear structure of a Roman shade. The starchy stiffness of the traditional mattress tickings – not so much those of a softer cotton weave – make up excellently into the neat structure of these shades. Insert borders of plain color or cut strips of ticking on the diagonal and use them as contrast edgings. Both these treatments will give an interesting optical effect to an arrangement that is essentially flat.

Ticking is quite heavy, so when using several widths – in full drapery for example – you should make sure that a suitably strong pole or track is adequately fixed to the wall. It should also be noted that most tickings are *not* pre-shrunk and the element of shrinkage can be quite considerable. Either wash the cloth before making it up or always dry-clean the finished item.

Dish towel fabric

Recently, the bright blue or red stripes or checks of dish towels have followed ticking into the best-dressed houses as window curtains or upholstery. Originally called glasscloths, some have the word woven into the textile in bold lettering along a broad central stripe. Dish towel fabric is woven in cotton or linen or a mixture of both. Despite the fact that it is woven in fairly narrow widths, these can easily be sewn together to produce wider fabrics for curtains or tablecloths.

Using dish towel fabric

Although a sophisticated look may seem at odds with its humble origin, dish towel's strong, crisp texture gives it a smart appearance, so it need not be dressed down or confined to kitchens. It looks especially good combined with colorwashed or aged painted furniture. Be imaginative with treatments; mix a larger check with a border of smaller, or vice versa, or pipe tie-backs with a contrasting check.

Dish towel fabrics can look smart and elegant next to a mass of floral chintz where the colors of each are complementary. Hang curtains instead of wardrobe doors – in narrow alcoves, for example. Or use the fabric to line and curtain an entire dressing room next to a bedroom decorated mainly with traditional floral fabrics.

The cool sophistication of these glasscloths is due largely to the heavy cotton or linen yarn used to weave them, and their monochrome coloring. A single panel can be hung over a narrow rod within a window recess. The panels may need to be

Dependable cloths – mostly stripes – in earthy browns, creams and grays can be brought together in a neutral interior or used to break up a more colorful palette. The creamy canvas-type fabric with a woven black line is soft and drapes well, its weight adding body to an arrangement. The tickings are woven with a beige ground, rather than the traditional white, and use a softer cotton yarn. All are strong enough to be used for upholstery, although their soft, matte surface does tend to attract dirt.

joined as most of these cloths are not very broad – some are only 18 inches (46 cm) in width.

One point to bear in mind when using genuine utility fabrics like dish toweling or ticking is that they are not pre-shrunk, so you must either wash them before making them up or incorporate a generous allowance for shrinkage.

Utilitarian-influenced stripes

Many straightforward stripes which feature clean lines of color against plain white or cream are influenced by utilitarian fabrics such as ticking, shirting or deckchair canvas. Like the originals, they are woven in cotton or linen, but unlike their utilitarian counterparts they have the advantage of being pre-shrunk, which makes fabric estimation easier.

Using utilitarian-influenced stripes

Strong and linear, these stripes look good for flat window shades – Roman or roller – and would work well as an upholstery fabric for traditional or modern chairs. Surprisingly, many of these cloths are less sophisticated than those already discussed. Many of them are woven in softer yarns, some in poorer quality cotton and in less vibrant colors, and all of this somehow reduces the formality. They can, however, be excellent choices as main drapery or upholstery fabrics in a room where elsewhere there is a considerable collection of ethnic textiles. The softer colors – terracottas, ochers, olive- and bottle-greens – work well as they neither dominate a room nor set up a striking theme from which all else should follow.

Many of these fabrics, like their utility counterparts, are inexpensive and can be used as "filling in" fabrics in places that are not the main areas of the house, such as stair windows, kitchen windows or spare rooms. They can be used on light upholstery, to cover or line an old trunk or chest and they are a practical choice for simple bed-covers.

Simple, two-color checks provide strong texture and pattern against the subtle surfaces of colorwashed plaster and old, peeling wood. Ginghams call for an understated curtain arrangement. Here, straight tabs of one checked cloth loop around a bamboo pole to hold the darker, denser main fabric in place, while the simple tie-back is practical and totally unfussy.

A crisp, cool interior decorated with stripes of the subtlest mint green and bright scarlet. The walls are striped with regimented rows of mattress ticking strips, held only from the top so that the merest breeze creates shifting flicks of shadow and light. This ribbon effect could be prepared on a temporary basis – to decorate a garden room for a special occasion, for example. For a more permanent arrangement, the strips could be stuck firmly to the wall using a suitable fabric adhesive. The starchy stiffness of ticking resists fraying, so strips can be unhemmed. Hardwearing cotton stripes are used for the seat cushions and the window shade. The gently rippling fabric scooped across the ceiling is a useful device for concealing a poor or unattractive ceiling finish. It can also be used to shade a glass roofed dining room, in a conservatory perhaps, from direct midday sun.

Sophisticated stripes

These designs are a more formal, decorative step-up from straightforward "utility" stripes. The change is partly due to the different fibers used. A ticking stripe woven in silk is bound to become sophisticated entirely because of the switch from basic cotton to much more luxurious silk. A stripe of the same simplicity will also be transformed if woven in wool. The textile will be heavier, which in turn makes it richer. And the distinction between stripe and ground will not be so clear because the yarn is thicker and gives more texture.

Another element which can transform a stripe from a basic to a higher plane is the introduction of other weave detail. For example, combining a stripe with a floral motif gives the cloth more decoration. And breaking the stripe with a small diamond will enhance the surface texture and pattern the cloth still further. This will make the textile richer and more luxurious.

Many sophisticated stripes are multi-stripe. In contrast to ticking stripes, which repeat the same stripe pattern across the cloth, they combine different widths, different weave structures to form a more complex cloth. Simply because of its weave structure, a damask or brocade stripe will have more sophistication than a plain canvas deckchair one.

Multi-colors, too, are used to add immediate sophistication, making the textile richer and more detailed. A black and white pinstripe may be dramatic, but a multi-color stripe has greater subtlety, especially if careful blending of shades and tones are used to produce complex intersections of pattern.

Using sophisticated stripes

Sophisticated stripes are often used in a formal manner, in swags for example. This tradition dates back to their popularity in early 19th century French interiors, a fashion which was thought to have been inspired by the striped bunting hung on buildings to celebrate Napoleon's victory. Use sophisticated stripes for elaborately swagged drapery, bed curtains or as close covers for Louis-style chairs if you want to recreate this other classic French style.

Striped cloths can be some of the most satisfying to use in an interior – in almost any situation. Stripes can have a particular interior design function, if used with care. For example, used vertically, they will give a room height. And if they are used horizontally they will widen a narrow window or room. However, you should be careful not to over-accentuate poor architectural features such as windows that are already too tall and narrow. Furniture too can benefit from the optical illusions a stripe can provide. Broad stripes, especially if colors are in the same tonal range, will diminish the apparent size of an over-large sofa. And narrow, contrasting stripes will highlight a finely detailed chair.

The more detailed and complex the weave structure, the greater the sophistication of the fabric. Because the vibrant checked fabrics are so varied, so too are their potential uses.

The effect of yarn

The fiber content of these fabrics will, to an extent, dictate their use. For example, one of the luxurious shot silk checked fabrics could be used for elegant (but expensive!) curtains and swags or to upholster a small, ornate chair or sofa which is simply intended for decorative use. However, for a piece of furniture that is subject to everyday use a tougher fabric is required. The addition of viscose to cotton yarn adds strength and luster, as in the fabric shown near left in the top row, and gives it more scope for use in situations where the fabric would undergo stress.

The effect of color

Vivid or unusual colorways, like turquoise and lime green or hot pink and bright yellow, are important in distinguishing a sophisticated check from its utilitarian counterpart.

*uxurious fibers, colors and weave
tail turn simple stripes into
phisticated ones.*

he effect of yarn
*corded yarn effect, where a thicker
rand of yarn runs through the fabric at
tervals, used on a stripe will
mphasize it and add texture. The
mbination of different weights of yarn
so adds interest, but can restrict the
ay in which the fabric is used.
The ground-breaking effect of a
oiré finish woven in a fine silk will
ften a stripe's usual crispness. Such a
bric is excellent for swags as the
adow and highlights created by the
lds will bring out the shimmering
oiré effect, while pleats will
mphasize the striped design.*

he effect of color
*ues can contrast – dazzling purple,
aret and green, for example – or else
subtle shades of the same color, like
ft blues.*

he effect of weave
*special weave like the ottoman will
mphasize a stripe's linear direction or
btly undercut it, depending on whether
e ottoman rib follows or dissects the
ripe. The weave structure of an
toman makes it a strong fabric for
pholstery. However, with a striped
ersion you will need to allow enough
bric for pattern matching.*

Sophisticated checks

There are two main characteristics that distinguish a checked or plaid fabric in this group from one in the gingham family, for example. The first is to do with the type of yarn used, which may give the textile a sheen or luster, and the second stems from the layout of the checked pattern – a complicated check or plaid will look more sophisticated than a plain dish towel-type check.

The weave does not have to be complicated, though; the choice of color will also, inevitably, have an effect one way or the other. For example, if a fabric is woven to the pattern of a gingham check in black and cream, but instead of cotton, silk is used, the resulting cloth will be infinitely more elegant, precious and expensive than its equivalent in cotton yarn.

Contemporary checks have moved on from gingham's earth and pastel shades to hot pinks, sharp yellow and acid greens. The scale has changed too; small checks have been joined by bold 2 inch (5 cm) squares which sit more happily on larger items like chunky sofas. When using a check or stripe for upholstery avoid styles of furniture which demand deep buttoning or heavy gathering as these will distort the pattern.

The number of colors used will add to the cloth's sophistication too, if jewel-bright shades are chosen. Some of the complicated silk plaids shown here incorporate several different colors in the weave structure; where they cross over, an additional vivid color is made. Very detailed and complex weave layouts also give wonderful richness to both sides of the cloth and make the textile feel luxurious. However, even simple changes of direction in the weave can give rise to an interestingly sophisticated surface.

Using sophisticated checks

A glorious sophisticated check will make much more of an impact seen flat, for example stretched across the seat of a day-bed or chaise, than hung, gathered in curtains or drapery. Strong checkerboard reds, blues and creams in a richly textured slubby silk would look marvellous on a Louis XV-style gilt chair. Across a bed, a wonderful rich patchwork of checks in colors that either tone or clash violently can be a marvellous way of displaying these patterns in their full glory.

It is not essential to use them flat, however. Loosely draped informal swags hung from a pole and intertwined with ornate tassels and ropes can be an effective use for these sophisticated checks. Graphic, monochrome plaids are wonderfully dramatic, especially set against plain, strong wall colors. While bundles of cushions heaped around a bay window seat are another way to display the rich variety of these cloths to full effect. Use different checks on the front and back of each cushion or combine pieces of them – cut on the diagonal perhaps – as inset borders, or piping.

stripes and checks

A single full curtain, caught back into a full drape with a heavy antique rope tie, displays the entire design of this magnificent striped fabric. Its detailed patterning, based in some parts on the paisley motif (see page 162), is combined with simple geometrics to form subtle, vertical striping. For contrast, a double swag in a much finer striping is used over the pole. The two fabric types are vastly different, yet they sit happily together, linked by color and tone. The subtle luster of the elegant moiré finish stripe used on the chairs suits the polished chrome frames and links with the metallic shine of the other decorative elements.

Woven Motifs

For a pattern to be identified as a motif it must be an isolated form, set apart against a plain ground. The motif, usually abstracted from a recognizable shape such as a natural form (for example, a leaf), will repeat up and across a length of woven cloth.

This section deals with motifs that are worked into the design at the weaving stage, in other words they are formed as the cloth is being produced. Of course, motifs can also be printed or painted onto a cloth – there is a section in the printed chapter which examines such fabrics (see pages 154-167). In addition, motifs can be added to a woven cloth in the form of embroidery (see pages 197-203).

A woven motif is formed either by varying the structure of the weave (see pages 8-9) or by changing the color of the yarn. More usually, it is a change in the weave structure that distinguishes a motif from the ground weave.

Floral damask fabrics contain woven motifs, but they are usually large and form part of a design that is read as an overall pattern. The individual elements of a damask design – for example, a pomegranate or stylized flower – are motifs, but as they touch or intertwine through other elements of the pattern they do not have the same effect as a conventional motif such as a small repeating diamond or spot would.

Unless a distinct color change is employed, woven motifs are less obvious than their printed counterparts. Some simple geometric motifs blend with the cloth as they are woven in the same texture and color, with only a variation in weave direction distinguishing them from the ground, while others stand out because they are woven in a different yarn and/or color.

Motifs are abundant in ethnic textiles (see pages 70-77 and pages 180-183). Beliefs and religions have always been an influential force in the decoration of textiles, and representation of gods, mythical creatures and fertility symbols, as well as more complex codes, can be found in many woven (and printed) ethnic motifs. These images are frequently incorporated as geometric forms, with amazing similarities in design between different cultures.

Among cultures with no written language, for example the pre-Columbian peoples of Peru and Bolivia, symbolism was used as a form of communication. A mix of old and new, pagan and Christian symbols and motifs were adapted as conquering civilizations brought influences into an existing language.

A fine collection of motifs has been developed within Islamic cultures. As well as geometric designs, the flat weaves of Central Asia and Asia Minor, Peru and North Africa show an abundance of floral motifs. These are either realistically portrayed or highly stylized. In a climate where spring is often short, dry and dusty, real flowers have a limited growing life and therefore it was thought to be important to capture their beauty in textiles.

The "tree of life" symbol which appears throughout Islamic cultures and has been adapted in European textiles, notably through the importation of Indian chintzes and other Eastern textiles, can be read, at its most basic, to be a model for the axis of the world. Although it is a more extensive pattern than most motifs, because it is so stylized, it is nevertheless a motif. However, because of its size it is not as versatile as a smaller less elaborate motif.

The effect of weave structure

Along with the variation in yarn – most of the fabrics shown here and overleaf are cotton or mixes of cotton with a synthetic fiber – it is essentially the structure of the weave that determines the clarity of the motif. A coarser yarn combined with a loose weave will tend to blur the motif. The weave will also vary the texture, so that some cloths are smooth, while others are much coarser. Where there is a particularly fine motif – the fleur de lys, for example (see bottom row left) – it is important to use the fabric in a situation where it can be shown to full effect – upholstery is an obvious choice, as are flat, panel cushions.

The effect of a light or dark background

A pattern with a light-colored background is unusual, although some examples are shown here, in that a woven motif is more usually woven light against dark. This is because the lighter version has the disadvantage of attracting dirt. Therefore if you want to use it for upholstery you should take into account the frequency of use the particular item will be put to before you purchase such a fabric.

Using woven motifs

Fabrics with woven motifs are a very useful means of definin[g]
shape. For example, a simple, small-scale repeating patter[n]
such as a diamond trellis with a central dot, or a small leaf [or]
berry, can be used in a great expanse across a large, imposin[g]
sofa. The shape of the sofa is not lost to the pattern, but th[e]
sheer size of the piece is contained by the "textured" effect tha[t]
the small-scale motif achieves when used in this way. An[d]
subtle-colored woven motifed fabrics are practical choices fo[r]
upholstery or chair coverings because their texture tends [to]
conceal dirt and general wear and tear rather better than th[e]
surface of a completely flat cloth does.

Small motifs will successfully break up any large areas, henc[e]
their perennial use on floor carpets, and their patterns have th[e]
further advantage that they do not distract from any large[r]
more rambling patterns, such as a floral chintz, used in othe[r]
areas of a room, for example at the window. Indeed, a small[er]
motifed fabric can be chosen to harmonize with other textiles [or]
patterns in the rest of the room. Some manufacturers produc[e]
small motifed coordinates for their floral or other patterns.

Motifed fabrics can even be physically combined with cloth[s]
woven in other patterns, or plain cloths. Bands of a motife[d]
design can be cut and inserted into the plain or patterned fabri[c]
as borders. Be careful to combine fabrics of similar weights an[d]
yarn content. Diagonally repeating patterns are better for th[is]
purpose than those that repeat on a basic grid pattern.

When choosing a motifed fabric, color is an importan[t]
factor to consider as it can greatly affect the impact that a fabri[c]
in this category may have. Some color combinations do n[ot]
work with all-over small motifs and should therefore b[e]
avoided. For example, when read from a distance a red motif o[n]
a green ground tends to be seen as brown because the color[s]
blend together and their effect is lost. With other suc[h]
combinations the density of tone actually causes a "buzzing" o[f]
the motif against the background, an effect which can pla[y]
havoc with the eyes.

*A collection of traditional motifs in heavy woven cloths, chosen because their textur[e]
complements the rough surfaces of the furniture and wall. The fabrics are similar i[n]
weight and texture and have small motifs which are sympathetic in style. The
collection of earth colors work with each other as a unified group, toning also with
the surrounding surfaces of wall, furniture and flooring. This group of fabrics can b[e]
an isolated group or one of the pieces may be picked up elsewhere in a room, for
example taken as a border for a neutral curtain.*

Translucent

ranslucent fabrics are those which are woven with an open weave that allows light to penetrate the cloth. All fabrics which are either sheer or semi-sheer fall into this category. Muslin, for example, is plain-woven in a finely spun cotton yarn, sometimes silk, which gives a soft, fine open cloth. Lace, too, is an open-weave fabric, worked by hand or machine. This quality is exploited in all kinds of net curtaining, sheers and so-called vision-nets. When hung at a window, they allow light through, at the same time diffusing the view to the outside, beyond the glass. When looked through from the outside, these cloths conceal the view from within.

These muslins, organdys, lace and similar translucent cloths, are generally hung as a single shade or curtain on their own or behind a main set of draperies. By their nature they do not require any form of lining. However, some of the most open lace patterns can be lined, for example in a shade, with a subtle color, so that the light diffuses through both layers and casts a gentle colored glow into the room.

Although these cloths are plain, they can be ornamented with cords, crammed stripes, spots and other designs. Mostly these decorative additions are woven. Swiss muslin, however, has spotted effects which are produced by embroidering the cloth after it is woven. Printed designs, spots or figurative patterns can also be applied onto the muslin.

These lightweight muslins and organdys and some less-patterned lace should be used with substantial fullness when hung as curtains. However lace fabrics, especially the highly decorative Victorian panel lace, can be hung almost flat, as originally would have been intended.

These translucent or semi-translucent fabrics can be used on their own for a light, soft effect – a long panel, for example, trailing to the ground from a simple window pole or entwined around four bed poles in frothy swags. If the fabric is to be used as a curtain on its own choose a type with a subtle texture – top left, small flowers on lace net, top right, inset stripes – to give more substance. Other translucent fabrics can be used as curtains or shades hung behind main draperies made up in a heavier, more solid fabric. Traditional patterns such as the figurative design (lower left) should be used with similar main fabrics. Use the sheer, sharp white cloths with more modern, perhaps geometric, patterns. Lace fabrics take on a different look if a colored lining in cotton sateen is stitched behind the fabric to give a subtle diffused color.

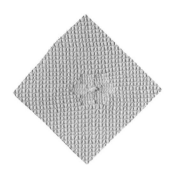

Machine-woven net, woven in cotton, with stylized flower motif. This is a traditional design for net curtaining.

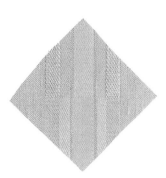

A modern striped design, incorporating several different weave structures that give opaque as well as translucent areas.

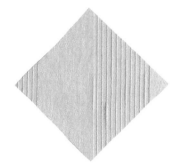

This fabric exploits the slub of the yarn to give textural interest and to form the stripe.

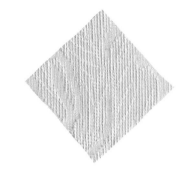

A mixture of fine and heavy yarn, each characteristic determined by the amount of spinning time, goes to make up this figurative design.

A fine translucent fabric liberally scattered with tiny dots.

Plain muslin woven in Egyptian cotton which gives it a fine, lustrous quality.

A subtle pattern on a sheer fabric.

Machine-woven lace with a traditional pattern that features seahorses.

This fabric is more opaque than some but appears sheer when light shines through it.

Although this lace is machine-made, it has an attractive hand-woven feel to it.

Lace

The word lace stems from the Latin *lacques*, meaning a noose, and the term covers a great variety of ornamental openwork fabrics formed by looping, plaiting or knotting. Although the majority of lace produced today is machine-made, its origins lie in a hand-worked process.

Hand-made lace was produced in one of two ways: with a needle and thread using buttonhole stitch (needle lace), or by twisting and entwining bobbins carrying threads around pins embedded in a pillow (bobbin lace). Hand-made lace was almost exclusively made in Europe and notable centers are located in the Devon town of Honiton in England, Chantilly and Lyon in France, Genoa in Italy, and Antwerp and Bruges in Belgium.

Silk, cotton and wool yarns are all used to produce lace, but traditionally most was woven from flaxen thread and was made for clothing or to decorate altar cloths and other church linens. Like brocaded textiles, designs reflected those used in other decorative arts such as porcelain or silver work. Florals were the most popular, but animals and birds were also widely used.

The earliest records of hand-made lace date back to 15th century Italy. Throughout the 16th and 17th century it was an expensive, luxury product. In 1763 the first machine-made net was produced using the *leno* or cross-weaving process (see page 8). Within a hundred years, hand-made lace had become a rarity and nearly all lace was made commercially.

Where lace starts and embroidery ceases is a blurred point. The subject of lace is greatly confused by centuries of French, Italian, English, Spanish and Flemish craftsmanship, with a mixture of terms, some anglicized, others not. Much of what falls under the general heading "lace" is in fact not lace, but a form of open-worked embroidery. For example, drawn-thread work and whitework are both often wrongly labeled as lacework. Both these hand-worked skills are looked at in more detail in the Embroidery section (see page 196).

The development of lace

Needle lace evolved in the mid-16th century from a kind of Italian drawn-thread embroidery used to decorate handspun woven linen altar cloths or bed hangings. Threads from the cloth were pulled together and small parts of the cloth cut away, leaving geometric spaces which were then stitched decoratively with a needle and white linen thread. From this, all kinds of openwork techniques were devel-

An Italian point de neige *needle lace border, dating from circa 1680.* Point de neige *derives its name from the shape of the tiny layered picots, which are thought to resemble snowflakes.*

oped and the skilled art of lacemaking spread across Europe, changing and evolving as different nationalities became involved in its production.

In design and pattern terms, lace-makers in Venice and the North of Italy were by far the most adventurous. Their marvellous flowing patterns began to appear at the beginning of the 17th century. One such was *Punto in Aria*, literally meaning "stitch in air", which involved the use of parchment patterns invented around the beginning of the 16th century. This enabled freer lace designs to be made by assembling threads along the lines of the drawn design, which were tacked into position (removed once the work was finished) to provide the framework for the buttonhole stitching. Outlining threads were overcast to make a kind of raised border.

Gros point, needle lace used on bed and table linens from around the middle of the 17th century, employed a similar technique, but needle-made tapes were used over the parchment patterns. The designs were grander, more free-flowing and more substantial due to the build-up of buttonhole stitches and thickness of the tape. A padded, raised effect, for which this lace is famous, is formed by more buttonhole overstitching. Stylized flower-heads that showed Oriental influences, for example marigolds or chrysanthemums, were linked by scrolling stems and tiny buttonholed bars (a device for holding the rest of the stitched design together).

Point plat (flat point) was similar to *gros point*, but without the raised effects, and was therefore more suited to draping. The design was also smaller, although still floral in origin.

The most intriguing kind of Italian needle lace, Venetian *point de neige*, was immensely elaborate and on first glance appears to have no controlled pattern. Again, it follows the style of *gros point*, but on a much smaller scale, using layers of tiny picots which resemble snowflakes, hence the name.

Spanish needle lace was strongly influenced by the *Punto in Aria* style, but incorporated Moorish geometric designs, such as the wheel and sun. These were often made with gold and silver thread. Narrow needle-made strips were inserted into widths of cloth and used for bed linen or table cloths. Both the Spanish and the Portuguese took lace to their colonies, notably to parts of South-West America. Lace decorated with scalloped edges, baskets of flowers, knots and ribbons, seen in profusion in these parts, is a legacy of Spanish lacework.

In France, as occurred in other areas of textile production, concern arose that too much French money was being spent on imported lace from other countries, mostly Italy. The French courts were quick to control the native production of lace. In the late 17th century, King Louis XIV appointed ministers specifically to establish a lace industry and Italian lace-makers were persuaded to move into France to aid this development Italian styles, therefore, formed the basis of the early French designs, but a lighter, more decorative style was developed which became known as *point de France*. This major move away from the formative Italian style involved the use of a background hexagonal mesh, formed by tiny picot lines. It appearance resembles an embroidered mesh, but all of the design, including the background, is worked as lace. During the 18th century fashion demanded much lighter lace, much of which was French-produced, and this seriously threatened the Italian lace industry.

The English needle lace industry blossomed when refuge Huguenot lace-makers reached British shores at the end of the 17th century. They colonized a part of Devon, where the firs Honiton lace was made. *Hollie point*, thought to derive from the word holy, was a fine version of flat needle lace made from tight rows of buttonholing, the design being formed from holes between the stitching.

At some point during the 16th century embroiderers abandoned the use of ground linen altogether and buttonhole stitches were worked over a grid of threads tacked over a parchmen pattern. Meanwhile, bobbin lace was emerging as a separate technique, developed from the plaiting and weaving techniques employed in making *passementerie* (trimming braids) (see page 118). From the beginning of the 17th century, lace made this way on a pillow with bobbins was being produced all over Europe. A technique known as *mezzo punto* combined the two types of lacemaking. Outlines of the design were made from bobbin-lace tapes and the fillings were needle-made. Perforated lace patterns were punched on rolls of heavy parchment paper which was then attached to a "lace pillow" – rather like a large, well-stuffed pincushion. Fastened to the pins which pricked the design were threads attached to bobbins. The lace patterns were formed between them.

In America during the 18th century a major center for hand-made bobbin lace developed in Ipswich, Massachusetts. By the late 18th century this area was producing thousands of yards of silk lace using this bobbin method. Most American lacemaking derived from European techniques, and imported examples were eagerly copied.

The development of machine lace

The English led the way in the production of machine-made lace, which began in the 19th century. The majority of production for domestic use was for lace curtains. These had exuberant patterns of hothouse flowers and other designs, largely based on 15th and 16th century fabrics. Panel-curtains, popularized by the Victorians, had elaborate borders to enclose the designs.

A section of late 19th century Irish crochetwork, imitating lace.

A detail of a 19th century French Art Nouveau linen cloth inset with needle, bobbin and filet laces.

A detail of a late 19th century Italian linen bedcover decorated with finely worked needle and tape lace.

A section of a 19th century Swiss sewn muslin curtain, imitating lace.

Nottingham machine-made lace was a cheaper alternative to the hand-made Brussels lace that was also used for curtaining at this time; it was a coarse cotton lace with patterns taken from 16th century European hand-worked lace.

Using lace

Today, antique lace in particular is much in demand for decorating windows and beds. Although a period treatment is the obvious use, the delicate fragility of period lace will not look out of place in a stark, hard-surfaced interior. An interesting tension can be built up between lace and old, worn leather, for example, and marble or glass surfaces work well with crisp, white lace. Smaller, more delicate hand-worked lace may be applied to other pieces of cloth to make curtains, pillows or bed-covers.

Modern machine-made lace can be "antiqued" to have its crisp "newness" softened. There are those who swear by dipping lace in cold tea or coffee, which does give the fabric a remarkably subtle, pale color. But a much diluted solution of standard dye can be equally effective and is probably less messy.

Patterned lace panels or curtains can add a rich but not dominant texture to a room. By draping two lengths of lace across the same pole so that they cross and overlap, a wonderful interplay of light and shadow can develop. In a room in which the entire color scheme is arranged around the subtleties of cream or white, the delicate texture of lace in the same color can cleverly introduce decoration without the heaviness of a solid fabric. The entire room, a bedroom or bathroom perhaps, can be bathed in glorious light.

Lengths of machine-made lace can be used for curtaining, either on their own at a window, or layered with heavier drapery as they would traditionally have been used. Different patterns – small, scattered sprigs next to large, swirling flowers – can be hung together and held with heavy, creamy rope tie-bands.

Heavy ropes with wonderfully detailed tassels will provide rich texture and weight to the fineness of the lace mesh. Natural-colored fringes or braids can be a simple addition to the leading edges of lace curtains, and will give definition to formal arrangements, such as swags or lavish, full-length drapery.

Using pieces of lace, old or new, inset into close-weave fabrics such as plain cottons or flat woolen cloths, mimics traditional drawn thread work by contrasting the fragile and translucent with strong solid areas. Known as panel curtain, this inset of lace providing linear borders, can be effective hung against an unattractive window, perhaps one with frosted glass. Panels of figurative lace, in any case, need to be hung flat in order that the full effect of the pattern can be felt.

Like glass, lace has a wonderful strength and beauty, shot through with brittle fragility which deserves to be displayed in floor-length curtain swathes or loose swags. Hung against strong sunlight or well-lit from the interior, the textured patterns have a magnified strength.
Although good lengths of antique lace are difficult to find, they are worth searching out to layer at a window with contemporary machine-made net. Contrast dense patterns with flatter, more open designs. Do not apply gathering tape at the top of the curtain length; instead, stitch a channel through which a pole can be slotted. Some lace can be extremely fragile, due either to its age or weave structure, so stitch with care.

Sheers

Two factors make fabrics sheer or semi-translucent: special weaving processes or the fineness of the thread used, or a combination of both.

Book Muslin

Traditionally, sheer fabrics such as muslin have been hung at windows or around beds in hot countries to filter light, prevent insects coming in through open windows and to give privacy in urban streets. Throughout the 19th century muslin was used extensively for undercurtains or "glass curtains", hung on simple rods next to the glass.

The term muslin originally referred to the cotton yarn itself, which was made exclusively in India until the late 18th century. By the 19th century the term was applied to the gauze-like, open mesh fabric often called muslin today. Occasionally, it is woven with a ribbed stripe or small motif to add texture. Muslin is mostly white or off-white, but it can easily be dyed – soft, pale colors work best.

Organdy is a slightly stiffer version of muslin, originally used as a stiffener for clothing or as an inner lining material which would give firmness to the main fabric covering it. It can be treated in exactly the same way as muslin, but because of its handle, it gives a more sculptural effect.

Other sheers

Unlike most woven fabrics, including muslin; which are made up of vertical and horizontal threads placed parallel to one another, many contemporary sheers are produced by cross weaving. In this method, also used for machine-made lace (see page 8), the warp threads are not parallel but cross over each other to form the weave. Termed "leno" or "gauze", these cloths have an open, perforated structure which allows more light to pass through. Many are made from man-made fibers for economy and ease of laundering.

Using sheers

The fact that these fabrics are so lightweight is a major advantage in that you can drape them in great swathes over a fairly flimsy window pole or bed frame. It has to be said that any drapery arrangement, formal or not, is only as good as the support structure on which it hangs or from which it is fixed. Working with lightweight fabrics will avoid the problems of having to construct rack-like supports on sturdy brackets or laths, as the possibility of the weight of a curtain pulling the whole arrangement off the wall is never going to occur, even with yards of muslin or other lightweight sheer.

The idea of tenting one's bed with layers of muslin seems to be sheer romantic fancy, but in hot countries it is in fact very practical. Whether it is shielding the sleeper from the sun or from insects, or is purely decorative, the idea of coolness and light is certainly conveyed by lengths of swathed or draped creamy white muslin.

Today, muslin can be used for its traditional purpose as an undercurtain or hung on its own. If you want to use it as a feature fabric you will need plenty of cloth to create a generous effect since it folds into fine pleats and in time will "pleat" still further. If you want a flat sheer choose organza – its crisp texture means that it works well made up into Roman shades, bordered with bright, plain cotton.

There is another aspect of sheer fabrics that is fun to exploit. By joining strips of diaphanous muslin between pieces of closely

Although corded, the muslin shade is intended to be left down for the most part. It has a central box-pleat to create some fullness and falls into scoops on the sill. Muslin is excellent choice if you want to screen windows for privacy without losing light, but its long-term practicality is limited. The dreamy bed drapes are impermanent gestures of fun or drama.

woven fabric, like poplin or damask, a web-like effect is built up. The tension between the opposing fabrics develops a movement of its own, like pieces of armour held loosely, but with freedom of movement. Although time-consuming and difficult to prepare because the muslin is inclined to fray so much, the finished effect of a large piece of this "new" fabric is quite wonderful.

Pastel sheers in lemon, pink or pale blue tones are so insubstantial that they should, I think, be ignored completely in favour of stronger or subtler colors. Use plaster-pinks, warm brass colors, or soft bluey-grays for contrast. Or dip muslin in tea or coffee solutions for a gentle "aged" effect.

Another use for sheer fabrics is to stretch them over screens that are used as room dividers. These could be free-standing or constructed along the lines of the traditional Japanese *shojis*, used to divide up their small houses without sacrificing light.

Make sure that light is allowed to travel *through* muslins and sheer cloths and is not directed onto them. This is because direct light will make a sheer fabric look opaque, which nullifies the fabric's special quality.

A dramatic effect can be created with the addition of a simple band of color, in this case brilliant red. A tied knot creates sculptural folds in the muslin, and could also be turned to a practical use as a means for holding the cloth up from the ground and swagging it around the poles of the bed.

Overleaf:
Filmy white muslin diffuses light and gives a feeling of calm and stillness. Muslin is a temporary fabric that can be used with panache in simple settings. By this I mean that it can be draped to hang in one way and then the length and arrangement changed with swiftness and ease. Although astonishingly cheap, it is not a long-lasting fabric; it will shrink drastically when washed, which makes it impractical in the long-term. When it is hung for a period of time, it will "pleat" itself like Fortuny silk. This may be a pleasing effect, but if it has been made up into a curtain designed to cover a certain width, pleating into half is not welcome. Therefore its best use is in casual arrangement like this.

på slätten var vi närmare döden, än vi ...
höver bli hädanefter, hoppas jag. Men nu har
vi det ju varmt och bra. Eh? Du är väl inte
rädd längre?

Han satte sig bredvid dottern och ... hur
varsam hand pälsverket kring knytet, hon höll
i sina armar. Då såg han lilla Joans röd...
blommiga kinder. Modern Joans ögon strålade
om stjärnor.

— Det var lilla barnet, som räddade ...
...de hon. Vargarna söndersleto hundar...
jag såg dem rusa på dig, men en av ...
... till släden — jag tyckte först, att ...
av hundarna, men det var en varg...
...t tag i våra pälsar, men det skydd...
skulle just hugga mig i strupen, ...
lla Joan och då stannade han sä...
oss, och jag tyckte alldeles sä...
r hund. Ögonblickligen gjorde...
ngs sedan emot vargarna i stä...
flyga på en som höll på...
...und, sade gamle Pierre, ...
id elden. De rymma o...
h slå sig ihop med va...
haft sådana hundar v...
en hund hat...

...ar kunna förändra hans natur — i längden.
...an kom med vargflocken — för att döda.
Men när han fann oss, sa...
— Han kämpade för oss, sa...
...högväxt och bie... ...anga kvin...
...för oss och bie... eldskene... ...stod där
...såg hur han sla... ...kämpade
...han skulle ligga o... ...on. Jag
Pierre Radisson r... ...ar, om
...ostning, som han ...
...den röda fläcken.
...cken. Pierre d...
Jag har tänkt
...kadad och
...se hä...
...han
...na upp...
...a livet. S...
...kroppar
...hundar...

Braids and Ribbons

B raids and ribbons are like miniature textiles or scaled-down versions of furnishing fabric. A braid is a narrow, woven strip, often hand-worked, with a detailed raised texture and fancy patterning. Braids are made in a range of light and heavy yarns, from wool to silk. A ribbon, although similarly narrow, is woven in a very fine weave and a lightweight yarn such as cotton or silk. For the purpose of this section, corded ropes and fringes have been omitted as they do not represent *flat* woven trimmings.

Much of the development of the braids and other narrow decorative trimmings that are used so widely throughout interior furnishings stems from the 18th century, the period when they were first in fashion, notably in England and France. At that time, the term upholstery referred not simply to

Braids and ribbons can be applied to curtains, valances or swags to add definition and texture. The exquisite detailing of the individual patterns and colors highlight specific edges or outlines of decorative furnishings. These miniature textiles can also be practical. Tied through rings attached to the curtain headings and then taken over poles, they can support curtains. Bands of picot braid or wide silk ribbons can be used to draw curtains back or hold loosely fixed full swags.

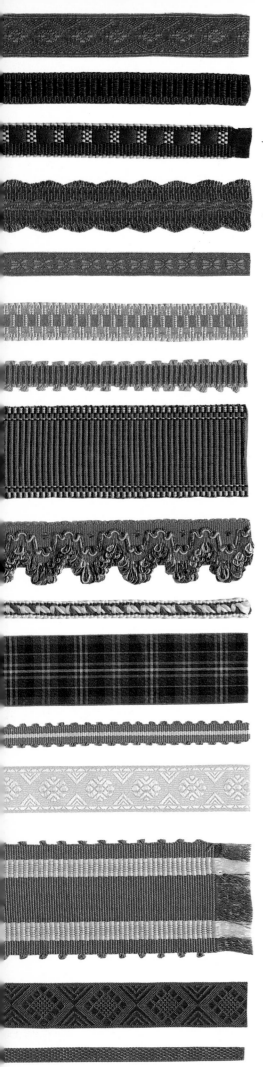

Flat picots and gimps, ribbons and knobbly, textured braids can be chosen either to coordinate or contrast with the fabrics to which they are applied. Flat braids may be applied inset from the edge of the curtain, correctly along the leading edge and base. They may also be used to form complete borders on panelled curtains – those which are hung like banners with very little fullness in the width. Double inset borders with two different types or scale of braid may also be employed to great effect on draperies and flat bed covers.

furniture, but to bed hangings and other formal draperies a well. The abundant use of all kinds of trimmings on thes furnishings heralded the establishment of a successful industry.

In the 17th century, because looms were not as wide as the are today, upholsterers had to work with narrow fabrics and therefore they had to join several widths for wider seats and backs. The frequent seams were disguised with trimming, and this became a decorative feature (later to be extended int piping). By the middle of the 18th century the decorative use o braid and tape in upholstery became very popular, and con tinued to be so, throughout the 19th and early 20th centuries In the latter half of the 20th century trimmings were out o fashion, but in the past decade they have enjoyed a revival.

Using trimmings

It is the attention to detail that makes any furnishing iten successful. Lack of attention is often shown up at the edges o items, where work isn't finished off properly, hems aren' neatly folded, pleats aren't gathered in evenly. The edges are a important as the main body of the item because the eye i inevitably drawn to the outer shape, even if the pattern of th fabric was what first attracted attention. The leading edge of curtain, the lower line of a shaped valance, the skirt of a chai covering are all major points of visual impact which shoulc never be overlooked. One of the ways in which these "defining lines can be made more dynamic, and serve to emphasize stil further the shape they outline, is with braids and trimmings.

Braids, ribbons and other trimmings are being revitalized i tandem with the demand for rich, traditional fabrics and forma curtain treatments. Added to the edges of draperies or used on cushions they create a strong visual border. They can also b more functional: use them to tie back curtains or hold up swa; valances. Ribbons can be used to hold pictures and to add decorative interest against plain or striped walls. Braids o ribbons can be used to trim the edges of fabric applied to walls They can also be used to hold swags of fabric onto a pole. I sewn to the top of curtains and tied around a pole or to rings they can be used to replace a taped heading and hooks.

The influential interior designer John Fowler was particularl adept at using trimmings and braids, experimenting witl unusual shapes and textures. For example, he had a specia trimming made up using the *Guilloche* pattern, a highl decorative neo-classical architectural ornament with interlockin; circles. Another decorative trimming he used was the Gothi gimp. This ran like a normal gimp along the top edge, bu hanging beneath it were cords in the shape of Gothic arches (Today, similarly shaped braids are available from Colefax an other suppliers.) Such special trimmings can add enormously t draperies or valances in plain fabrics.

A collection of exquisite silk furnishing borders. These braids date from the late 18th through to the mid-19th century.

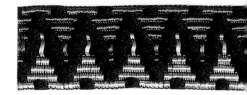

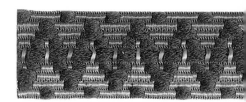

These are all old ribbons and braids, dating from the early 1900s, mostly 1920s with some startlingly graphic Art Deco ones (top 3). The delicate pink and gold Victorian braid (6th one from the top of the page) imitates the stronger contemporary picots. The three floral ones are unusual in that they are "cut-outs", probably machine-embroidered on vanishing muslin which is then ironed away, leaving the design intact. A braid with a particularly complex or beautiful design, or one of which there is only a small amount – perhaps just such a piece of antique trimming – can be used to border a small, square cushion cover.

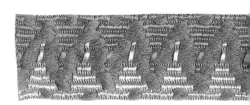

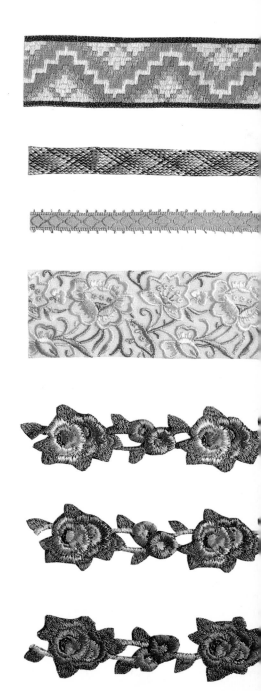

Pieces of a late 16th century medieval linen braid with silk embroidery from Hardwick Hall, Derbyshire, England.

Pictorial toiles

Classic toiles are used to enliven plain surfaces, where their patterns can be displayed to full effect.

Modern pictorials

Humorous prints that tell a story will cheer a nursery or garden room.

Florals

The widest choice of classic and contemporary print designs is found in this popular category.

Birds and animals

Realistic or stylized, these designs are as varied in their imagery and application as the beasts that inspired them.

Motifs

Despite their strong colors, the symmetry of the repeat means that motifed fabrics decorate without dominating.

Motifs

A simple motif from a Provençal-inspired pattern can be used on small items such as cushions.

Motifs

The most elaborate of motifs, a paisley print will enrich any interior.

Trees and cherries

Abstracted trees and cherries form strong silhouettes on this simple print for drapery or upholstery.

Stripes and geometrics

These fabrics form a "bridge" between plains and prints in many decorating schemes.

Abstract

These colorful, individual designs need careful selection as they can easily dominate an interior.

Ethnic

Rich and graphic, ethnic prints can be used in modern or period settings.

Hand-printed

One-off hand-printed (or painted) designs like this batik demand a furnishing scheme that is planned around them.

Printed

The surface of any textile can be colored by various methods, known collectively as textile printing. This form of decoration has been in existence for at least two thousand years. Methods have developed from simple hand-crafted skills, first invented thousands of years ago, to today's sophisticated computer-aided processes.

Although there is growing interest in hand-painting fabric (see page 188), most printed fabric is mass-produced, using colored dyes to obtain the color and pattern, by either roller printing, blocking, screen printing, or resist printing (see pages 10-11). This chapter includes some of the most well-known and widely available mass-produced home furnishing textiles – floral chintzes, *toiles de Jouy*, Provençal and paisley prints – as well as some more unusual hand-produced designs.

The principal virtue of printed, as opposed to woven, patterned cloth is that printing technology allows a number of colors to be introduced into a design relatively cheaply. A further advantage to a printed textile is that a perfect copy of a particular object – for example, a faithful representation of a flower – can be obtained. With today's sophisticated color printing processes, accurate and fine detailing can be achieved, and, more rarely, subtle color changes where one color overlaps another. On closely woven cloth areas of pure color, unaffected by woven texture, can be produced.

Pattern is the unifying factor for all these fabrics. Large, open printed patterns would suit full-length draperies or an expanse of upholstered seating – any situation where the large pattern repeat would be shown to full effect. While smaller patterns – for example the stylized motif-flower or *fleur de lys* –

may be used with larger areas of varied color or pattern. These could be small individual items, like a chair or pillow, or perhaps a narrow border for a curtain or swag. Dense all-over patterning can give a printed fabric a woven appearance.

The size of the pattern is determined by the equipment used to print it. Large-scale patterns, while impressive, can turn out to be extremely expensive to use, as a lot of fabric is wasted obtaining a pattern match in situations where several lengths of fabric are employed, as in draperies.

When buying printed fabric, you should always check that the print pattern is straight to the grain of the fabric and that it is printed centrally on the width of the fabric, and fits within it.

Most printed cloth is mass-produced inexpensively but the costly and beautiful hand-printed cloths deserve to be hung with the kind of special respect usually reserved for paintings.

In general, printed cloths are lighter in weight than their woven counterparts. This can have advantages when considerable quantities are required and the sheer weight of some woven cloths could be too heavy for some curtain supports to hold. On the other hand, the lack of thickness of most printed cloths means that they are not so suitable for upholstery situations, where durability is the key factor.

The range of printed cloth is vast, from sophisticated chintzes – old and new – to ethnic tribal cloths. Of course the quality of the cloth will greatly affect the printed design – for example, flatter, smoother cloth will allow a clearer show of color and pattern definition. Similarly, the texture of the cloth will also affect the finished design, with some rough-surfaced cottons often giving an effect of woven cloth.

Pictorial

The subject matter for the fabrics in this group – human endeavor and images of the human face or figure, realistic or mythical – is more usually the domain of the painters, sculptors and engravers whose work is of a figurative, rather than abstract, inclination.

Many of the fabrics included here, such as the detailed 18th century *toiles de Jouy*, have printed designs which are complete scenes, depicting hunting, fishing or other pastoral activities. Beautifully drawn, many of them are detailed reproductions of human activities – "little masterpieces" which tell a story.

Other fabrics in this group are inspired by artefacts – coins, plates, combs or other everyday objects. Architectural elements, such as columns or arches, are frequently used, either standing on their own or incorporated with figures or scenes.

Some pictorial fabrics repeat the same image in the form of a motif. Some of these "motifs" then merge to form all-over patterns with their own pattern rhythm, thus making the original image less important.

The particular appeal of these pictorial fabrics is threefold; the first reason being simply to do with the production. The *toiles du Jouy* appeal to me for example, not so much because of their subject matter, but because of their fineness of line and exquisite detail and coloring. The amusing nature of some of these fabrics is my second reason for liking them. To come upon a quirky fabric showing people crammed into deckchairs, oddly clad in layers of clothes (for a *British* summer beach scene!) will appeal to a certain sense of humor. The third aspect of these designs that I enjoy is the fact that they are such strong images that they can be used as pictures – flat and in isolation. In other words, they do not need to be gathered up into folds or swagged into elaborate pelmets. It is the *image*, not necessarily the cloth, that immediately appeals.

These very strong images, especially the magnificent Timney Fowler backdrop, need settings where their drama can be fully felt. Hang them as panel curtains, with headings held with loops of black braid, or feature them in bold swags decorated with heavy tassels. They could also be used to upholster prominent items of furniture – a gilded day-bed or an unusual wing chair – or applied flat to cover entire walls. The patterns need to be "read", so avoid excessive gathering or situations where the pieces used are too small to show the pattern properly.

Toile de Jouy

To most people, the term *toile de Jouy* conjures up carefully drawn pastoral images, in pink or blue, on a white ground. The term comes from the fabrics created in 1770 at the Jouy factory in the small village of Jouy-en-Josas, near Versailles, using copper-plate printing techniques on imported Indian calico. The factory, set up by two German brothers, called Christophe-Philippe and Frederic Oberkampf, also produced block-printed patterns of bold chintzes and tiny flowers (see page 140), but the pastoral images are the ones with which Jouy is popularly associated.

So successful was the Jouy factory that production expanded rapidly, and in 1806 Christophe-Philippe set up his own cotton mill in France, when French government policy restricted imports of Indian cloth.

In 1810 the brothers visited England to obtain information about workshops and machinery involved in the production of printed textiles. They smuggled out the infor-

mation using an ingenious method of invisible writing. The information was written on percale (a type of cotton) with a alum solution tinted by red dye. The dye disappeared whe dipped in vinegar, leaving the colorless alum solution on th cloth. When the treated cloth was immersed in madder dye, th writing reappeared.

The pigments used to colo the *toile de Jouy* fabrics wer the natural ones of madde (for the familiar pink/re colors) and indigo and woa (for blues), although othe vegetable dyes were also use for patterns in less well-know colors. The cloth itself, orig inally imported unbleache and later manufactured in th factory's own mill, wer through a series of washing and bleachings before it w ready for printing, and it wa also calendered (passe through giant rollers) smooth it.

The origins of many of t traditional Jouy patterns l in the events of the time. F example "*Le Ballon de Goness* (c. 1784) was inspired by t

A quilted cotton panel depicting dancers and musicians, probably Mulhouse, dating from the mid-19th century.

"Départ d'Elodie pour Nancy", *a design engraved by Marcus Rollet who produced work for the Orange factory, dating from circa 1820.*

"Les Comédiens ambulants", *a copper plate engraving from Toiles de Nantes, circa 1800.*

"Esther et Ehaseus", *a Jouy design dating from 1810.*

Another section of the Robert Jones design, "Peacock in the Ruins".

"Peacock in the Ruins", *a French copy of an English design by Robert Jones, 1761.*

One of a set of four late 18th century quilted cotton hangings, printed in rose madder.

first hot-air balloon ascents by the Roberts brothers. The American War of Independence (1775-83) was commemorated in a design known as *"La Liberté Américaine"*. Mythological and classical subjects were also popular sources, notably *"Motifs Pompéiens"* (c.1808) and *"Medaillons et Cartouches à l'Antiques"* (c.1800). One of my own favourite designs is that of *"Louis XVI, Restaurateur de la Liberté"*, printed in 1789.

A more unusual print, although it forms a style much imitated by designers today, is one based on the legend of Cupid and Psyche. Called *"Psyche et l'Amour"* (c.1810), it shows a series of scenes set in panels, arranged vertically against a background pattern composed of lozenges and scales.

Similar printing techniques and an absence of copyright regulations allowed straight copying from engraved designs to cloth, although without dated documents it is difficult to ascertain whether the copying was from print to cloth or the other way around. There are certainly also wallpaper patterns which are similar to those of printed textiles. Given that they are used for the same purpose, covering walls, it was inevitable that they should have similar properties as they were designed to harmonize with the furniture and architecture of a room.

Many later designs contain series of geometric panels, often diamond- or lozenge-shaped, rectangular, circular or sometimes octagonal. These panels are frequently ornamented with elaborate frames, comprised of smaller motifs such as urns, leaves or fruit. The design within the panel will either be light on dark or the other way round. It may be a single motif – a carved head, for example – or a more complex design incorporating classical figures or ancient buildings. The medallions or cartouches were sometimes framed by allegorical figures, scrolls and trophies of arms.

The designs which were not printed against a plain white ground had backgrounds in-filled with an even pattern of grids, rosettes, lozenges, circles or smaller decorated medallions. The punch and spilled roulette was a printing device which was used to create many of the fine net-like backgrounds. Oberkampf demanded of his designers that the most striking objects within the design should be equally distributed over the width of fabric so as not to appear too dominant. Neither should they form too regimented a band down the length of the design. It was important, visually, that they were not perfectly symmetrical. The ground patterns were often gridded, and resembled papered walls, with the parallel designs looking like framed prints hung against them. The pictorial or motifed scenes inside these panels were often linked by scrolling flowers or wheat passing through rings above each panel. It is easy to see the similarities between these particular *toiles de Jouy* and papered walls hung with framed prints or engravings.

Using *toiles de Jouy*

These fabrics, more than most, are either loved or loathed. The original ones, in particular, are most unusual textiles as the designs are specific and highly pictorial, rather than decorative and so do not fit comfortably into many of today's interiors.

Traditionally, these *toiles* were used in abundance, covering walls, windows, beds and many interior furnishings. Creating a *toile de Jouy* room is still popular today. In general, the prettier, less austere and architectural patterns are used. In the main, the softer prints are best suited to bedrooms, although the heavier, darker prints can also work well in an appropriate environment. The best *toile de Jouy* prints are on beautiful soft cloth – toile – which handles and drapes well.

If you are covering the walls with the fabric, you may be wise to employ an interlining between the wall and the cloth, which should be supported with wooden battens. This is because the cotton cloth is quite thin, and the wall surface behind may otherwise show through. Similarly, you should avoid using strong, dark colors to line pale-colored toiles. The pattern will need careful matching if the lengths have to be sewn together. Ideally, the main parts of the pattern should be positioned centrally on the wall, but try to ensure they are not chopped in half by window architraves or fireplaces.

Another option is to hang single lengths in straight panels from supporting poles. The panels can be placed at intervals around the room or in particular places for emphasis, such as in alcoves or above a fireplace.

Some of the patterns which incorporate bordered panels, rather like framed pictures, can be used to imitate a Georgian print room, with the lengths hung from simple rods against the walls. The high decoration and pattern of *toiles de Jouy* need to be contained using simple fixtures – plain iron or wooden rods – rather than anything too lavish.

One of the reasons that *toile de Jouy* fabrics were originally used as flat vertical wall panels was so that the pattern, or story, could be fully appreciated. For similar reasons, excessive gathering for curtains or bed hangings should be avoided and ideally the fabric should always hang vertically, rather than being pulled up into a drape. If you are hanging the fabric over a pole or in a half-tester bed drape, for example, make sure you join two lengths of fabric at the top, so that both sides hang correctly, the right way up. Choose a complementary *toile de Jouy* or else a plain type of pale fabric to line the inner sides of bed drapes.

Although different patterns can be mixed together – for example, for pillows on bedcovers or cushions on sofas – any combinations should be carefully thought through to ensure that the colors and patterns work well together.

The placing of a prominent part of a larger pattern – the green/cream toile *known as*
Louis XVI, Restaurateur de la Liberté *– on the contained space of chair seat is one*
way of featuring the pattern of a toile *so that it can be appreciated at close hand.*

Overleaf:
Original patterns mix with modern designs whose motifs take their inspiration from
traditional toiles de Jouy. *By keeping the same pink tones together, completely*
contrasting patterns can be used side by side. The red-madder and pink-on-white are
most commonly associated with pastoral and historical depictions. The fabric itself,
although relatively thin for use as seat coverings, can take on a decorative appeal
on items that are intended more for display than active use. You can either cover the
entire item with the same pattern so that it "reads" as a full story, or you could extract
a single motif or segment of the pattern and display it centrally on a cushion or chair
seat for example.

Modern Pictorial

Even the most contemporary-looking printed fabrics have their roots in the designs of the past. Flowers and birds naturalistic or stylized forms are constantly a subject and are seen in abundance in both Western and Eastern prints throughout the centuries. Among pictorial images, classicism and, in particular, architectural images have been a major source of many of the best textile patterns in recent years. Rimney Fowler's black and white "Urns and Drapes" and "Small Roman Heads" are both immensely striking designs with a strong contemporary feel, yet both are derived from classical images. Pillar prints, extremely popular around the early 1800s, are now back in fashion in contemporary textiles, often most strikingly in monochrome shades.

The re-use of patterns has recently been exploited to bring humor into textiles, sometimes subtly and sometimes more overtly. Janet Milner's hand-printed beehive hairstyle fabric (see page 186) is a 1960s-inspired design, which avoids vulgarity by the choice of fabric – in this case linen – and a sophisticated color palette.

The crude brightly colored designs popular in the 1950s, when they were used primarily for kitchen or bathroom furnishings, have been worked into contemporary textiles by a company called Reputation, who have recreated them in a new tongue-in-cheek approach. The results are funny and attractive, although their lifespan is probably quite short because of their strong fashion element.

Some mainstream furnishing companies have exploited the contemporary desire for an individual, artistic look by mass-producing pictorial prints that appear to be hand-printed. For example, Designers Guild, in collaboration with the textile designer Isabel de Borchgrave, have produced just such a collection. Although machine-printed, these highly successful fabrics retain a distinct hand-printed feel that echoes de Borchgrave's earlier, hand-printed collections.

Using modern pictorial prints

Like their traditional forebears the *toiles*, modern pictorial prints are best used flat. Furnishing uses such as Roman shades, bedspreads, flat panel curtains or walling are the most appropriate ways to display their patterns to full effect. Bear in mind the size of the pattern too – some designs have a very large repeat that will restrict its use. You will find that smaller designs, like the jewellery-patterned fabric shown top left, are more adaptable.

The novelty prints like the Red Indian design, bottom left, are probably best restricted to use in children's rooms, especially when they are printed in bright colors.

For those among you who want a "wacky", humorous patterned fabric for a dramatic or unusual situation, then one can be found from these original designs. There is a tradition of "kitchen" printed fruit and vegetable designs which came with bathroom counterparts depicting fishes and seaweed. These updated versions are covered with highly 20th century images – for example, the rows of deckchairs, the razor blade or the perfume bottle.

Floral

Flowers and foliage, more than any other symbols, have dominated textile design. Throughout the centuries, floral motifs or patterns, including leaves, stems, nuts, fruit and berries as well as flowers, have been used on every kind of textile, woven, printed or embroidered. Nature has long been one of the noblest sources of inspiration for decorative artists, and in medieval times nature was meticulously copied by the craftsmen of the day.

Although flowers, stems and leaves were a popular subject for woven and embroidered fabrics, particularly Italian damasks and Jacobean crewelwork, it was in printed textiles that the subject came into its own.

During the 19th and 20th centuries, when the manufacturing process took over, floral and related images were among the prominent pattern designs. The type of flower used in the design often related directly to the fashions of the time. When an English country feel was in demand, for example, roses, lilies and tulips predominated in fabric patterns. When a more oriental style prevailed, the floral images changed to chrysanthemums, bamboo or forsythia.

The Arts and Crafts Movement (see page 146) was committed to the use of natural images such as flowers in its textile patterns. William Morris was particularly fond of traditional English garden flowers and he also drew widely on his knowledge of wild flowers. Of his own flower designs, Morris maintained that the flowers should be rendered with "a degree of conventionalization to suggest to the viewer not only the part of nature which to his mind ... they represent, but much which lies beyond that part".

Many of today's designers acknowledge their debt to nature as the source of some of their most inspired designs. Tricia Guild, for example, uses floral imagery as a major, positive force in her design, particularly for the way in which it allows her, as a designer, to bring nature into the house.

These fabrics are suitable for living rooms and bedrooms. Although traditional in feel, they do not necessarily dictate the use of antiques or period-style furnishings in the rest of the room.

Linen mix
This yarn gives more weight to the fabric than the usual cotton used for florals.

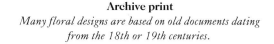

Archive print
Many floral designs are based on old documents dating from the 18th or 19th centuries.

Glazed chintz
The overall background pattern is found in several chintzes and may be sold as a separate coordinate.

Two-color floral
Designs like this make a refreshing change from traditional multi-colored patterns.

Arts and Crafts design
Intricate patterning characterizes the floral designs produced by artists from the Arts and Crafts movement.

Glazed chintz
The pattern is clearly defined against a plain cream ground.

Double outline print
The blue ground color outlines the floral image; this is reinforced by an inner black outline.

Faded floral
Coffee-brown backgrounds and "faded" print colors are produced today for an instant antique look.

Linen union
A slightly faded document print on tough linen union is the classic choice for English country house slip-covers.

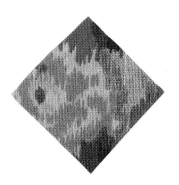

Outline prints
In an outline print the ground color – the red here – surrounds the floral image.

Chintz

The term chintz generally refers to a cotton fabric on to which a floral design is printed in several colors onto a white or light-colored ground. Often, but not exclusively, it has a shiny, glazed finish. Although the vast majority of chintzes use floral patterns, other designs, using motifs such as fruit or intertwined foliage are sometimes incorporated.

The origins of chintz

In 16th and 17th century Europe, the art and skill of interpreting elegant floral designs had been the weaver's province and little was known about how to print color on cloth that would stand repeated washings. Textiles had been painted, or more usually block-printed, with crude pigment which lay on the surface of the fabric, rather than being impressed into it. The rough surface prevented the fabric from being washed, as it would have been damaged in the process.

The techniques of painting patterns onto cotton cloth using dyes and pigments, with mordants to bind them, were first practised in India. Cheap cotton cloth had been widely available for centuries and to make up for the poorer quality of the calico, vivid designs and detailed patterns were applied to it.

Painting calico is generally thought to have been a widespread craft in India for

An Indian painted cotton palampore *(bedcover) from the Coromandel coast of Eastern India, dating from circa 1800.*

several centuries before it spread to other parts of the Far and Middle East. At the beginning of the 17th century the European market was introduced to small quantities of these painted calicoes. The East India companies, founded in Holland, England and Denmark in the late 17th century, developed the trade much more vigorously. In France the painted calicoes were known as *"chittes"* and in England as "chintz", derived from the Mahrati word *chit* and the Sanskrit *chitta*, meaning "speckled". In France painted calicoes also acquired two other names, taken from the points of importation: *perses* for textiles from the Middle East and *indiennes* for those imported directly from India.

Although the textiles at this time were largely hand-painted, some involved elements which were hand-blocked. The designs were mostly of flowers or fruit, in stylized patterns using many colors. As trade increased the colors and patterns were modified to conform to a more restrained European style.

With the development of the trade from the Orient, chintz became an established feature in European bourgeois homes, both for apparel and furnishing fabric, in vivid contrast to the previously used formal and monochromatic damasks.

Later, with the advent of an indigenous cotton manufacturing industry in Europe, the patterns that decorated the painted and resist-dyed Indian cloths began to be created in the West. The patterns began to change as they moved away from their roots. Images from imported Chinese textiles, porcelain and lacquer work were mixed in with those of Eastern textiles, in patterns that were a subtle blend of European, Chinese and Indian elements.

French chintz

The French were the first to develop the Indian techniques in Marseilles to create their own *indiennes*. Many of the patterns decorating these forerunners of Provençal prints were inspired by the printed calicoes of the Levant as Armenian refugees had come to Marseilles and found work as pattern designers.

Later in the 17th century, the infatuation with chintz apparently posed such a threat to the manufacture of woven silks, wools and linens, long the basis of the flourishing French textile industry, that its importation into France was prohibited by a decree of the Royal Council of State in 1686, which also prohibited the production in France of imitations.

Other European manufacturers, many already associated with textile production, sought to imitate the delightful Indian floral patterns, in spite of continual measures by the rulers of the day to repress their output in attempts to protect the older, established textile industries.

In addition to producing the magnificent mainly monochrome pictorial prints from engraved copper plates, the Oberkampf factory at Jouy-en-Josas near Versailles was also responsible for many thousands of multicolored floral designs in the Indian style, printed by woodblock. The level of production at the Oberkampf factory was prolific and the woodblocked printed designs (chintzes), which were used for both fashion and furnishings, underpinned the factory financially.

The quality of the printed calicoes produced under Oberkampf's guidance, had much to do with the strength of the colors used and the superior quality of the dyes. Oberkampf was a perfectionist, using the most skilled workers and talented artists in addition to the best products.

The sharpness of the print depended on the correct consistency of the mordant used. Prior to mordanting, the cotton cloth was thoroughly washed and beaten. These two processes were largely responsible for the smooth surface of the cloth.

The patterns often comprised several different colors. Dyes used included madder, woad, indigo and cochineal, which came from Mexico. One Oberkampf floral pattern, *"Fleurs Indiennes"* (1788), was block-printed on cotton in eight colors on white ground and consists of several swirling, stylized flowers. The design was inspired by an Indian textile. Another design,

colored like a chintz but consisting of a layout which closely resembles the panelled *toile de Jouy*, is called *"L'enfant au Dauphin"*. It has classical ornamentation, scrolling flowers and cornucopias, which surround pictorial lozenges in each of which is depicted the child on a dolphin from which the name of the design is taken.

Oberkampf produced many Indian-inspired prints, commissioned from individuals for apparel or furnishing use. Many of the stylized floral patterns were devised from actual plants in the Ile-de-France region. As the cloth became more sophisticated, so too did the printing methods. An intriguing print called *"Roses chinées"* (1774-78) has irregular contours, caused by the cutting of the block, which gave the effect of silk.

Flowers appeared in all kinds of forms, strewn across a solid or dotted ground, in garlands, bouquets or scrolling vines. The designer was able to call upon a personal knowledge of botanical elements as well as drawing from the numerous publications available on exotic, hot-house flowers.

Early English chintz

In England, in 1676, William Sherwin patented a technique based on the true manner of printing and coloring cloth in India. Most subsequent printing was carried out around London, the tributaries of the Thames supplying the abundant clean and fresh water needed for the process. By the early 18th century the weavers in England had begun to complain that the printed cotton industry was putting them out of business. As a result of their lobbying, by 1721 an Act of Parliament was passed forbidding the manufacture of English calicoes and chintzes for the home market.

In the 1730s the cotton printing industry was allowed to go back into partial production using a linen and cotton cloth called fustian. By the 1770s English chintzes had become sufficiently popular to allow a much increased range of prints and colors to be manufactured, and in 1774 all-cotton cloths were once more produced. By the middle of the century copperplate printing began to revolutionize the industry, and English chintz started to cross the Atlantic.

American chintz

Although the Americans were originally happy to import their chintzes from England, by the end of the 18th century they were successfully manufacturing their own, largely as the result of English printers setting up their own design and manufacturing businesses in the New World. Many of the most influential settled in Philadelphia, which formed the base for the industry. One former English textile printer, John Hewson, found considerable success in America. When he died, in 1822, he bequeathed his "largest India Chintz bedquilt" to his daughter Ann; it is now in the textile collection of the Winterthur

Museum. Although this particular quilt was not one of his own manufacture, the handsome bedspreads and quilt centres (for inserting in the centre of patchwork quilts) that he produced were of a quality which had very few parallels in 18th century American textiles.

Glazed chintz

The improvement of roller blinds by 1825, and their ensuing popularity with Victorian households, helped create a huge upsurge in demand for heavily glazed chintz. Victorian chintzes were so stiff and hard that they were, in fact, extremely difficult to sew.

The heavy glaze was originally achieved using a "flint lock" which consisted of a large lump of flint with a polished surface, set in a wooden casing. It was suspended over the fabric and worked like a rocker across the stretched surface to buff it - the friction produced the required gloss on the finished material.

Originally, children were employed to do the work in the British textile mills, but when the much needed reforms initiated by the Earl of Shaftesbury in the middle of the 19th century took place in the factories, machinery took over the job.

19th-century chintz

One of the major factories producing chintz in England in the 19th century was the Cummersdale company, Stead McAlpin, which was established in 1835. By this time the English had acquired a reputation for the production and export of quality cloth. Stead McAlpin exhibited in the Great Exhibition of 1862 and were awarded a gold medal for their class. Two of the principal designs were floral chintzes that featured bold roses on a pale ground.

A designer who had gained much of his experience in Cummersdale, Harry Wearne, went to the States and opened a studio in New York. His hand-blocked designs were printed in the Cummersdale factory and imported to the USA. They were largely responsible for the huge upsurge of interest in chintz in America around the turn of the 20th century. One of his

An English printed cotton, dating from the early 1830s.

A typical English hand-blocked printed chintz design that has formed part of Warners' range since the late 19th century.

designs, "Old Vauxhall", portrayed leading theatrical, artistic and literary figures like Dr Johnson, Fanny Burney, Oliver Goldsmith and Hogarth in conversational groups.

In the late 19th century some of the most popular designs were printed by G.P. and J. Baker and depicted naturalistically drawn flowers, a style which the company continues to this day. Many Victorian designs were named after the flowers depicted on them, such as "Convolvulus and Seedpod", a G.P. and J. Baker textile of 1898 which illustrated scrolling acanthus leaves and flowers in shades of green, blue, white, violet and yellow.

This particular design was purchased in 1895 from the Silver Studio, the design company founded by Arthur Silver which produced many floral Arts and Crafts fabrics (see page 146).

Recent developments

By the 1950s chintz had lost a lot of popularity to the new abstract and geometric patterns, but in recent years it has begun to arouse renewed interest. One company in particular, Colefax and Fowler, which was established in 1938, sustained its popularity throughout that fallow period and is still in the forefront of fabric fashion in chintz today. Primarily an interior design company, it is nevertheless best-known worldwide for its distinctive range of fabrics.

The company was set up by interior decorators Sybil Colefax and John Fowler, but the inspiration for the designs of the fabrics is largely John Fowler's. Like many interior designers, he amassed a collection of objects like tassels, pieces of frayed ropes, corners of old wallpaper patterns and samples of old fabrics from which he drew the ideas for his designs. Among his stock of chintzes were prints from the old established textile manufacturers, Warners, that he first used in the 1950s, with images of faded flowers, leaves and urns. The designs, known as "Bailey Rose", "Hampton" and "Passion Flower", were reproduced for Colefax and Fowler, and are still widely in use in today's homes.

The subtle, barely discernible floral patterns of these and

other antique textiles attracted Fowler, who combined them with his own distinctive taste for plain or striped woven fabrics. Other Colefax and Fowler fabrics adapted the ornate designs of the Indian Tree of Life cloths to a more English idiom, using traditional English cottage garden flowers – roses, briars, lilies of the valley, in small sprigs and garlands.

The delicate and refined patterns fitted in especially well with English country house architecture, and gradually these light, printed chintzes began to be seen in grander settings – as part of formal bed tester arrangements or swagged valances. A feature of the Colefax and Fowler style was the use of one fabric and pattern throughout a room. For such a look to work well, it needs to be contrasted with large areas of plain color, whether for the walls, floor or upholstery. Although the Colefax and Fowler hallmark is to use the same fabric for an entire room treatment, many people prefer to contrast the heavy pattern of chintz with plain fabrics, or those with smaller-scale patterns, to give the room a greater feeling of space.

Other more recent designers have taken up chintz, notably Tricia Guild, whose printed floral chintzes have a freshness and vitality in their original use of color. Her earlier water-colored fabrics that were produced in pale pastel shades have given way to stronger colors, but all her floral designs, past and present, are based squarely in the chintz traditions of the last two centuries.

Using chintz

Whether glazed or not, chintz is best suited to curtains, bed hangings or tablecloths, or small items of upholstery, such as chair seats or stools.

The more delicate the design, the greater the care needed to position it to best advantage in the house. The most beautiful chintzes tend to be of softer cotton, with less glaze, such as those in Percale Persan.

Old pieces can sometimes be found, although they are rare and subsequently expensive. They can, however, be used inserted into other fabrics or as borders. In fact, many of the *palampores* (the Indian painted calico bedspreads popular in Europe several hundred years ago) were not discarded when they reached the end of their useful life, as the unworn parts of fabric were cut out and applied to new backgrounds.

Chintz is as popular today as it was in its heyday and is still a staple fabric in English country house style. Its use, though, is much changed from its original applications. In the 18th century chintz was generally preferred for slip covers in sitting rooms; today, its prime use is in the bedroom. Many 19th century patterns and colors remain virtually unchanged and it is just this timelessness that creates its chief attraction. Although the more modern designs can sometimes be very effective, they

What profusion of color and flora! From the dark and densely-patterned to finer-detailed fabrics set against parchment and off-white backgrounds.

Background patterns
In some of these florals, the main patter has the effect of being laid onto a background of all-over secondary pattern, which in some examples is quit detailed. This has several advantages. will give depth to a fairly flat pattern and adds texture. It can also be used to introduce an additional color – useful for contrasting fabrics.

Overall pattern
While some chintzes are faithful to the growing characteristics of the flower or foliage they represent, others are rambling and more concerned with a stylized design and general pattern. The most successful all-over patterns are those which are broken by the pale parchment color of the background. This gives clarity to the design and formality to the fabric.

A delightful mix of glazed floral patterns which fall under the general term "chintz" (although not all are patterned in the style of the original chintzes). Lively contrast between small- and large-scale pattern is displayed on these box coverings; an excellent use for this type of fabric. Lining the inside of drawers with fabric revives an old tradition. Closely resembling paper, but being much stronger, chintz cloth works exceedingly well as a wall covering. Pattern-matching and calculations would be the same as that for paper, with the additions of turnings.

The appeal of this fabric has to do with its subtlety of color and a particular quality that a printed linen possesses – the older it becomes the more pleasing it is. Indeed, the designs printed on coffee-colored linen appear slightly old and faded straightaway, and they have the advantage that, when put all together, there is not one pattern that dominates. The "English Country House" look, itself an enduring concept, relies on fabrics like these. The flat pattern of the "all-over" floral works well on the wall and the same colors and tones continue into the curtain fabric, patterned with a defining vertical stripe and tiny flowers.

do not recreate the feeling of faded charm which is so much part of the prized English country house look.

Fabulously patterned chintz, notably those designs with traditional origins, should be used in abundance, but not necessarily on all and every surface. Walls could be covered and then a single color from the design could be picked up in a painted line of a cornice moulding or a skirting to define and contain the patterned area. Flat braid could, perhaps, be used instead against skirtings for added textural interest.

In large, well-lit sitting rooms, a backdrop of boldly printed chintz on the walls makes a dramatic but not claustrophobic contribution to the decor. In bedrooms, where a more muted effect is required, a softer, gentler, chintz pattern is more appropriate. Reducing the color palette of the entire decor of the room to two or three colors at most creates a calmer, quieter atmosphere.

In dining rooms, libraries or studies, where the emphasis on natural light is less important, the color range can be darkened, and greater use made of fringes and tassels on heavy swags and draperies. When a formal period style is needed, selecting the correct fabric is of paramount importance. Aim for one of the traditional patterns, many of which are based on archive designs or are actually faithful reproductions of them.

To add variety, consider using printed striped cotton fabric for linings to chintz swags or draperies, in colors that link or tone with the main fabric.

The formality of the majority of chintz patterns contrasts well with the colorwashed furniture or dragged paintwork that is so popular today. A colorwashed wardrobe with glass doors, for example, would look effective with simple slot-headed gathered chintz curtains behind them, or a dragged cupboard could have its shelves and interior covered in a chintz.

Chintz, especially if not too heavily glazed, makes up well into window curtains and bed hangings. It is often used to cover furniture, either for padded seats for dining chairs, or for slip covers for armchairs or sofas. It is not hard-wearing enough, however, for situations that attract a great deal of daily use and is too thin for a satisfactory upholstery cloth.

Arts and Crafts

The setting up in England in 1888 of the Arts and Crafts Society (which gave its name to an existing movement), stemmed from the fact that the Royal Academy refused to include the work of decorative artists – illustrators, textile designers and ceramicists, for example – in their exhibitions of fine art.

William Morris, the most influential designer and craftsman in the movement, was deeply critical of a system that had allowed British craftsmen's work to be pushed aside in favor of the technically brilliant but often dull products emerging from the manufacturing industry. An architect by training, he had moved over to painting and then to revolutionizing the art of house decoration and furnishing in England.

The arts of medieval England and France had an important influence on the work of William Morris, as did the Italian woven fabrics of the 15th and 16th centuries. Another influential source were the Indian textiles that Thomas Wardle, a skilled printer and dyer with whom Morris worked, imported, printed and sold through Liberty's in London.

With the object of creating a new range of textiles, based in the traditions and techniques of the past, Morris started up the firm of Morris, Marshall, Faulkner and Company, later known as Morris & Co., which was to become highly successful. With the help of Thomas Wardle, Morris conducted detailed experimental work on vegetable dyeing and revived the dying art of hand block-printing.

The manufacture of printed textiles had changed drastically in Morris's lifetime. Roller printing grew in importance from the 1790s and by the 1840s, not long after Morris was born, it dominated the English textile industry. Morris chose to ignore so-called progress, and preferred to block-print his cloths which he rightly felt had a far superior quality.

The palette of colors in his prints was probably influenced by Persian textiles, and to achieve the same purity of color he resorted to the process of vegetable dyeing, which had largely been abandoned in favor of chemical dyes. According to Morris, "There is an absolute divorce between the commercial process and the art of dyeing. Anyone wanting to produce dyed textiles with any artistic quality in them must forego the modern and commercial methods in favor of those that are at least as old as Pliny, who speaks of them as being old in his time."

The use of vegetable dyes

Morris's use of, and enthusiasm for, vegetable dyes, lends unique quality to his prints. He said himself, "They all make in their simplest form beautiful colors. They need no muddling into artistic usefulness when you need your colors bright .. they can be modified and toned without dirtying".

Once he was satisfied that he had produced a sufficiently large palette of unfading, clear bright colors to carry out his designs, he set to work and in 1876 set up a dyehouse at Queen's Square. By 1881, in conjunction with Thomas Wardle, he produced first 16 fabrics and then went on to create a further 28, which he printed in the printworks and weaving workshop he had established in 1881 at Merton Abbey, Surrey, England.

For all his enthusiasm for natural dyes, Morris did not entirely eschew chemical colors and in "Daffodil", one of his last designs for a printed chintz, the yellow of the flowers was achieved with an aniline dye.

Known as "Salanum", this fabric is screen-printed on cotton. The design was drawn by Ann Lynch from an original design by the Arts and Crafts architect Charles Voysey.

Known as "Tiger-lily", this pattern was block-printed on linen in 1896 to a design by L. P. Butterfield. The design is reproduced by G. P. & J. Baker in 1990.

A pattern of waterlilies designed for a printed textile. More naturalistic than the design below, it was produced by the Silver Studio in 1892.

A stylized floral design for a printed textile, produced in 1907, by Harry Napper.

Known as "Waterlilies", this watercolor design was intended for use on a printed linen. It was produced in 1905 by Harry Napper.

Known as "Lynham", this design in watercolor was produced for a printed textile by artists from the Silver Studio in 1898.

The effect of color

Compared with the bright, vivid colors of the chintz samples shown on page 143, these Arts and Crafts fabrics are printed in much earthier colors – duck egg and navy blues, moss green, gray, brown and crimson. This is because the designers of the original Arts and Crafts textiles deliberately chose natural, rather than synthetic, dyes. These softer colors are much more versatile to use and are also less dominant in a room than the chintzes are.

The colored patterns printed on a light ground are a little more stark. The two self-patterned fabrics with the light-on-dark print effect (top row left and near left) have a more textured feel than the other designs. And because of the use of a subdued single color, they are even more versatile than the multi-color versions.

The effect of pattern

The formal style of the popular Lodden (bottom row, left), with its highly stylized pattern, works well on a period-style piece of furniture that is closely in keeping with its character. The patterns which display flowing foliage would be better chosen for flowing draperies, where the pattern can travel. All these fabrics are cottons and the flatness of the cotton contributes to the crisp, clean lines of the printed patterns.

Morris's influence

Morris was not the only British textile designer in the Arts and Crafts Movement whose influence has lived on. A younger designer was Charles Voysey (1857-1941), also an architect by training. Voysey's designs for houses inspired much of the English vernacular architecture of the first half of the 20th century. His influence on the ordinary domestic home extended to its furnishings – he created many designs for wallpapers, and for woven and printed textiles, and carpets. He sold his designs to British companies such as G.P. and J. Baker and Liberty, and became known for his flowing patterns incorporating birds, animals, hearts, flowers and trees.

Another successful designer of the period was Lindsay Butterfield (1869-1948), whose crisply depicted flowers, foliage and fruit were particularly striking. A typical fabric print was "Tiger Lily", manufactured by G.P. and J. Baker and sold through Heal's at the end of the 1880s, which depicted the flower with a very linear stem and foliage, the brilliant orange flower-head contrasted against a deep blue-black indigo ground, with the whole pattern outlined in gray.

Butterfield was also commissioned by Liberty's in the 1890s, as was Arthur Silver. Silver had already opened his own design studio, known as the Silver Studio, and their good-value range of fabrics for the new store brought exciting designs within the grasp of a much wider public.

Although Morris died in 1896 and the Arts and Crafts Movement continued after his death, his influence was the most profound and the most far-reaching. His designs, with their superbly balanced colors and their rich and well-controlled elaborate patterns, were seen as the epitome of good design in both England and the United States. Morris's designs have lived on as classic furnishing textiles, and have enjoyed a popular appeal throughout much of the 20th century.

The American Arts and Crafts Movement

Morris's products, and those of the Arts and Crafts Movement, certainly appealed greatly to the Americans, and by the 1880s, Morris fabrics and wallpapers were sought after in many parts of the States. An association formed in the United States, Associated Artists, founded by Louis Tiffany, Samuel Colman, Lockwood de Forest and Candace Wheeler in 1879 used the basic principles of the English Arts and Crafts Movement.

Despite the fact that the partnership was dissolved in 1883, Mrs Wheeler kept the name and between 1883 and 1907 she and two of her children printed and designed woven textiles, many of them produced by Cheney Brothers in Connecticut. Although her firm closed in 1907, it spawned many smaller societies round the country whose aim was to use simple and familiar design sources to create practical products.

Birds
and
Animals

Although there are numerous bird and animal motifs in woven antique textiles – for example, birds and beasts of a heraldic nature feature in the Renaissance woven cloths and in the originals from which these fabrics were copied – the image of a living creature is much more widespread in printed textiles.

One of the reasons, perhaps, is that it is much easier to print a complex design than to weave a stylized flower-head or the rich and complex colors in a peacock's tail. A design drawn first on paper can be transposed to a fabric by printing so that the printed image is an exact copy of the drawn design. As a result, not only is it possible to achieve total accuracy in pattern and line, but there is also complete control of color matching as well.

In a few of these examples the bird or animal element is almost incidental to the design (for example, in the floral fabric shown in the top right corner), whereas in many others the main image or motif concentrates on the particular characteristics of the elephant, the rabbit or more whimsical creatures. On the butterfly print fabric the effect of the glaze on the fine cotton ground heightens the sense of sheen and luster on the colored wings. The stiffness of the linen yarn used for the blue and white fabric makes the cloth more sculptural and allows more of the pattern to show.

Peacocks, partridges, herons and birds of paradise have long been popular subjects. The more exotic birds emanate from Chinese artefacts, and to a lesser extent, from Indian textiles, although not many appeared on early painted calicoes. English and French designs in the late 18th and 19th centuries made use of birds for their decorative chintzes.

Animals featured in some of the highly detailed prints from the Jouy factory (see page 128). In *"Le Ballon de Gonesse"* there are galloping horses and barking dogs throughout the print. The scene is drawn with a clear indication of

From the whimsical, nursery images of the little armadillos and their painted friends to the detailed, realistic observations of the twittering birds, from the black silhouette of the cat to the richly textured cockerels – all of these printed fabrics have a marvellous energy and vibrancy.

A block-printed linen from the G. P. & J. Baker studio, dating from 1914.

The effect of pattern

Highly stylized little animals can form a series of stamped motifs set within a bold framework, in the example of one fabric shown here, of different intersecting ears of corn. This formal framing device highlights each animal, with the result that they won't be lost if the fabric is used in a large, hanging arrangement. It also forms a link pattern across the cloth.

foreground and distance, as though the onlooker is part of it. Another print from the same factory, *"Les Chinois"* features cranes and herons, but in a less realistic style. In this print, the bird is the size of a small child.

The exponents of the Arts and Crafts Movement in the late 19th century (see page 196) were much drawn to the natural world for their imagery. A great deal of effort was spent on detailed drawings of botanical specimens and much was made of the patterning elements that could be devised by flattening an image of a plant, taking its separate sections and relaying them to form a

The effect of color

Color can be incidental in any design or it can be used to make a striking impact, in which case it will form a major part of a room's overall style. Paler colors soften the design, while bold shapes in strong colors, like the cat silhouette shown here, help make strong graphic statements.

recognizable motif. This allowed the characteristics of the particular plant or flower head to be maintained, while emphasizing its style. Similarly stylized patterns of animals are to be found among some of G.P. and J. Baker's prints, in particular "Pekin", with its dragons and scrolling flowers. Birds, too, were drawn from every conceivable angle, to exploit their design potential. The peacock, in particular, is a frequently chosen subject. Arthur Silver, the founder of the Silver Studio in 1880, was very fond of using it in his designs, and in 1888 he designed a peacock feather

A formal French chintz that combines floral arrangements with a stylized exotic bird.

pattern called "Hera" for Liberty & Co., which became their trademark. Birds were a popular subject with Arts and Crafts designers, often appearing among foliage or with fruit.

Designers at that time were also much influenced by Japanese design, and the stylized, symmetrical shapes of paired birds in the textiles of the period, owed much to Japanese images. Chinese peacocks, dragons and phoenix were also popular. Many of the early 20th-century block-printed English linens referred to the painted designs on Chinese scrolls in the Victoria & Albert Museum for their source material.

The traditional device of "texturing" the background is picked up in the toile shown on this page (2nd row, left). Here it outlines the main image of the animal and gives clarity to a very detailed print. This monochromatic toile pattern and those shown 4th row left and bottom left, take their inspiration from traditional designs. The blue on cream toile (bottom left) is based on archival documentation.

The effect of pattern
The patterning of the toiles is clear and easy to "read"; one color on a light ground can be useful for monochromatic or highly colorful situations. The relatively formal patterning of all of these fabrics perhaps makes them especially suitable to formal rooms and arrangements.

The effect of color
The fairly subdued coloring of these fabrics plays down the intensity of the design; the effect is subtle, allowing a more successful mix with other types of fabric.

Motifs

All printed motifs base their designs on a single repeating pattern arranged in an ordered fashion across and up the length of a piece of cloth. For the purpose of identification, a motif is defined as an isolated shape. A printed pattern may be composed of repeating shapes, but if they touch or merge into one another, then the design is termed an overall pattern and not included here. Some paisleys are an exception to this rule, but paisley is so inextricably linked with the history of motif printing that all paisleys are included in this section.

There may be more than one pattern of motif featured on a fabric design; for example, a small floral sprig and a solid geometric shape. Looked at from a distance, both these motifs together form a small, all-over pattern against the plain background. A large rose spray, not immediately obvious as a motif because of its dominant size, may repeat across a fabric where the background is composed of a series of small dots each set in a square. The dot and square are both motifs; so too is the rose spray, although less abstract in design. This patterning device is very popular in chintz collections, and often the background design is included as a toning fabric that can be used as a contrast lining or border.

Natural subjects are frequently the source for printed motifs – stylized fruit, flowers and leaves can all be found. In addition, architectural patterns and simple geometric shapes such as the diamond, or lozenge, are seen on many textiles. Heraldic devices are also popular motifs for textiles.

Some motifs are historically inspired, perhaps culled from old fabrics or wallpaper. For example, the logo of the interior decorating company Colefax and Fowler is a motif called "Berkeley Sprig", taken from an old wallpaper found by John Fowler on the walls of a London house he was decorating.

As with graphic and linear fabrics (see page 84), the subject of scale is very important when considering any of these fabrics for interior furnishing use.

These fabrics illustrate the small all-over patterns which are so useful in furnishing schemes because they never dominate. Although some seem traditional and others modern, none of them stridently dictate where they should be sited.

*Note the device for shading the motif and the random
dots of the background, both of which add texture.*

A simple "cut-out" paisley motif effect.

*Stylized flower on a "sponged effect" background,
which adds depth.*

A series of dots form a trefoil motif on a plain ground.

*Another example where dots form an illusion of a
defined pattern.*

*Two colors printed to leave the ground cloth
"highlighting" the pattern.*

*An oakleaf motif set against a shaded ground and
printed in four colors to display a rounded shape.*

A motif printed in gold over a patterned ground.

*Art deco style shells form a secondary motif in the space
between them.*

A small maple-leaf design on a simple cotton fabric.

Heraldry

Within the broader subject of motifs and symbolic patterns, there is a special category that deserves to be looked at separately – that of heraldry. It is important as a subject in its own right and has been much studied, both in relation to textiles and countless other decorative arts. A love of symbols goes back to tribal emblems (see page 70). Although this fondness for pictorial or sculptural signs is of such ancient origin, it was not until the first half of the 12th century that the system we call heraldry really started. Reaching its zenith in the early 13th century, it was a powerful visual language used to communicate a bearer's identity. Distinctive personal devices were employed on shields to identify the armored participants in jousts. The hereditary significance came about because marks of the head of house were used by descendants, adapted to distinguish generations. From such labeling, coats of arms grew up.

Since the 17th century heraldic patterns have been used in textiles. Although sometimes, certainly in the earlier textiles, they were incorporated for their symbolic meaning, nowadays the meaning of the symbol itself is not significant; its value rests solely in the beauty of the pattern it creates.

The common images fall into two main groups, and patterns which derive their design from these groups can be identified throughout many of the categories of this book. The first group comprises human figures, "monsters", beasts, birds, fish, reptiles and insects. And the second includes vegetation and inanimate objects. This group includes one of the most popular heraldic devices – the *fleur de lys*. This ancient symbol is most closely associated with France and acts as the country's emblem or badge.

Another frequently found device that has its origins in French heraldry is the bee. It served as a sign of the Napoleonic Empire, and replaced, for a time, the *fleur de lys* as the most common decorative symbol in France. It was used on draperies, banners, flags and battle-dress of Napoleon's armies.

One more important device originated in France: the chaplet. Taken from the French *chapelet*, meaning rosary or garland, it consists of a circular wreath of leaves, with four flowers, usually roses, at the north, south, east and west points of a cross.

Geometric devices are numerous in heraldry, and many are incorporated as patterning devices in textiles. For example, the diamond-shaped lozenge is frequently used as a background pattern for *toile de Jouy*.

A Watts & Co., fabric, featuring elaborate fleur de lys *alternating with a chaplet enclosing a floral motif.*

Provençal

rovençal prints are now universally known and admired for their brilliantly multi-colored and almost kaleidoscopic patterns of floral and geometric motifs. Originally, the dyes were obtained from natural materials and each color in the highly complex design was applied with a separate woodblock impression.

Few factories survived the mechanization of the textile industry. One well-known company, based in Tarascon, France, is owned and operated by a member of its founding family, Demery. It trades under the name "Souleiado", a Provençal term taken from the works of the local poet, Mistral, meaning "the rays of the sun that pierce the clouds". The factory has retained more than 40,000 of the original fruitwood blocks from which the original prints were taken, and they form the basis of today's successful production. Such is the appeal of the Provençal prints that there are now several factories and workshops in the region reproducing the original designs.

The colors in a typical Provençal print reflect the sun on the local countryside – hues of yellow, rich blue, earthy chestnut brown and indigo. Many of the prints, while using strongly contrasting colors, have a similarity of tone that gives them a remarkably solid appearance, even though the cotton itself is quite thin. The prints hang as well at windows as they do over tables and beds, or they can be used for cushion covers. The most classic, and most prized, product today is the Provençal *boutis*, or quilt.

The history of these ever-popular Provençal prints can be traced back to Marseilles in the 16th century. As early as 1580 Marseilles had imported the first *indiennes* into France, and the inhabitants developed a passion for these painted cloths. T first recorded manufacture of these *indiennes* in France, usi carved wooden blocks, is in Marseilles in 1656. T manufacture of the *indiennes* was prohibited in France, except Marseilles and Avignon, which were part of a papal sta outside the jurisdiction of the French government. A eventually in 1692 an edict prohibited their importation fro the papal state into the rest of France. This was because the fabrics had become so popular and were so much in demar among fashionable Parisians that the traditional weavers' trad was threatened, resulting in the ban.

The oldest known manufacturers of *indiennes* in Marseill were Benoit Ganteaume and Jacques Baville. They manufacture the cloth in Ganteaume's house, where they also printed playin cards. By 1660 demand for their fabrics had increased enoug for Ganteaume to employ not only his son-in-law from Roue but three apprentices as well. Ganteaume's other daughte married printers, and along with two other printers, Franço Chambon and Jean-François Attingan, they formed a brothe hood of designers and manufacturers known as *les Trois Ro* Apart from this first company, later manufacturers of tl typical Provençal *indiennes* were scattered throughout tl region. The existence of one such factory is recorded at Avign in 1675, but there were undoubtedly many others in the are By 1773 there were 24 workshops that were producing *indienn* in Marseilles alone.

With the increasing competition from mass-produced print textiles in the 19th century the industry declined, althoug small operations remained in Tarascon and St Etienne-du-Gre

Made of lightweight cotton cloth, with simple floral motifs inspired by the patterns of the original indiennes *imported from India into France, these fabrics are delightfully bright and lively, in strong, primary colors based on dye colors closely associated with the Provençal region.*

The effect of pattern
The scale of the pattern will affect the use to which the fabric is put. For example, the tiny motifs can be incorporated as an overall pattern in an large room treatment or used in narrow borders to larger patterns or on small, single items. The larger, flowing patterns can be used more exuberantly.

The effect of cloth
The lightness and thinness of the cotton cloth restricts the usage to hanging or draping arrangements, rather than upholstery.

However, the tradition stayed alive and was passed on from generation to generation. Fortunately, it is enjoying a new-found popularity today. Paisley patterns, romantic flowers, trailing garlands and small geometric patterns, in rich, deep colors, typify the prints from Provence now available.

Using Provençal prints
The modern Provençal fabrics are created using chemical dyes, rather than the vegetable dyes of the original textiles, although the colors simulate those produced by the old dye recipes.

In general, the colors are bright, with the strong "sun colors" predominating, and the patterns small and busy. As a result they tend to dominate other textiles no matter where they are placed. Because they do not mix well with other fabrics, the best effects are achieved by making a feature of their pattern, and using them *en masse* – for curtains, bed hangings and pillows, for example.

The patterns do, however, combine successfully with other Provençal prints – for example, the small geometric patterns work very successfully with the larger floral motifs, either inserted as borders or employed as edgings. Some of the most successful applications of Provençal designs have been in patchwork fabrics – for quilts, cushions and tablecloths.

The fabrics are not grand or formal, nor are they tough enough for conventional upholstery use. However, they make ideal curtains – preferably interlined to give them more substance, so that they hang better – and bed covers. Their rich, earthy colors look particularly attractive when combined with the dark patina of antique wood, especially in French country-style rooms with wooden or terracotta-tiled floors.

provençal

Simple arrangements allow the fabrics to speak for themselves. Bright, delightfully cheerful patterns demand to be used en masse, *with small- and large-scale designs set together. Warm but dark colors – deep yellows, reds and blues – call for the room to be treated with the same palette, providing the light is good. Here, simple wall stencils have been used to link the walls with the motifs. The cloth is thin, so if you are using it for curtains, you should line it with a toning plain color or another Provençal pattern. The quilt or* boutis *is an antique Provençal piece.*

Paisley

Today's printed paisleys take their name from the Scottish town of Paisley. They have an involved ancestry that can be traced back to twill-woven shawls exported to Europe from Kashmir in India in the 18th century, which in their turn had been influenced by illustrations from imported European herbals. Indian shawls were copied all over Europe, and the term "paisley" includes all paisley shawls, regardless of where they are made. It is used to refer to an entire shawl, the characteristic design motif and the patterns that use this motif.

The paisley motif has been variously described as a cone, mango, pine, teardrop and pear. Most frequently referred to as the *pine* or *cone*, the motif's source is thought to derive from illustrations of the growing shoot of the date palm found in European herbals sent to the East. In India the motif is known as *buta*, meaning "flower", and was incorporated into textiles, carvings and tiles. Over the centuries, the paisley shape has appeared extended, compressed, intertwined and elaborated in every conceivable way, while still remaining completely recognizable. Modern printed paisley patterns still resemble very closely earlier printed ones, which themselves were modeled very faithfully on their woven sources.

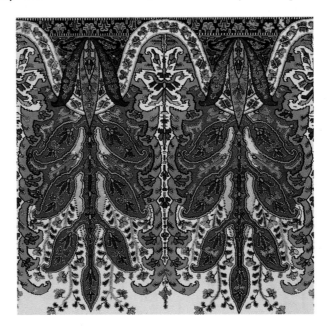

A painted design, for a paisley shawl dating from circa 1850, stamped "Carter, Hyland, Hudson and Purnell, Designers, Paris and London."

Kashmiri shawls, produced in India from the 15th century became popular in Europe at the end of the 18th century, when they were imported by the East India company. However, they were very expensive and scarce, so European manufacturers began to weave cheaper imitations. At first, these were known as imitation Indian. In Britain, craftsmen from the Spitalfields silk industry (see page 37) turned to weaving silk shawls that copied the Kashmiri patterns. Paisleys were first woven in Spitalfields, Norwich and Edinburgh, from around 1780 before they were produced in the town that gave them their name. Paisley was a center not just for weaving but for printing, dyeing, embroidering and fringing, and it became a major producer of imitation Indian shawls in the 19th century.

But although Paisley gave its name to the pattern, the developments in pattern design were actually led by French manufacturers, who commissioned leading artists to design imitation Indian patterns to the European taste. And the development of a new weaving loom in 1801 by Frenchman, Joseph-Marie Jacquard (see page 10), revolutionized pattern design, making even more complex designs possible, enabling greater adaptation of the paisley motif.

A fragment of an early 19th century woven Kashmir shawl. The traditional paisley motif first reached the West on woven Kashmiri shawls like this one. Made up of numerous stylized floral images within its own clearly defined border, the paisley is usually set on a plain-colored ground, as here.

A detail of a British glazed furnishing cotton with a printed paisley motif, dating from circa 1830. Printed paisleys were initially produced by block-printing, but by the end of the 19th century roller printing had taken over.

The French industry began in Paris at the beginning of the 19th century, and by the mid-19th century a large center had also grown up at Lyon. By the 1840s many British manufacturers were weaving copies of the French imitations of the original Kashmir shawls. France and Britain were not alone; a thriving paisley shawl industry grew up in Vienna early in the 19th century. All three countries exported their products to other European countries and to North America.

The printed paisley

Although all Kashmiri shawls were woven, the European industry produced printed shawls as well as woven ones. During the mid-19th century, many shawls were block-printed with paisley motifs on a lightweight cotton or silk gauze. Some designs imitated the woven shawl so precisely that the blocks also printed small diagonal lines to imitate the original Indian twill weave. These printed paisleys were cheaper and faster to produce than the woven versions were, and because they reached a wider market they have exerted a profound and continuing influence on printed textiles worldwide.

By the end of the 19th century printed paisley furnishing fabric was being produced in Europe and America using the roller printing method. From woven shawls draped over tables, the furnishing uses blossomed as infinite lengths of printed fabric became available.

Using paisleys

The paisley motif is an exotic one and the coloring of paisley-printed textiles is usually rich and vibrant – oranges, reds, ochers – which gives the fabric an Eastern feel, particularly if the richly colored motif is set against an equally bright ground. Vivid colors aren't essential however. Some paisleys are set against a white or cream ground, which produces a cooler, more summery mood.

In a sophisticated interior the color and pattern of the design can be highlighted by using one paisley print on a single sofa or item of upholstery. Despite the fact that paisley is such an exuberant design, it can still be used very successfully *en masse*, for example in a pile of cushions, as long as the various patterns and colors combined in the scheme are selected carefully.

Some contemporary designers have used the paisley motif, yet have moved completely away from its traditional associations. Notable among these is Celia Birtwell, whose crisp white cottons are decorated with printed paisley motifs in strong primary colors. These monochromatic fabrics, with their white backgrounds, can be used against, or surrounding richly patterned fabrics. Equally they can be put with other geometric patterns to create a very graphic overall effect. Many of Celia Birtwell's prints are negative and positive in the same colors, and such fabrics can be cleverly combined in one item, with a negative border on a positive curtain edge, for example. She also produces sheer fabrics printed with paisley motifs, either in a subtle white on white, or in colors on a sheer white ground. These sheers are very effective if combined with a coordinating paisley printed on an opaque ground. For example, a black motif printed on a white sheer could be combined with an overdrape of black cotton printed with a white motif. This free adaptation of a traditional motif provides greater scope for its use in modern interiors or in situations where you are not restricted by theme or period style.

The effect of pattern

Paisley patterns all have such rich attention to detail, with exquisite detailing within the motif itself, as borders, or simply swirling against a plainer ground. Design elements like borders can be very useful to edge curtains or bedding.

The effect of yarn

All these examples are printed onto cotton cloth except the moiré finish one, which has viscose added. The fineness of the yarn will produce a better quality finished cloth (bottom row right) that most closely resembles the palampores.

The effect of color

The change of color range has a direct effect on the level of sophistication of the cloth. For example, the combination of strong blues, greens and reds (top row right, 2nd row left, bottom row right) helps to give clarity and strength to a very busy all-over pattern.

The rich variety of the paisley pattern is shown to full advantage. The layered curtains are held in simple scoops and draped asymmetrically. A dark red-on-red paisley print on the seats is a good choice; a contrasting print might have distracted the eye from the chairs.

Modern Motifs

*L*ike modern pictorial prints (see page 134), modern motifs are influenced by designs from the past, but they have a strong contemporary feel. For example, Osborne and Little's very successful "Romagna" collection, which came out in 1988, made use of the pageantry and rich ornamental patterns of the Renaissance, the influence of which is also evident in the clever use of gold effects. And some geometric motifs owe their origins to the repeating patterns of Persian paintings and ceramics.

Modern motifs can be abstracted forms of more traditional patterns or mere marks, like those made by a paintbrush. With the exception of a few, most are highly stylized and therefore merge to form a close, all-over pattern or "texture" when viewed from a distance. Some merge or link to form a secondary pattern. Most are done on a diagonal line on a print repeat, which is less grid-like in appearance. These stop at each edge of the width of cloth (at each selvage) which can be easily matched with the corresponding one when fabric pieces need to be joined.

In most examples the motifs are printed onto a plain ground, light on dark or vice versa. Some patterns are created by "outline" printing. This technique involves printing all but the motif. Similar effects may be achieved by various resist methods. Separate motifs can overlap in a visible way to form "shadows", or, alternatively, two entirely different sets of motifs can overlap to create another pattern.

The patterns are usually chosen according to personal taste rather than with their suitability for a particular purpose in mind. The room scheme is then planned around the fabric rather than the other way around. In general, they tend to look best in stronger, darker colors which can make a statement - pastels can seem insubstantial.

The smaller motifs on these fabrics (13, 14 bottom row far left, near left) create an overall 'texture' when seen from some distance and when gathered up, for example, in a curtain. Smaller motifs are best used on items that mix against larger, more solid areas of pattern or color. For example as cushions, in different colors, against a sofa. Almost like marks from a crayon or paintbrush (3, 5 top row near right, 2nd row near left) these motifs 'skim' across the surface of this cotton fabric. Most of those shown here are abstract forms representing leaves or flowers, trellises (9) or shells (1).

Stripes and Geometrics

$\mathcal{W}$hile floral images remain strongly associated with English textile design (although their use is universal) the geometric patterns that were popular in the 1950s and 1960s stem mainly from European and American designers.

A geometric pattern is one that is best described as mathematically derived, and can be woven or printed. Printed geometrics, however, occasionally merge with those that can be more readily described as loosely non-figurative or abstract.

Stripes can be woven or printed. The printed solid stripe has less depth of color than its woven counterpart, but a greater density and strength. A printed stripe is unaffected by the texture of the weave unless the cloth is particularly rough and the dye very thin. The glazing of some cottons will catch the

A glorious display of rich colors, interspersed with strong black and white. Their visual impact is strong, both as individual fabrics and as a group. Striped designs are good as "defining" fabrics – to break up pattern. The addition of a glaze will give a rich luster to this straightforward cloth. The splendid gold-printed fabrics are designs taken from Renaissance pageantry and should be used dramatically – to "tent" a room or space, to swathe a cornice or tall window, for example. An intriguing and very clever use of the stripe as a device for displaying inset broken pattern is deployed in the black/white "figurative" stripe.

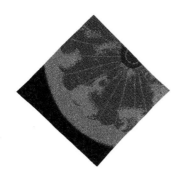

A detail of the rich patterning achieved with the addition of gold print.

Intricate detailing set into the stripes, gives broken texture as well as considerable visual interest.

Solid plain stripes, with a heavy glaze, give drama and definition.

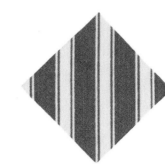

The simple addition of the thin lines flanking the wider one gives an illusion of cream stripe on grey ground or vice-versa. The strength of either may be exploited in decoration.

The geometric shape of the square is created by single 'crayoned' lines, stacked in alternative directions.

A detail of the gold print against strong plain areas.

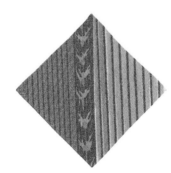

A more intricate stripe with patterning set between.

Bold geometrics set in stripe formation, in a strong hue.

A formal stripe in sober shades for more traditional interiors.

Dynamic black and white solid stripes can be used for dramatic effect in full width or to border plain hues.

light and affect the appearance of the printed stripe. Stripes can be used in almost any style, whether formal, grand, plain country or ethnic; in any situation, from nursery to bathroom, kitchen or conservatory and with fabrics and furnishings of any period from 18th-century French to 20th century modern.

Stripes can be made up of plain bands of color or from small patterns, most commonly geometric ones. One of the most successful fabric designs combining geometric patterns with stripes is Timney Fowler's "Design Stripe", which has tiny images or scenes repeated vertically in each stripe, resembling a strip of film. Printed in black on white, the dye density is varied so that some of the stripes appear faint, while others are strident and solid.

The geometric patterns that swept into popularity in the 1950s and 1960s were largely European in origin. Contemporary fabrics in this category are produced by Baumann Kendix, a Swiss company, which specializes in just such bold geometric patterns made up of small squiggles, triangles, dots and squares. Owing much to Op Art for their origins, these designs have to be considered carefully in an interior because they can sometimes be hard on the eye.

A strong influence in geometric patterns emanates from the East. During the Middle Ages, these influences were absorbed so thoroughly that they have become almost indistinguishable from Western decorative design. Later, in the 19th century, there was considerable interest in the architecture of the Islamic world and many Western authorities made detailed studies with intricate drawings, which then influenced all kinds of decorative work, including textiles. Eastern influence, this time involving China, Japan and India, was equally prominent in the 19th century, but no-one at that time paid much attention to the geometric designs of ethnic peoples in Africa or in South America, for example. Darwin encouraged the belief that culture and art developed in a progressive, evolutionary sequence and, with this background in mind, the precise geometric patterns of these peoples were regarded in the West as the uninformed marks and drawings that a child might make.

It was not until Owen Jones published his greatly influential book, the *Grammar of Ornament*, in 1856, that primitive patterns and decoration began to be taken seriously. His work has provided an invaluable source-book for generations of

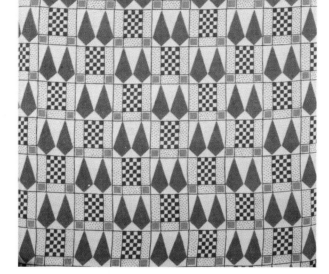

A block-printed linen design purchased by G. P. and J. Baker in Vienna in 1908. The Wiener Werkstätte designs like this one have had a profound influence on modern geometric prints.

textile designers ever since. For example, you will find that some of John Stefanidis's contemporary geometric prints closely resemble Owen Jones's "Melanesian and Polynesian Bark Fabrics", dating from 1856, even if they were not directly influenced by them.

Throughout the history of textile design, artists whose main work lies in another medium have turned to designing patterns for textiles. Geometric designs have gained from the involvement of modern artists like Dufy, a painter who, at the Beaux Arts in Paris was a fellow student with Braque. Dufy produced many influential textile designs in the 1910s and 1920s. He was commissioned by a leading French silk firm, Bianchini-Ferier. Some of these designs were based on stylized floral patterns, but many had roots in strong geometric shapes. Dufy was influenced by the cubist preoccupations with form and space, an approach to design that was helped by the wood-block printing methods he used.

Another Frenchman who worked with, and also commissioned, Dufy, was the fashion designer, Paul Poiret. Poiret opened a school of decorative arts in Paris in 1911. Students were encouraged to work from nature and they produced designs for wallpapers, carpets, embroidery and furnishings as well as for fashion fabrics. Some of the designs incorporated strong geometric patterns or bold stripes, often combined with abstract floral forms.

Another early 20th century artist whose work embodied geometric design was Sonia Delauney, a painter who was born in the Ukraine but lived and studied, from 1905, in Paris. Along with her husband, the painter Robert Delauney, she researched and developed theories on color, relating to form, space and movement. Sonia Delauney worked with strong colors, blocked shapes and lines. She was reputedly much influenced by a traditional Russian patchwork quilt which suggested "space and movement".

Sonia Delauney produced fabrics for fashion items (using cheap Japanese silk), theater costumes, screens, furnishings and other textiles, bridging the gap effortlessly between fine and applied art. By the 1930s she had resumed her painting but continued to produce designs for carpets and wall hangings.

Using printed stripes and geometrics

These patterns tend to suit flat, linear arrangements. For

example, the Roman shade with its rectangular shape and linear structure is ideal for displaying a simple printed vertical stripe or geometric pattern well. For such shades choose narrow stripes for wide windows, and where a window is considerably taller than it is wide, use a wider stripe unless you particularly wish to accentuate the height. Borders, set on the outside edges of a Roman shade, or inset a little, can incorporate contrast colors of the same stripe – set at right angles to the main striped fabric. Additionally, the structural rod pockets of these shades, normally placed out of sight on the back, can be positioned on the front if made from a contrasting stripe. Narrow and wide stripes – of the same or contrasting colors – can be used in the same item. When working with striped or geometric fabrics you must take care not to strike optical illusions which may be disturbing in some interiors.

Bedcovers are another essentially flat item which provides potential for using linear borders. When joining the necessary fabric widths for a large bedcover, incorporate contrast strips of fabric at the seam joins. Single pieces, or "patchworked" elements, can be inserted at these seams so that rich pattern detail contrasts with a plain ground fabric.

If covering a large expanse of glass – for example, a wide, flat bay window – using different but coordinating geometric patterns can often be successful. In a modern interior a series of flat Roman shades can feature small and large scale geometric patterns sitting side by side.

Valances and cornices, originally devised in the 18th century to hide curtain rods and fittings, are popular again. Their flat, box-like form, which contains the curtain headings, is perfect for geometric shaping – edges can be either scalloped, square, castellated or with pronounced Gothic forms. Bold stripes or a pattern that combines both geometric design with subtle, broken striping, looks particularly effective when used to cover a box cornice.

These fabrics are all cotton and with the exception of the glazed stripe (bottom row, third from the right), they are all printed with a flat, matte finish. The effect of the glaze is to highlight the linear pattern, which is very modern.
Printed stripes may be simple designs (bottom row, far left) that imitate the woven versions, or they may take advantage of the qualities of print to introduce an effect like the broken stripe (bottom row, third from the right), which could not be achieved in a weave.
Some geometric prints imitate hand-painted results, like the fabric on the far left in the bottom row, reproducing the effects of brushwork.

Striped fabrics may be cut on the cross to give an interesting diagonal pattern. You may choose to do this for a design effect, or it may be necessary for technical reasons. An outer edge fabric border for a circular tablecloth, for example, would need to be cut on the bias for ease of stitching.

In curtains, striped fabric borders applied along the leading edge and base allow for additional color, or sometimes pattern, to define or enhance the main fabric of the curtain. If the color combination is correct, a geometric pattern can cleverly contain a busy, floral one.

Insetting borders across the entire width of a curtain or set of draperies provides another opportunity for using flat, linear or geometric pattern. In this way printed (border) and woven (main) fabric can be successfully mixed. The opposite can also be effective – geometric or striped fabrics interspersed with borders of floral pattern. When you see only a few inches or centimeters of border, a pattern is diminished and reads as a clever blur of color.

Striped fabrics, especially printed ones, are a popular choice for slip-covers on chairs or sofas, and especially on dining chairs when an entire cover is to be made. The very linear pattern enhances the formal shape of the piece of furniture. Traditionally, "summer" or "daytime" slip-covers were made for upholstered furniture. The choice of fabric was often a simple, inexpensive printed stripe, or sometimes a gingham (see page 86).

Color will have a strong influence in your choice of stripe. For example, black and white stripes are dramatic and strong. While black combined with a color of a similar tonal strength – bottle green, dark red or navy for example – has a formality and elegance that it does not have when it is combined with a lighter or brighter color.

Abstract

An abstract pattern is, broadly, any pattern that is not figurative. For the purposes of this book, however, I have treated geometric and linear patterns separately. Unlike floral images, the development of which can be charted with comparative ease through the centuries, abstract pattern has a very short history and woven types are rare. Abstract prints came about early in the 20th century, when the textile industry absorbed the Modern art movements that were just beginning. Many of the designs of the time are reminiscent of other design disciplines, in particular furniture, sculpture and architecture.

The fashion for abstract prints was at its height in the 1950s. Stylized shapes based on real objects were used, but not in the tradition of motif-patterning, which relies on balance and

The abstraction of the image in some of these fabrics is quite extreme, the resulting pattern being an array of indeterminate shapes or lines. Others, however, choose recognizable motifs as the basis for their design – the paisley, for example — and then alter one's perception of it. Abstract patterns tend to be printed in bold, bright colors and are therefore best used for fun items, like children's play-boxes or hammocks, or a shade to brighten up a dull window.

harmony. A lemon cut in half, for example, is a starting point for a shape that cropped up consistently in 1950s furnishing fabrics. However, the abstract shape doesn't immediately bring to mind cut lemons, or indeed any fruit in natural form, as it is used in such an unrealistic, irregular fashion. Some patterns are simply marks across a surface – circles, lines or dots – that resemble paintbrush lines. Each shape bears little relationship to another, except perhaps in a color-coded way, and although the pattern repeats, it appears to meander, to run off the edges of the cloth.

A well-known 1950s abstract fabric, which was reputed to have captured the spirit of the age and was exhibited at the Festival of Britain in 1951, was decorated with similar irregular shapes, far removed from their original inspiration in nature. This award-winning design by Lucienne Day was called "Calyx" and was screen-printed on linen for Heals. The color range was as avant-garde as the pattern – it was printed in lime-green, turquoise and white on black, and brown-gray, orange and white on mustard-yellow, among others.

Most 1950s fabric designs, which today only appeal to a minority of enthusiasts, were commissioned for use in large modern public buildings where they complemented the scale and style of the architecture. On the whole, abstract designs are not as easy to live with in the home as the classic, traditional patterns like florals or stripes, and therefore they are today less widely used in a domestic context.

However, in recent years certain designers, notably Susan Collier and Sarah Campbell, have produced some very successful contemporary abstract printed fabrics. Many of Collier Campbell's textiles are inspired by the Fauve art movement – for example, their *Côte d'Azur* design owes much to the work of Matisse and Dufy. Dots and dashes, squiggly lines and other indeterminate shapes in bold colors abound in their work. And, unlike the 1950s prints, their patterns have a balance and coherence that makes them a versatile and popular domestic choice.

Using abstract prints

Modern patterns are very difficult to incorporate into houses with a strong period feel. They suit modern design — large, open rooms with flat walls and picture windows.

By their very nature, abstract printed patterns do not relate to a specific use or placing in a domestic interior. The large abstract patterns, which were often originally commissioned for bland, open public spaces, do not sit easily in the more intimate environment of a home. Neither are they fabrics that evoke great passion in the way that a richly decorative chintz or striped silk taffeta might.

It is not easy to mix these patterns together, unless they are

A selection of brightly colored contemporary abstract designs.

Combining patterns
As is evident here, these patterns tend to clash violently and are therefore best used singly, set against a plain backdrop.

Pattern and color
In my opinion, some of the most successful of these fabrics are those patterned in monochrome colors, like the black and white fabric shown in the bottom left hand corner. Otherwise, I find that jewel-bright primaries are preferable to wishy-washy pastels.

from the same designer or manufacturer and therefore link well in terms of style. For example, you could select a good overall pattern that can be used to cover a very large piece of furniture such as a couch, and combine it with a simpler geometric in the same colorway for the curtains.

Bold, brightly colored abstract designs can be fun to use in a light-hearted context. For example, you could make a print up into a garden hammock, using a bold, brightly colored lining on the inside to contrast with the abstract pattern.

Some of the old 1950s fabrics, or those of the 1960s in the style of the earlier ones, can still be found. Used on small items – perhaps a box cushion for a low bench or a pair of bolsters on a plain daybed cover – these non-specific patterns can have some impact. For small rooms or dens, try using them in place of wallpapers – above a dado, for example, with bright paintwork on the wall beneath.

Although a traditional shape, the sofa's square lines are suited to the modern graphic pattern of the fabric. Behind, an entire wall of curtain displays a single fabric design, swept up to show the contrast lining. The leading edge of the curtain is bordered with rich shot silk which acts as a strong contrast to the glazed surface of the boldly patterned fabric. The curtain could be broken up into several different complementary patterns; printed geometric patterns could be worked together, perhaps even cut and joined as contrast stripes, inset across a plain fabric.

Ethnic Prints

As with woven ethnic textiles, it is impossible to cover all the various methods and origins of the world's printed ethnic cloths in such a limited space as this, so what follows is simply a general overview.

Although the volume of ethnic printed textiles imported into the West today, notably from India, Korea and Thailand, is vast, the production of most items remains at a domestic level, albeit large scale. These countries lack the technical development which has led to the sophisticated mass-production of screen-printed textiles in Western countries. The printing methods remain fairly basic and, in most countries, they are a continuation of age-old traditional techniques, found throughout Africa and the Far East. The most common of these are resist techniques such as tie-dying and batik.

The *adinkra* cloths of the African Ashanti are one of the few examples of printed ethnic textiles where the actual designs are placed directly onto the cloth. The designs are stamped into a plain, often white, ground cloth which traditionally would have been woven locally, but today is more usually imported. The stamps are made from pieces of calabash cut to different designs, with a small handle made from sticks.

Ethnic textiles are creeping into all kinds of interiors as useful fabrics in their own right. Once merely displayed as collectors' items, today they are used as highly sophisticated drapery arrangements, worthy of inclusion alongside more traditional Western furnishing fabrics. The textured detail of the "tie-dyed" cloth (right) contrasts with the stark black and white print which takes as its inspiration woven African kente cloths (see page 71). The clear blue colors, seen especially in the stylized motifed pattern (middle left) could mix with a formal floral chintz or could be used in a more ethnic setting.

Some of the fabrics shown here are printed using a traditional method, notably the batiks in indigo and white. Others imitate traditional ethnic cloths whose patterning devices are based on woven configurations. The African Kente cloths (see page 71) are the inspiration behind the two at the bottom of the page. The one at center left closely resembles the blurred lines of a woven ikat cloth (see page 73).

The effect of pattern

The eye-catching, bold designs of the printed "Kente" cloths (bottom row) take on a much more modern, contemporary feel than their woven counterparts. Use them to contrast with the smooth, uncluttered lines of a cool, modern interior or as a single splash of color in an otherwise white room – as a bed canopy perhaps. The batik and resist-dyed cloths display the simplicity of a hand-drawn design.

The choice of weave

Note the effect of the cloth that the ikat and the multi-colored designs are printed on. The slubby texture in all three, but especially in the printed ikat, gives the appearance (as well as the strength) of a woven cloth.

Blue-and-white printed fabrics from Java make a lavish display of cushions and throws over a plain calico-covered chair. Since these fabrics are very thin they should be used in situations where they don't receive a lot of wear.

sing printed ethnic textiles

t is relatively easy to locate importers of inexpensive printed thnic cloths, in particular those with a batik or other resist-dye nish. The quality of the cloth is often not very good, but the rength of pattern makes up for this shortfall. As many of these ontemporary ethnic cloths are made of lightweight cotton, one f the most obvious uses is as curtains or other window angings, such as shades, either in a modern or traditional nterior. The graphic patterns, of an "ikat" or batik print for xample, can achieve a very modern effect and work well in ool, pale interiors where there is minimal furniture or other ecorative items.

These cloths can be made into simple slot-head curtains to sit behind a glass panel in a wardrobe door. Their depth of color and pattern makes a refreshing change from the expected "chintz" appearance.

A central band of cloth can be displayed across a long table for decoration, or a larger piece draped over a single cloth on a round, informal table. A selection of printed cloths can be loosely draped over a large sofa in order to display a range of matching or related designs or colors, while smaller, single pieces may be used as antimacassars or simple throws over plain-colored upholstered furniture. More robust cloths, woven from a thicker cotton yarn, may be used to cover entire walls; they may either be stuck like wallpaper or left hanging loosely from ceiling-level fixed points.

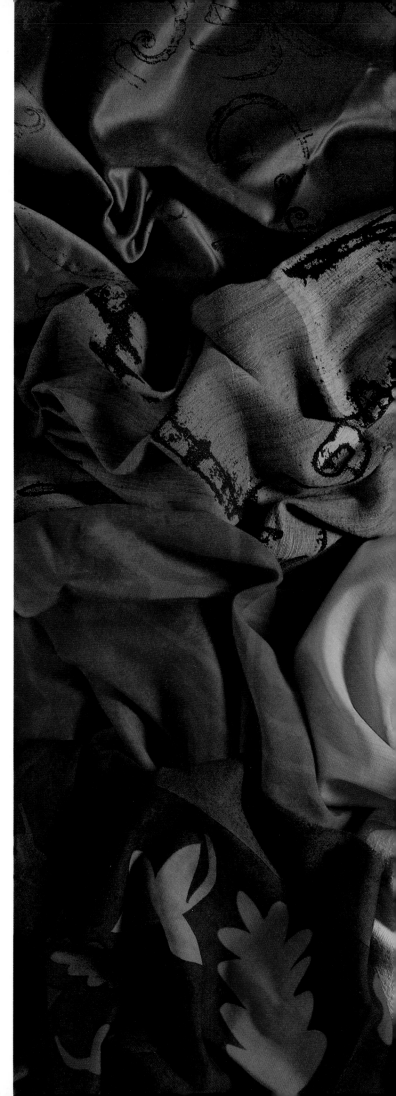

Hand-printed

Many textile designers today are shunning mass-produced industrialized printing techniques in favor of age-old traditional ones like hand-blocking because the latter gives them the opportunity to create individual "one-off" textiles. Not only does hand-blocking give the designer more scope for experimentation, but another advantage over industrialized techniques is that it ultimately allows greater control over the final design. And for aspiring designers hand-printing can be a low-cost route into manufacturing.

Hand-printing can take several forms – from simple cut-outs to large repeat patterns. The simplest tools can be used for the printing, including potatoes, corks, or lino, and the simple geometric prints produced using such basic blocking devices can have a refreshingly naive quality. More commonly, hand-blocked fabrics are produced from carved wooden blocks, just as the original cotton prints like Provençal (see page 156) and chintzes (see page 138) were.

Discharge or resist printing and screen printing are other methods of hand-printing patterns onto cloth. And some textile artists are reexploring traditional hand-printing methods such as the skill of batik.

Whimsical and sophisticated, these hand-printed fabrics cover a range of possibilities and are a refreshing change from the products of mainstream furnishing fabric companies. It is interesting to note the use of gold in several of the cloths shown here. The inclusion of the gold pigment creates an impression of luxuriousness and richness, akin to some woven fabrics. The inspiration is broad – from ethnic (ikat) to 1950s textile imagery – and the cloths that these designs are printed on range from silk to cotton sateen.

Most hand-printed fabric requires some form of pre-drawn design, however simple, together with careful positioning of the blocks to organize the repeats, although some designs are organized in an arbitrary way across the surface of the cloth and much of the charm of fabrics printed in this way derives from the random nature of the design.

The renewed interest in hand-printing has produced some excellent fabrics in recent years, and lifted the craft of textile printing to new heights.

Some mainstream furnishing fabric companies have brought out collections which imitate hand-printed (and hand painted) effects. Some of these are based on earlier hand-printed designs; the best retain the essence of the originals.

Janet Milner's delightfully funny printed images parade across a simple piece of furniture. The totem-pole arrangement of heads and hairstyles on the drapery fabric looks almost hand-painted with its heavy black-inked "brush" marks. The simple use of sophisticated color – black, cream and caramel – transcends the comic imagery and gives these fabrics a lasting appeal.
The flattened leopard floor rug is also worth noting – it is crewel-worked.

Hand-painted

*I*n the past, many textiles were hand-painted – for example, the beautiful 18th century Indian calicoes – and a number of some ethnic fabrics have maintained this tradition. In the West, hand painting has been revived as an art form. Like hand-printing, hand-painting gives the designer a unique opportunity to create a one-off textile. As it is almost impossible to reproduce hand-made marks precisely, each hand-painted piece assumes an identity of its own, and consequently a greater value than printed fabric. Individual involvement and expression of this kind automatically pushes the textile designer closer to the role of the fine artist.

Hand-painting can take a number of different forms, from carefully formulated stencilled images to freestyle paint splattering. Brushes, palette knives or other tools can apply the paint or dye thickly or thinly.

The most obvious use for these hand-painted textiles is as wall hangings. However, they can be used to upholster chairs, hang at windows or cover beds. Bear in mind that their surface may be more delicate than is the case with some other textiles, so avoid uses where abrasion wear will be heavy or where frequent cleaning is necessary.

Stencilled, resist-painted, or simply decorated using a brush soaked in dye, these fabrics have a special quality – an individual, one-off appeal.

Overleaf:
Hand-painted textiles like these by Carolyn Quartermaine are works of art and should be the collectable classics of the future. The cloths shown here are not inseparable. One chair would stand out as a solitary splash against a plain white wall. And the hangings could be incorporated into a less austere interior, mixed with contrasting styles of fabrics.

APPLIED TEXTILES

A rich display of old and new. Note the use of a silk damask ground decorated with scrolling flowers and foliage in cream in the formal valance. This antique valance could be a marvellous starting point for a window treatment. The large needleworked panel could be used as a cloth for a large table or as a panel curtain, hung with curtain clips rather than a standard sewn-on tape. The deep colors of the felted pieces are somber but dramatic; smaller pieces are set in to make a pattern.

Embroidery

Machine- and hand-worked embroideries (pages 197-207) provide decorative embellishment to furnishing schemes, usually on small items like cushion covers.

Crewelwork

Rich, dark stitchwork decorates this ground cloth in familiar crewelwork style. Scrolling flowers are depicted against a light ground.

Needlepoint

Concentrated solid stitching, like small fragments of a whole, builds up to create a detailed colorful pattern. Both texture and weight are emphasized in this cloth.

Quilting techniques

Quilting, patchwork and appliqué methods (pages 208-213) layer different fabrics for decorative and practical effect. Their main use is as bedcoverings.

Patchwork

Unusually, this is patchwork by the yard! It is Indian made from fragments of madras shirting (see pages 78-9). It is colorful and lightweight, suitable for bedcovers.

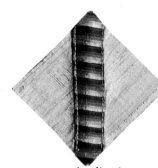

Appliqué

A tiny piece of cloth is attached to a machine woven semi-sheer fabric. There are some fabric suppliers who have taken the art of appliqué into machine-production, and this is one such fabric.

Felt

Much underused, this non-fraying material (pages 214-217) is effective for curtaining and wall hangings.

Applied

All but one textile in this chapter is included under the heading "applied" for one simple reason – they feature stitchery. Applied textiles involve the stitching of a pattern or image, usually by hand, into or with existing woven fabric. The work may involve the creation of a new cloth from existing pieces, as in quilting, patchwork and appliqué; or it may cover an entire existing cloth, leave large parts of the background visible or be used minimally as a border. In cloths that are not newly made up, the key factors in tackling applied work, are the design and the degree of skill involved in the embellishment. The ground is of secondary importance except to support, visually or otherwise, the appliquéd or stitched design.

The term embroidery covers a variety of skills which use the stitch as a major patterning device. Crewelwork and needlepoint (sometimes, incorrectly, called tapestry) come under the larger heading of embroidery as do numerous other techniques such as whitework and beading, all of which are skills in their own right. One related needle skill, lacework, is dealt with in the Woven section as its machine-made contemporary versions are woven rather than worked with a needle.

Unlike embroidery and quiltmaking, needlework is not essential to the production of felt. In fact, felt is the odd one out in this entire book because it is not a woven cloth at all. Nevertheless, it is a fabric and one which plays a part in interior furnishings. Felt is unusual in that it possesses all the qualities that other textiles have – softness, malleability, durability and a definite texture, but it is not woven. It does not rely on any stitching, although stitched lines are often applied to its surface. However, it is a traditional hand-worked skill, and is therefore perhaps most appropriately included in this section.

These textiles are, by their very nature, labor-intensive and some do not translate into machine production very easily, if at all. This means that they tend to be used for small items – bedcovers, small cloths, valances – and individual hangings. Also, because these skills are dying out, many of the textiles in this category that are available today are often antique. However, a growing number of craftspeople are reviving applied textile-making skills and interpreting them in new and exciting ways.

There is applied textile work throughout the tribal world. (see also page 70-1). Patchwork, for example, is an ancient craft and one closely associated with Central Asia. Throughout the Indian sub-continent, the colorful art of appliqué can be found on anything from items of dress to animal and household decoration.

From embroidery to quilting, through the most sophisticated needlepoint to simple patterning of some tribal appliquéd cloths, the essential element is human, the emphasis, individuality. It is interesting to note that when looking at quilts, for example, some of which were made in the last century, it is still possible to learn who made them and to whom they were given, by examining the way in which the fabric pieces were applied – the way they are cut and patterned on to the ground cloth often reveals individual quirks particular to the maker of the textile. In quilt-making, more than any other area within textiles, the production was geared towards the presentation of the finished work to someone else. The social aspect – and this is true also of many applied tribal textiles – is of great significance.

Embroidery

All embroidery, from the Bayeux Tapestry through canvas work to samplers, uses stitches to apply a design or pattern to a textile rather like drawing with thread. The success of the embroidered image depends entirely on manual skill. Even machine embroideries need dexterity and a good eye to transpose the design through the manipulation of the sewing machine onto the cloth.

Until the 16th century, most embroidery was produced for the church. As people became more wealthy, the privileged classes were also in a position to patronize embroiderers and many households would have an embroiderer on their staff. And embroidery also became a pastime for ladies of leisure.

Embroidery, like other forms of needlework, continues to be worked by many people as a hobby. Small items, such as tablecloths, cushions or borders, are the most commonly and easily produced embroideries at this level. On a larger scale, the embroidered picture, still the most popular form of

The stitch as decorative patterning device has been used here in many different applications. The beautiful green-on-cream design, worked in one stitch, can be read as a formal pattern and resembles a woven or printed fabric. Its use, like the crewelworked length beside it, could be for curtaining or simple swags.
The beaded piece is decorated with gold stitches; it is quite beautiful and would demand pride of place in any interior. Suitable curtain fabrics could be found to hang beneath the embroidered valance. Small lengths of special textiles like these can be used as borders for plain curtains or bed-covers.

displaying original stitched designs, is frequently worked today. Longer panels are also made. These are designed to be hung from poles on walls. For precious or antique pieces, simple fabric slots can be attached to the back of the piece so that the embroidery itself is not damaged.

Embroidery and the Arts and Crafts Movement

The Arts and Crafts Movement (see also page 146) was an important influence on the revival of the craft of embroidery. Still very much the domain of women, embroidery was produced professionally by the wives, daughters and sisters of artists and craftsmen of the period. At first they made items for their homes, but later they produced commercial work, known as "Art Needlework".

Notable among domestic output was the bed cover for William Morris's bed at Kelmscott Manor made by his wife, Jane Morris, to a design by their daughter, May. It has an overall "ribbon" grid, with formal floral motifs embroidered between it. The accompanying hangings, which resemble crewelwork, were woven by May and two assistants who worked for Morris & Co.

Many of the embroideries were worked as large panels, hung alone or used on screens, to be exhibited at the great exhibitions. One example, exhibited in 1888, is a six-panel wooden screen designed by Arthur Mackmurdo, with embroidered panels in silks and imported Japanese gold thread.

In Britain, the Royal School of Art Needlework, as it was then called, was started in 1872, and much of its earl[y] commercial work was embroideries of designs by thos[e] involved in the Arts and Crafts movement.

Art needlework was taken up enthusiastically by many wh[o] perceived it as a new form of interior decoration. This wa[s] fashionable with the upper classes. The simple stitche[s] encouraged by Morris and Co.'s embroiderers – which ha[d] taken great interest in peasant textiles in order to recreat[e] simplicity of design and traditional use of materials – were eas[y] to learn, and this tended to encourage amateur involvement i[n] embroidery.

Samplers

The fashion throughout Europe and America for producin[g] samplers began in the 17th century and lasted until the earl[y] years of the 20th century. Samplers fulfilled several function[s] they served as a record of stitches and designs, a testbed for ne[w] threads and a practice ground for apprentice embroiderer[s] Toward the end of the 18th century samplers began to b[e] worked to commemorate particular events, such as coronation[s] and dates or mottos were included in the design. Embroidere[d] samplers produced today, or antique ones in good repair, can b[e] framed and hung on walls. It is particularly pleasing to se[e] several hung together in a group. If they are quite flat, they ca[n] be put under a piece of glass to make an unusual, decorativ[e] covering for a table.

Some of the most beautiful and detailed of embroidere[d]

A silk shawl from Yazd, Persia (Zoroastrian people), dating from the 19th century.

Part of an East European embroidered gold on silk window curtain, dating from the 19th century.

An embroidered silk panel, or hanging, from Agra or Delhi, India, dating from circa 1875.

amplers are to be found in the Netherlands. The earliest surviving examples date from the beginning of the 17th century. There is extensive flax farming in parts of the Netherlands and many of the ground cloths were woven in linen and worked with linen threads. Madder, extensively cultivated throughout the Netherlands since the 15th century, was one of the dyes used to dye imported silk threads when these were required.

The main ground fabric was covered in a series of small motifs, often arranged in block form. The patterns consisted of contemporary themes — for example, tulips are shown in some of the early samplers. These flowers were a relative novelty in western Europe at the turn of the 17th century, the bulbs having been introduced from Constantinople only a few years earlier. Other flowers, windmills, animals and biblical themes were also incorporated into the designs.

Crewelwork

Crewel is a strong, two-ply, loosely twisted worsted yarn that has been extensively used for domestic embroidery since the 11th century, particularly for bed-hangings in Europe. The worsted wool thread is applied to a linen or cotton twill ground cloth. Chain stitch is most often used, but herringbone, back, running, stem and speckling stitch are also found. Due to the thickness of the wool, detail is less fine than in other embroidery techniques.

Contemporary crewelwork is imported from India and uses a softer, fluffier yarn than the hard, almost glossy crewel wool that was used in period crewelwork. However, contemporary crewel fabrics still favour the traditional designs of scrolling flowers and leaves which were influenced by figured silks and Eastern textiles. Usually they have pastel or earthy colored stitchery on a creamy ground. Some are self-patterned — the thread is the same color as the background cloth. These types have a particularly beautiful effect when hung against the light (see page 211).

Crewelwork cloth, which can be bought by the yard or metre in a wide range of colors, makes lovely soft curtains. Keep the cream on cream for window curtains and use those embroidered with brightly colored wools on areas such as bed drapery or archways between rooms, where double curtains can be hung. These fabrics are highly textured and, as hand-worked cloths, display pleasing irregularities in color or pattern which does not seem to affect their attractiveness. The present-day commercially produced crewelwork fabrics are not as formal as their historic counterparts, and can be used successfully in most contemporary interiors.

Whitework

White-on-white embroidery was used extensively throughout Europe from the 16th century onward. Garments as well as church, bed and table linen were decorated, and it was often used in conjunction with lace.

A lull in the fashion for lace at the beginning of the 19th

A late 19th century silk floss embroidery with couched threads and sequins, in the 17th century style.

A Russian or Polish embroidered silk altar frontal, dating from circa 1800.

Embroidered cloth is silk chain stitch, early 18th century. It was made in India for export to Portugal.

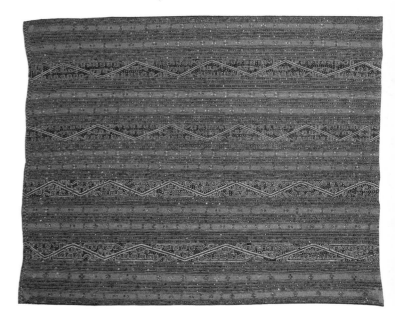

Woven and embroidered "Tapis" (young girl's wedding skirt) from Sumatra, Indonesia circa 1875.

century led to the production of what was known as "sewed muslin", a form of whitework. From about the middle of the 18th century Indian muslin was imported into Europe along with a technique known as tambour work (so-named because of the circular, drum-like frame over which the muslin was stretched). The technique produced all-over designs, mostly floral derivatives, which were worked in white thread into white muslin. A hook was used instead of a needle to form a continuous chain-stitch. This form of whitework was worked on small areas and edgings, but was also available by the yard. Tambour·work to an extent imitated lace, because the fineness and open-weave of the muslin allowed the stitchwork to pull the fabric apart, forming open areas.

Another, related, form of whitework that uses cut or open patterns is *broderie anglaise*. Most of this work was produced for apparel, although the Swiss machine-made embroidery of the late 19th century, which imitated *broderie anglaise* and other whitework techniques, was also used for curtaining and various linens. Today, machine-made *broderie anglaise* can still be bought. In a furnishing context this fabric is usually used for bed linen.

Antique whitework can be found, but most pieces are too fragile to use for hanging. It is better to combine them with a stronger cloth to which smaller pieces of white or openwork can be applied — on pillow covers, for example.

Goldwork

Gold and metal threads were used extensively in all forms of English and European embroidery. The metal threads were stiff and resistant, but by couching them down from the underside of the canvas — an innovative but difficult process requiring much skill — they were made more flexible. This process, which pulled tiny loops of another thread through to the back of the cloth, thus securing them, produced a uniformly smooth front to the metallic surface.

The technique, developed in Flanders, was called *or nue*, or "shaded gold". A detailed picture was built up by using couching threads in colored silks to fasten horizontally laid gold threads. The couching stitches were densely placed where the shadow in the picture was deepest, and more widely spaced where the gold thread was highlighted. A highly realistic image, close to that produced by painting, was built up in gold light and colored shadow. The straight gold threads also gave an impression close to weaving, so that the textile resembled tapestry.

Turkish embroidery

Turkey is a notable country for all forms of textile production. It is a bridge between Europe and Asia, and has been hugely influential in the development of textile traditions and in trade between the two continents.

Since the 16th century, Turkey has exerted a strong influence on embroidery, primarily seen in representations of flowers, cones and the tree of life symbol motifs which have become popular all around the world. Turkey exported madder, originally introduced from India, in great quantities to western Europe where a truly fast red was "Turkey red". A black made of indigo, vinegar and iron was also a dye used by Turkish embroiderers, notably to outline motifs.

Silk production had been established in Constantinople

An embroidered hanging (by Mrs Beale) from a William Morris design. It is in Standen, Sussex, England.

An embroidered damask cloth which was used for the antechamber to the Queen's room, in Ham House, Surrey, England. The stitching is exquisite.

A detail from another embroidered panel in Ham House – the stitching is goldwork.

Istanbul) in the 6th century and silk is still farmed there today. Turkish embroidery is largely done with silk threads on a linen, cotton, silk or sometimes a velvet ground. The work is typified by scrolling floral shapes, outlined in black with in-fills of chain and other stitches. The work is similar to crewelwork (see page 199). Narrow borders, with similar floral devices, often surrounded main motifs. Narrow silk cords were also used for borders, couched down with satin stitch. The embroidery was traditionally worked by women for domestic use or apparel. Some of the work, in particular metalwork, was assigned to professional male embroiderers. Popular in Turkey and areas of the former Turkish Empire, metalwork was worked with silver or gold threads on silk or linen or, more unusually, velvet or soft leather.

Ethnic embroidery

The source for much of the ethnic embroidery that is commercially available in the West today is the Indian subcontinent, where embroidery has been practised for centuries to decorate textiles for temples, houses, apparel and animals. Muslim peoples employ geometric motifs derived from symbolic images of flowers and other natural forms, while the Hindu embroiderers incorporate more figurative images. And small pieces of mirror are often embroidered onto the cloth.

Ethnic embroideries, antique or contemporary, can be bought from Western dealers or by traveling to the countries from which they originate. The native uses for them are not just practical, many of the textiles have symbolic and traditional purposes. Researching these will provide clues as to how they might be used in decoration far removed from their original habitat. Many of the display ideas for woven ethnic textiles (see pages 70-7) can be adapted for embroidered ones.

Machine embroidery

Commercially produced machine embroidery began in Austria and Switzerland in the latter half of the 19th century, and the industry was firmly established by the beginning of the 20th century. The Swiss had developed multi-needle automatic machines capable of imitating hand-produced stitching.

Nowadays, however, machine embroidery is exploited for its own sake rather than setting out to imitate hand-embroideries. Machine embroidery can exploit the running stitch with speed and ease – "drawing" with the thread across a large surface. Specialist techniques can be used such as stitching spidery, criss-cross lines into vanishing muslin which, when ironed, disappear, leaving behind the web of stitching. The resulting fabric resembles lace. There is still a tradition among the Swiss for making nets or sheers decorated with small machine-stitched motifs, as well as high-quality machine-embroidered whitework and scalloping that is mostly used for table and bed linens.

Some machine-embroidered fabrics with detailed and rich patterning will be lighter in weight than the hand-embroidered equivalent and therefore can be adequately used for curtains or bed drapes. Antique hand-embroidered curtains may still be found – and look wonderful hung as panels, with tabs held over dark wood poles with ornate finials. Lightweight sheers, of which many have a machine-embroidered element, may be used for 'net' curtains (see pages 106-7). Small elements of embroidery – used like flat braids (see pages 118-121) – can be incorporated into plain lengths of fabric.

embroidery

Crewelwork is like fine embroidery, magnified in scale and color density. The colored patterns are visually very strong and need plain, restful surroundings or the whole effect will become too "busy". Cream-on-cream crewelwork fabrics are instantly enlivened when hung against the light – note the difference between the piece at the window and that draped over the table. The texture of the woven cloth itself is also affected by light diffusing through it, helped here by the fact that the curtain is unlined. The top cloth on the table is stitched solidly; the cream background is composed of fine-textured chainstitch. This produces a much stiffer fabric than those with unstitched grounds and is therefore better suited to floor or furniture covering than it is to window arrangements.

Needlepoint

Canvaswork or needlepoint is a form of embroidery in which the stitching is closely worked into an evenly woven cotton or linen canvas to cover the entire ground. The embroidery is usually worked in woolen thread (although silk is sometimes used), mostly in tent or cross stitch. Needlepoint is sometimes, incorrectly, called tapestry. (Although similar in appearance, tapestry is a woven fabric while needlepoint is produced with stitches.) Tapestry and needlepoint often sit well together in interior furnishings.

In the 16th century, upholstered furniture was rare, and the hard wooden seating commonly available was made more comfortable by needlepoint seat pad. At around the same period, needlepoint was also used to create bed hangings, often with large scale pictorial designs.

Needlepoint became a popular pastime for the women in well-to-do households in both the 18th and 19th centuries. Small decorative objects, like footstools and firescreens, were often covered in needlepoint. In the latter part of the century the patterns were often worked by the lady of the house and were taken from the popular magazines that circulated in middle-class households.

Needlepoint pictures were also popular, particularly in North America, where there was less in the way of a heritage of paintings, sketche and prints with which to cover the walls.

In every century, designs have reflected the decorativ fashions of the time, and so recurring trends like chinoiserie rural themes and floral images are the most abundant. Screen and small decorative objects such as footstools, pictures, fire screens and cushions were the most popular uses. And th Victorians also inserted bands of needle point as borders on tablecloths an curtains of velvet or wool.

Needlepoint rugs

It is possible to find 18th century or 19t century rugs of the English needlepoin type. The earlier ones, now quite rare are referred to as Turkey work, an imitated the Persian or Oriental carpet popular at the time. Old ones will b expensive and very often too fragile, o precious, to use underfoot. In response t the demand for antique rugs, ne versions have been made in the style c the original pieces, and these may b either decorated with period-style design or with direct copies of the 19th-centur motifs and patterns.

Modern developments

The uses that can be made of needlepoin today are still broadly the same as the were. Needlepoint textiles, owing to th

Original needlework on an early 18th century English wing armchair.

A French needlework valance, dating from the late 16th century.

An English needlework picture, dating from the late 16th century.

An English needlework in the Chinoiserie style, dating from the early 18th century.

olidity of the canvas on which they are created, are unyielding nd stiff, and so they have to be used flat. It is just this solidity hat makes them ideal for upholstering drop-in seats or stool overs, as well as covering screens and cushions.

As no machine has ever been able to reproduce the exact ffects of needlepoint, its greatest quality is its individuality; nd many of today's most talented textile designers are treating as a fine art, creating one-off pieces, which are framed and xhibited in the same way that an oil painting would be.

Because the needlepoint stitches are worked on the clearly visible squares created by the warp and weft of the canvas, its geometric formation makes it easy to translate a design for needlepoint by drawing it first on graph paper, each square of which represents a square of the canvas. As in embroidery, there are many different stitches that can be employed to create particular effects, although often the most successful designs are worked in one stitch, such as tent stitch, and rely solely on the design and colors for their effect.

needlepoint

One of the more interesting applications for needlepoint is to create a version of the wooden "lambrequin" – an elongated valance arrangement that sits round the top and part of the sides of a window. Valances are now popular again, and a needlepoint lambrequin could make an effective contribution to an otherwise fairly plain window treatment. Simple geometric designs, taken from Persian tiles or Provençal fabrics, would be easy to copy in this way. The curtain tie-backs could also be needlepointed in the same style.

Beadwork

This was widely introduced into Berlin wool work from the mid-1880s. First used to highlight details in the design, beads were later used for its entirety, with just the background worked in wool.

The beads were applied in place of a stitch, with a bead in every square of the canvas. The earlier bead designs were brilliantly colored, but the later ones were principally worked in black, grey and white beads. Grisaille (shades of gray) motifs were set against a plain ground of a single strong color. Beadwork was not solely decorative: on screens, banners or valances, the weight of the beads helped the textile to hang well.

Berlin work

This is an early 19th-century forerunner of today's popular canvas kits. The 18th-century embroiderers would draw out designs on their canvases themselves, copying published engravings. In 1804 in Berlin the first patterns were produced, printed on squared paper with hand-painted colors applied square by square, corresponding to those of the canvas.

Correctly matched colored thread would then be used to create the canvas picture. Originally the wide range of Berlin wools was dyed in the city, where a long established dyeing industry had operated successfully, but the popularity of Berlin work spread to other parts of Europe and the wools and patterns were soon produced in other countries.

Berlin work was often framed for hanging as pictures but it was also adapted to cover every conceivable household object, from footstools and chair seats to carpets and cushions. A specially manufactured canvas, in silk, permitted single motifs to be worked in the centre, leaving the remaining canvas plain.

The mass production of these printed patterns caused a resurgence in canvas work and embroidery, which had undergone a decline in the latter part of the 18th century with the rise of neo-classicism, which favoured lighter techniques such as whitework.

Antique pieces of needlework look very fine used in a traditional setting. All are richly textured, but their colors are subdued, even faded. The lambrequin is interesting and very imposing; it could be incorporated into a period interior, using other suitable fabrics beneath it.

Quilts

Quiltmaking has evolved over the years from a functional craft to a highly skilled and decorative art form. Today, the term quilt is generally used to refer to a bedcovering (though quilt-worked textiles have many other uses) which may have been produced in several ways. There are three main techniques involved: quilting, patchwork and appliqué, and these may be used singly or together on one quilt. Quilts have traditionally been made at home, and often the making of a quilt, or the quilt itself, was to commemorate an important or significant event such as a birth, a wedding or a death.

Nowadays quilts may be made by machine as well as by hand; both techniques have their own advantages. Machine sewing is clearly stronger and faster, but is less versatile. Hand stitching may be less even and is certainly more time consuming, but it is a better technique to use if the design is very detailed. Machine- and hand-sewing can be combined in one quilt.

Quilting

A traditional quilt consists of an entire cloth backed by padding and an underlining, with a pattern that is formed by stitching lines through the layers of fabric and padding. The fabric may be plain or patterned, pieced or appliquéd. Quilting flourished in 18th and 19th century Britain and America, and patterns were distinctive to different regions.

There are two specialized variations on the basic method of

There is only one example here – the creamy calico piece – that uses quilting alone as a means of decoration. Its stitching, taken through all the layers of cloth and wadding, forms a geometric pattern, with small floral motifs set between. The other pieces shown use patchwork and quilting – the indigo-dyed, rolled-up quilt, for example – or combine quilting with appliqué. On the black and white quilts the stitching is used like embroidery in addition to its function simply to quilt. The brightly patterned appliquéd quilt (bottom right hand corner) is decorated with geometric shapes and its scalloped edge is bound with a bright red fabric, crudely stitched in place. The dark blue and black cushion cover (top right) uses very graphic shapes which are appliquéd to a cream canvas ground. The appliquéd triangles that decorate the quilt that forms the background to all the others are further stitched and quilted onto the white fabric ground cloth which itself is made from pieces of joined cloth, each one decorated with different quilted patterns.

Quilting is usually worked on fabrics already cut to size for an intended use, nearly always bedcovers. However, machine quilting is available by the yard/metre. All the fabrics that are shown here, with the exception of the black and white ones, have been hand-sewn.

quilting. One is Italian, or corded, quilting, which relies on a method that dispenses with wadding altogether. Instead, two parallel stitch lines are used, running across and through two layers of fabric, to form a design. On the back of the quilt, cord is inserted to pad out the stitched channels. Being unpadded, this type of quilting is not very warm and is therefore a decorative rather than a functional device.

In the second method, known as Trapunto quilting, the stitched pattern is made through two unwadded layers, then a hole is made on the back of the hollow fabric "sandwich" and padding is inserted. The hole is sewn closed to hold the padding between the stitched areas. In this way the stuffed areas become like a sort of sculptural relief, with the emphasized patterns physically standing out from the flat areas of the quilt. Trapunto was popular in Europe in the 17th and 18th centuries, when the wealthier classes wore clothes ornately decorated with this style of quilting. In America its popularity reached a peak in the early 19th century, again predominantly amongst the wealthy.

Appliqué

A rich and ancient historical tradition of appliqué – stitching of pieces of cut cloth and other decorative objects such as beads or tiny mirrors to a plain ground cloth – exists. Distinctive examples are found all over the world, from Egyptian funeral tents to Hawaiian *luma-lau* quilting. In India, for example, appliqué and quilted work is closely associated with village embroidery. From Gujarat and Rajasthan come wonderful, brightly colored and vividly decorated appliqué hangings, covers, household and animal trappings. The village people use a wide range of materials and motifs and also combine appliqué with solid-color quilting. The technique of applique originated as a way of decorating and strengthening poor-quality cloth with left-over scraps of rich fabric. Not only did it have the advantage that it made economical use of fine fabrics, but it also proved to be a very decorative patterning alternative to embroidery that was far less time-consuming to produce. In 16th and 17th century Europe many great houses were decorated with applied work bed-hangings and tapestries. And when the

highly prized Indian cotton *palampores* came to the end of their usefulness as bedcovers, they were cut into pieces and the best bits then applied to a new ground.

Traditionally, in Europe and America, central motifs or patterns on a plain, light ground were surrounded by successive pieced borders. This was sometimes combined with the use of additional decorative stitching. The most usual motifs were flowers, fruit, leaves, birds, animals and people. The motifs used often had symbolic meaning. For example, the pineapple, which was a symbol of hospitality, was much used in Pennsylvanian appliquéd quilts. As with quilting, the designs were often pictorial representations of important events in the community or historical scenes.

Patchwork

From a modest beginning, where pieces of fabric were used literally to patch worn cloth, patchwork has evolved into a highly decorative art. Unlike appliqué, with a patchwork quilt there is no ground cloth: instead the pieces are joined side by side to form an overall pattern and a new fabric.

The range of patterns is vast; however, most tend to be geometric. Colors are coordinated, and darker fabrics can be cleverly used to form shadows and give a spectacular three-dimensional effect. A notable example of this is the American Log Cabin pattern, which represents the sides of a log cabin.

Some patchwork quilts are the framed or medallion type, where a central shape is surrounded by plain or patterned borders. These quilts were worked from the center. Others produce an all-over design, such as mosaic or strip patchwork. In America, where patchworking became almost a national obsession in the mid-19th century, block-style designs evolved, incorporating repeated blocks of a single geometric pattern. This type of patchwork is now the most popular.

The Amish community in America's Mid-West have a long tradition of producing beautiful quilts in powerful, bright colors and strong, uncomplicated patterns such as designs of diamonds and stars or even simple rectangles and squares. Originally hand-worked, their quilts are now pieced on treadle sewing machines. The Pennsylvanian Amish are a religious sect,

An American pictorial quilt made by Phoebe Cook of the Edison Township, Morrow County, Ohio.

An American quilt made by Mrs Caroline Brockmeier Engelman in the late 19th century in Christian County, Illinois.

A traditional appliqué patterned quilt, Princess Feather with oak leaves, made in 1850 in Kentucky by an 18-year-old slave named Mahulda Mize.

One of the many friendship quilts made throughout the 19th century. This is an album quilt, dating from the 1840s, and includes many typical motifs.

This quilt, in the pattern known as the "Double Wedding Ring", was made before World War II in Ohio. The rings are patchworked, the ground quilted.

This eye-dazzling "Pineapple" (or "Windmill Blades") patchwork quilt was made in 1880 by a woman from Buffalo, New York.

and their laws prohibit the making of quilts in anything other than abstract designs. Solid colors are preferred to patterned fabrics – mostly dark blues, greens and purples with bright, clashing colors such as red and fuschia. The designs are large-scale, but simple. The quilts made by the Amish community – even those produced in other areas of mid-western America which were influenced by the work of other, non-Amish, quiltmakers – are easy to distinguish from non-Amish quilts.

In mid-19th century America the making of "album" quilts became hugely popular. Each quilt would be made by a number of people, many of whom would be linked to the person to whom the quilt was given. Like the friendship album popular at the same period, these quilts were a form of remembrance, a going-away present or a wedding gift.

Using quilts

A quilted, patchwork or appliqué textile does not have to be used simply as a bedcover, although there is no doubt that this is a perfect combination of the quilt's functional and decorative properties. Many old or antique quilts which perhaps are too fragile to use as bedcovers where they would be handled daily,

could be hung over the top of the bed, like a canopy, supported by rods and held by fabric "tubes" attached carefully to the sides of the quilt. You could then view the quilt when lying in bed! Or a precious quilt could be hung on the wall, like a painting, displayed in its full beauty.

Floral patterned fabric, often chintz, tends to dominate many of the traditional patchwork quilts. A general floral theme may seem restrictive, but from a distance these tiny pieced patterns read as colorful designs. There is no reason why a quilt cannot be made – indeed they often were – from pieces of heavy cotton damask, richly figured silks or *toiles de Jouy* for example, in order that they work within an interior already containing such fabric. Colorful quilts can be used as throws over sofas – and in fact they can be quite useful, if thickly wadded, flung over upholstered furniture that is beginning to deteriorate.

There are some ethnic appliquéd quilts which contain strong, emblematic designs in plain colors. These can decorate all kinds of spaces and styles of interior – on the walls of children's rooms, hung over mantels or above beds, or even used as soft floor cloths over carpets.

An English patchwork quilt in the "Grandmother's Flower Garden" design, in patterned chintz, dating from circa 1825-30.

An embroidered cotton quilt from Bengal, Eastern India, dating from the middle of the 19th century.

An English medallion daybed cover, circa 1820, the design formed by cut-out chintz patterns, appliquéd onto a plain ground.

English patchwork, circa 1815-20, with a central medallion printed with a trophy of arms to commemorate Wellington's victory at Waterloo.

A delightful English patchwork cover, circa 1830, made from pieces of old chintz, which form a splendidly rich pattern.

An English strip quilt with a central medallion, printed in 1810 to commemorate George III's 50th Jubilee.

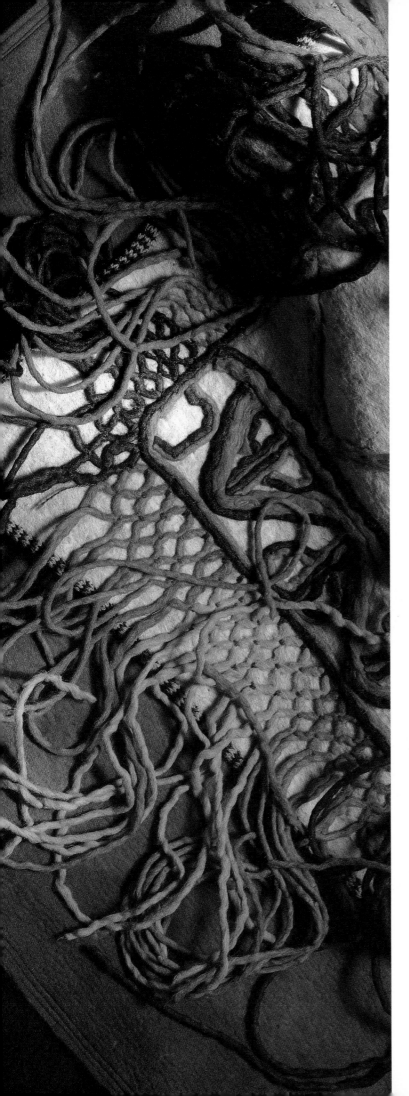

Felt

The word textile has its root in the Latin for weave, and therefore, strictly, is only used for woven fabrics. However, the literal meaning of the word fabric, again from the Latin, is to make or build. Although felt is a fabric, it is not a textile because it is not woven from spun yarn but made by matting unspun woolen fibers together.

How felt is made

The structure of the wool fiber, or staple, contributes to the ease with which, in certain conditions, wool will felt. The staple is made up from a series of overlapping scales that have a serrated edge. If the staple of wool is subjected to friction or pressure, it will behave rather like a spring, coiling up on itself. If many fibers are rubbed together, they will all coil up and tangle together. This is the beginning of felt-making. The other elements that must be present, in addition to friction and pressure, are heat and moisture.

To make felt the unspun, washed fleece is untangled by hand – teased – and then carded. Carding is a combing process which organizes the fibers into a parallel manner. The carded pieces are then layered on top of one another, each subsequent piece at right angles to the previous one, until the desired thickness is built up. This is then secured in a cotton covering of calico and canvas, held by stitching through the cloth.

Next follows the hardening process, which mattes the fibers together. Hot water is sprinkled onto the fabric-covered package, at the same time as even pressure is applied. It is important that the water is hot as it is the combination of heat and pressure that causes the fibers to matte together. The milling stage, where pressure is applied with a roller, repeats this process, but with the canvas covering removed. The fibers shrink during this process, and the more that they shrink the stronger the felt will be. Finally, the felt is dried and pressed flat with a steam iron.

This motley collection of felted items illustrates the delights and diversities of this tactile material. The type of wool used and the extent to which it has been spun affects the textural appearance of the felt. The deep colors are bright and cheerful and would make good floor rugs or decorative wall-hangings.

The fleece can be dyed before carding and colors blended together during the carding process. Colors can be layered to produce different effects, and other fibers, such as spun yarn or silk fiber, can be placed onto the carded layers to build up decorative patterns.

The history of felt

Felt-making is an ancient craft; some of the earliest felt remains found date from around 700 BC and originate from the frozen tombs of nomadic horsemen in the Siberian Atlai mountains. The tribe made clothing, saddles and tents from felt. Because felt is very strong and resistant to wet, snowy weather it was even used to make dwellings. Large sheets of felt would cover structures made from poles. Felt has also been used for centuries to make hats, to line instrument carrying cases and as part of the workings of pianos.

Using felt

Putting felt on walls, either for all-over walling techniques or simply as a single hanging, will greatly improve heat insulation, as well as acting as a soundproofing device.

Because felt is so densely compacted, it is difficult to burn (see Directory) and therefore is worthwhile considering as a top cover for upholstery. But it should not be used on items that undergo daily use as it will wear through.

The combined softness and strength of felt makes it a good choice for a floor-covering. Although a rug will be harder-wearing if it is made from a harsher, coarser fleece, the hardness makes it difficult to felt, so a mixture of soft and coarse fleece is probably the best solution.

Felt is not just a craft process – it is manufactured, and you can buy any color of smooth, flat felt by the yard. It is a greatly under-used cloth in furnishing situations, perhaps because people believe it will not last long. For curtains, however, it is a beautiful material to use as it is wonderfully soft and drapes well. Use its solid colors in great swathes – try bottle green against pale lemon or scarlet with navy blue.

Because felt does not fray like woven cloth, one of the major advantages in using it for soft furnishings is that you do not have to sew hems! You can, of course, join lengths together as required. It can be applied as a flat or fringed border to a curtain or valance edge and, similarly, no fraying will occur. Some ethnic rugs use a form of twisted felt as a fringe, which gives a wonderfully heavy and tactile edging.

Felt is undoubtedly a difficult fabric to use in an interior. The patterned pieces are visually strong and, like paintings, should be incorporated with care and much thought as one piece may easily dominate a room. The size of the design and the colors used in it will dictate where it may be hung to best effect. Plain felt, bought by the yard or metre, can be easily applied to entire walls. It is a great insulator, as well as playing a part in soundproofing!

Fabric
Directory

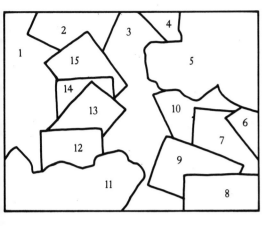

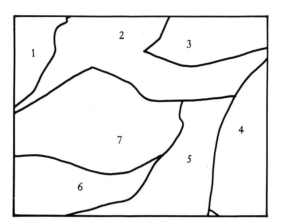

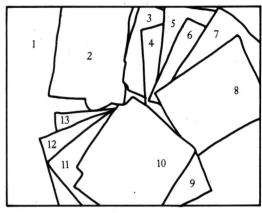

BLACK & WHITE p.18-19

1 Belgravia, Ian Morris
2 Indian Silk, 5079, McCulloch & Wallis
3 Arches, Timney Fowler
4 Olivia, Noir, 4288-95, Manuel Canovas
5 Gonfalonière, 10, John Stefanidis
6 Lyme, Noir, 4289.100, Manuel Canovas
7 Pali, Noir, 11146-99, Manuel Canovas
8 Peekaboo Bows, Celia Birtwell
9 Printed and Applied Pillow, Sarah King
10 Quilted piece, Manuel Canovas
11 Indian Silk, 5079, McCulloch & Wallis
12 Bellecourt, Noir, 4286.100, Manuel Canovas
13 Pramin, Noir, 4221.100, Manuel Canovas
14 Constance, 4287.96, Manuel Canovas
15 Indian Silk, 5079, McCulloch & Wallis

SINGLE COLOR p.24-25

1 Dúlverton, C7586-111, Parkertex
2 Stripe, Linen, NF242, Pallu & Lake (Interior Selection)
3 Knot, Ivory, Ian Sanderson
4 Star, Pearl, NF230, Pallu & Lake (Interior Selection)
5 Tavistock, Natural, 4016/01, Colefax & Fowler
6 Erbas Trellis, 128, Marvic
7 Mullion Twill, J0070/100, Baker

RICH p.34-35

1 Tintoretto, Gold, Kab
2 Pivots Tapisserie, 4951, Henry Newbury (Pansu)
3 Woven Wool Cloak from Mzab, Algeria, collected prior to 1909 (Joss Graham)
4 Strapwork, 991/09 (Brick), Hodsoll McKenzie
5 Tartan, NCF 202/05, Osborne & Little (Nina Campbell)
6 Tremolat, 4281/5 (Framboise/Jaune), Manuel Canovas
7 Velours Infroissable Gaufrage Montesquieu, 15121 (Cardinal), Percheron (Edmond Petit)
8 San Marco, 1220/11, Percheron (Rubelli)
9 Faille Padolle, 1826/3 (Moutarde), Pierre Frey
10 Darum, 4299/345, Clifton Textile (Zimmer Rohde)
11 Blue Ikat, Conran Shop
12 Bukhara, RF 3713 (Sage), Romo
13 Junction Stripe, Thorp

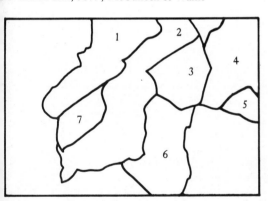

WOVEN p.20-21

1 India Song, 5068/839, Percheron (Chotard)
2 Oregon, 12652, Sahco Hesslein
3 Ellice, 12627, Sahco Hesslein
4 MacLachlan, M2796-64, Parkertex
5 Coutil Stripe, 2023, Jamasque
6 Silk Plaid, F300/01, Osborne & Little
7 Coutil Stripe, 2024, Jamasque

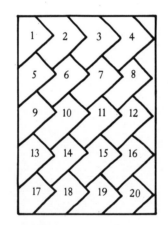

BASIC WEAVES p.28

1 Dobby Weave, FDW14, Osborne & Little
2 Isuna, 32, Baumann (Rudolf Volland)
3 Poncho, 4727, Tissunique (Rudolf Volland)
4 Mantilla, 4858, Tissunique (Rudolf Volland)
5 Valone, 10, Baumann
6 Park Stripe, 2, Ian Mankin
7 Sands of Time, 2458.01, Clifton Textiles (Jack Lenor Larsen)
8 Crocus, 228, Baumann
9 Holliday Ti, col. 209, Baumann
10 Relief, 840-2008, Boras Cotton
11 Diamond Stitch, F116/02, Designers Guild
12 Togo, 4932, Tissunique (Rudolf Volland)
13 Island, 4456, Tissunique (Rudolf Volland)
14 Park Spot, Ian Mankin
15 Tayside, Jo153/130, Baker
16 Linea, C220, Baumann
17 Campus, 243, Baumann
18 Shalimar, 8456-01, Clifton Textiles, Jack Lenor Larsen
19 Park Stripe, 1, Ian Mankin
20 Polkadot, M7604/90, Parkertex

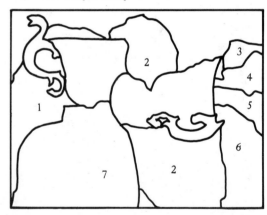

FIGURED SILK p.40-41

1 S6851, Gainsborough
2 San Marco, 1220/11, Percheron (Rubelli)
3 Almohada, A3110/450, Tissunique (Ardecora)
4 S6853, Gainsborough
5 Granduca, A3100/400 (Ardecora)
6 Bellini, Green/Spice, Watts & Co
7 Holbein, Red/Gold, Watts & Co

fabric directory

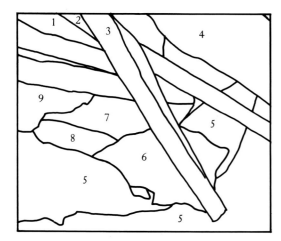

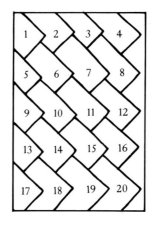

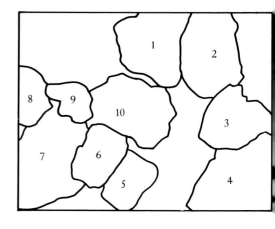

MODERN SILKS p.42-43

1 Thai silk, 199 014, Mary Fox Linton (Jim Thompson)
2 Taffeta, 107, Osborne & Little
3 Colette, 12, Osborne & Little
4 Thai silk, 190 226, Mary Fox Linton (Jim Thompson)
5 Silk Plaid, F300/08, Osborne & Little
6 Thai silk, 119 004, Mary Fox Linton (Jim Thompson)
7 Thai silk, S-4003, Mary Fox Linton (Jim Thompson)
8 Taffeta, 12, Osborne & Little
9 Courtisane, RS66832, Percheron (Rubelli)

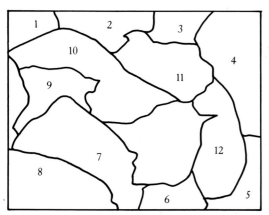

DAMASK AND BROCADE p.48-49

1 Vivant Damask (Pompeian red/Buff), T849003F, Warner
2 Rosette Stripe (Umber/Egyptian red), T853002F, Warner
3 India Song, 5068/600, Percheron (Chotard)
4 Fortrose Damask (Crimson/Rouge), T834/3, Warner
5 Percier Damask (Rich gold/Stone), T850009F, Warner
6 Lineate, 7153/117, Jab
7 Trevise, 15334/2, Percheron (Edmond Petit)
8 Magda (Rouge), F716, Designers Guild (Les Impressions)
9 My Lady's Garden, M5562/83, Parkertex
10 Elice, 12627, Sahco Hesslein
11 Fountain Damask (Antique Gold), GWC 89121, Warner
12 Florentino (Amber with Emerald), GWC 89530, Warner

TAPESTRY p.56

1 Brive, 6590 (Marine), Chanée Ducrocq
2 Crecy, Belinda Coote
3 Bukhara, RF 3711 (Navy), Romo
4 Prince Noir, 6792/3, Percheron (Rubelli)
5 Petit Point, ST 1911 (Red/Green), Pallu & Lake
6 Hampton, 2769/2, Marvic
7 Blois, Belinda Coote
8 Mougins, 6584 (Marine), Chanée Ducrocq
9 Martigues, 810/03, Lelièvre
10 Brive, 6591 (Rouge), Chanée Ducrocq
11 Tabriz, Belinda Coote
12 Tapisserie, ST 1933 (Gold/Red), Pallu and Lake
13 Cluny, 836-02, Lelièvre
14 Jumet, Belinda Coote
15 Carrouges, 813, Lelièvre
16 Conde, 6595 (Rouge), Chanée Ducrocq
17 Tapisserie, ST 1936 (Peach/Green), Pallu & Lake
18 Cross-Stitch, 310-05, Osborne & Little
19 Conde, 6598 (Abricot), Chanée Ducrocq
20 Petit Point, ST 1916 (Peach/Green), Pallu & Lake

PILE p.62-63

1 Malabar, 3051/3, Colefax & Fowler
2 Festival Velvet, T831/14, Warner
3 Velours Fiesole, 6357/3, Percheron (Rubelli)
4 Gonzague, 645/92 (Rouge/Vert), Chanée Ducrocq (Christian Lanzani)
5 Gaufrage Malesherbes, Red, Jab
6 Cellini, France, 12207, Percheron (Edmond Petit)
7 Velours Coton, Gaufrage Medicis, Vieil 02, Percheron (Edmond Petit)
8 Velours Tintoretto, 1012/1, Percheron (Rubelli)
9 Velours Quadrille, 27/524, Percheron (Tassinari & Chatel)
10 Velours Infroissable Gaufrage Montesquieu, 15121 (Cordial), Percheron (Edmond Petit)

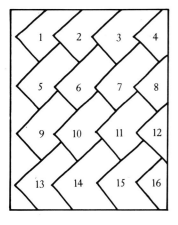

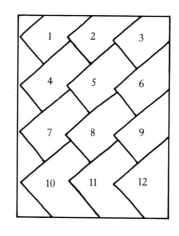

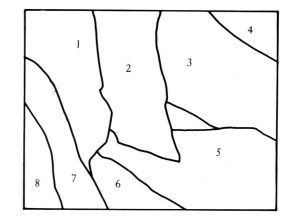

PILE p.65

1 Arson, 2398-774, Clifton Textiles (Zimmer Rohde)
2 Iseo, 6407 (Bleu), Chanée Ducrocq
3 Ravenne, 6344 (Bleu), Chanée Ducrocq
4 Alsace, 685/10 (Bleu/Beige), Lelièvre
5 Westminster, 9387-04, Clifton Textiles (Jack Lenor Larsen)
6 Montaigu, 107 (Bleu), Chanée Ducrocq
7 Ariana, 2333-974, Clifton Textiles (Zimmer Rohde)
8 Cortina, 6252 (Nattier), Chanée Ducrocq
9 Arda, 2428-689, Clifton Textiles (Zimmer Rohde)
10 Cézanne, 2590 (Campanule), Chanée Ducrocq
11 Albano, 9972 (Bleu), Chanée Ducrocq
12 Clearwater, 938402 (Moonstone), Clifton Textiles (Jack Lenor Larsen)
13 Velour Imberline, 2194, Percheron (Burger)
14 Gorgias, 2438-968, Clifton Textiles (Zimmer Rohde)
15 Gatinais, 368/12 (Jean), Lelièvre
16 Fourrure Zèbre, 612/1, Lelièvre

IKAT p.75

1 Ikat, AA368, Nice Irma's
2 Ikat, AA60, Nice Irma's
3 Eye Cat, VTX3, Bernard Thorp
4 SDS, 19423, St. Leger
5 Caretta, 945202 (Smoke Drift), Clifton Textiles (Jack Lenor Larsen)
6 Ikat, AA13, Nice Irma's
7 Thai silk, K4017, Mary Fox Linton (Jim Thompson)
8 Indo Ikat Lloseta, 36278-04 (Green/yellow), Colefax & Fowler, (Gaston y Daniela)
9 Ikat, A13, Nice Irma's
10 SDS, 9051, St. Leger
11 SDS, 19498, St. Leger
12 Ikat, AA34, Nice Irma's

TARTAN p.81

1 Ancient Hunting McRae, Ben Nevis
2 Ancient Douglas, M 2797-62, Parkertex
3 Black Watch, Ben Nevis
4 Hunter, Scotch House
5 Tartan, USA, Blue/Green, Payne
6 26-236NC (Twill), Anta
7 Ross Hunting, M2792/74, Parkertex
8 Silk Plaid, F300/03, Osborne & Little
9 21/2106 (Twill), Anta
10 34/236NC (Twill), Anta
11 Silk Plaids, F300/01, Osborne & Little
12 23/236 (Twill), Anta
13 Red MacAulai, Scotch House
14 Gordon, Ben Nevis
15 McNab, Ben Nevis
16 MacDonald Lord of the Isles, M2795/44, Parkertex

GRAPHIC AND LINEAR p.84-85

1 Tricastin, 276/12 (Biche), Lelièvre
2 Coutil Stripe, 2017, Jamasque
3 Stellar, 6664, Jamasque
4 Chemise, 18 (Sepia), Osborne & Little
5 Safi, 11, Osborne & Little
6 Banbury, 1303/17, Colefax & Fowler
7 Zig Zag, FZZ03, Osborne & Little
8 Park, Pewter, Ian Sanderson

STRIPES AND CHECKS p.88-89

1 Ticking I, Olive Green, Ian Mankin
2 Grande Rayure, France, 9892/88, Nobilis Fontan
3 Milleraie, France, 9893/96, Nobilis Fontan
4 Pelham Stripe, 1365/20 (Taupe), Colefax & Fowler
5 Garnachie Check, Green/Yellow/Red, Thorp
6 Pym Stripe, Turquoise, Ian Sanderson
7 Belur, 7978/133, Jab
8 Tassy, 4261/41 (Vert), Manuel Canovas
9 Milleraie, 9893.97, Nobilis Fontan
10 Ticking II, Air Force, Ian Mankin
11 Grande Rayure, 9892.90, Nobilis Fontan
12 Neuilly, 4263/60 (Bleu), Manuel Canovas
13 Ticking I, Pink, Ian Mankin
14 Grande Rayure, 9892/91, Nobilis Fontan
15 Ticking II, Dusty Pink, Ian Mankin
16 Pym Stripe, Brick, Ian Sanderson
17 Belur, 7978/125, Jab
18 Vitry, 4262/02 (Bois de rose), Manuel Canovas
19 Pelham Stripe, 1365/17 (Pink/Coral), Colefax & Fowler
20 Berber, Rouge, Elizabeth Eaton
21 Neuilly, 4263/08 (Rouge), Manuel Canovas
22 Tremolat, 4281/58 (Marine/Rouge), Manuel Canovas
23 Nantucket, ST3481 (Amethyst), Pallu & Lake
24 Pelham Stripe, 1365/19 (Amethyst), Colefax & Fowler

fabric directory

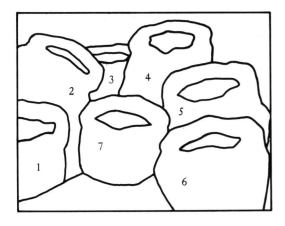

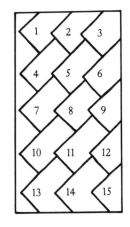

UTILITY p.90-91

1 Coutil Stripe, 2005, Jamasque
2 Mondria, 154/01, Kendix
3 Ticking stripe, Beige/Cream, Ian Mankin
4 Eclipse, 5605, Jamasque
5 Wide Ticking Stripe, Brown/Cream, Ian Mankin
6 Ticking stripe, Black/Cream, Ian Mankin
7 Coutil Stripe, 2017, Jamasque

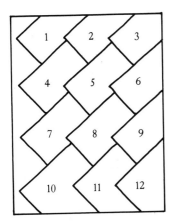

SOPHISTICATED CHECKS p.97

1 Asiago, F205/06 (Cornflower), Designers Guild
2 Tempo, 14378/73, Marvic (Deschemacher)
3 Istrana, F211/02 (Aquamarine), Designers Guild
4 Madison, 12512, Sahco Hesslein
5 Biscaya, TT6598, Tissunique (Tissard)
6 Millerton, 37834 (Cactus), David Ison (Payne)
7 Papageno Mu, 121, Baumann
8 Castiglione, 6721-3, Percheron (Rubelli)
9 Bronte Plaid, 41053 (Burgundy), David Ison (Payne)
10 Fulham Check, 37791 (Hunter), David Ison (Payne)
11 Cooper Plaid, 33489 (Emerald), David Ison (Payne)
12 Emmy Lou, 4512/5, Marvic

STRIPES p.98

1 Georgian Stripe, T840/17 (Cream/Soft Rose), Warner
2 Benares, C 6584/30, Parkertex
3 Mayence, 9796/87, Nobilis Fontan
4 Rigoletto, col. 39, Anna French
5 Rigoletto, col. 49, Anna French
6 Indira, 1740/6 (Rose/Mordore), Pierre Frey
7 Misa Moiré Stripe, 5635/3, Marvic
8 Leander, U6595/62, Parkertex
9 Coutil Stripe, 2018 (Clichy), Jamasque
10 Misa Moiré Stripe, 4330/4, Marvic
11 Chevrons, 4183/05 (Vieux Vert), Lelièvre
12 Azucena, 6863 col. 2, Percheron (Rubelli)
13 York, col. 3, Textra
14 Aurora, 08634, Sahco Hesslein
15 Leander, U6595/76, Parkertex
16 Ottoman Scozzese, MC4438, Alton Brooke (L. Marcato)
17 Opera Stripe, T854026F (Cream/Sung Green), Warner
18 Bellini, 4168/3 (Vieux Rose), Lelièvre
19 Orphée, 750/01, Lelièvre
20 Calèche, 9775-92, Nobilis Fontan
21 Ottoman Rigato, MC4440, Alton Brooke (L. Marcato)
22 Bossa Nova, 4201.4, Lelièvre
23 Cambridge, col. 6, Textra
24 Rigoletto, col. 29, Anna French
25 Gardone, 08631, Sahco Hesslein
26 Mapping, F138/03 (Claret), Designers Guild
27 Paul Stripe, ST3312 (Aqua), Pallu & Lake
28 Coutil Stripe, 2023 (République), Jamasque
29 Cascadio, 50118, Sahco Hesslein
30 Gonzague, 7012/2, Percheron (Laver)
31 Liberty, 12665B, Sahco Hesslein
32 Calèche, 9775-90, Nobilis Fontan
33 Roman Stripe, 606 4391, Alton Brooke (Bises Novita)
34 Turkoman, 839405 (Aubergine), Clifton Textiles (Jack Lenor Larsen)
35 Armani Moiré Check, 42116, David Ison (Payne)
36 Thai silk, 182 002, Mary Fox Linton (Jim Thompson)

MODERN WOVEN MOTIFS p.103

1 Chimu, 4273/56 (Nattier), Manuel Canovas
2 Star, 1350/31 (Delphinium Blue), Colefax & Fowler
3 Vine Leaf, FVL03, Osborne & Little
4 Céleste, 7005/14, Percheron (Lauer)
5 Hambledon, 073 779 413 (Navy), Laura Ashley
6 Laski, 2370/577, Clifton Textiles (Zimmer Rohde)
7 Lunes, TT6476, Tissunique (Tissart)
8 Meteor, 12717, Sahco Hesslein
9 Orsini, 9910-5, Tekko & Sawbra (Farois)
10 Berkeley, DH 928/02, Osborne & Little (Farois)
11 DR 1276/5, Turnell & Gigon
12 Napoli, DH 922/03, Osborne & Little (Farois)
13 Amalfi, 12508, Sahco Hesslein
14 Pine Tree, 515/25, Marvic
15 Tourette, 4309/27 (Paille/Marine), Manuel Canovas

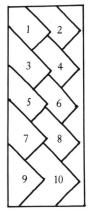

TRADITIONAL WOVEN MOTIFS p.104

1 F8886, Gainsborough
2 F8415, Gainsborough
3 Gothic Weave, NCF 200/12 (Coral), Osborne & Little (Nina Campbell)
4 Acorn Weave, 466 155 (Red/Beige), Osborne & Little (Nina Campbell)
5 Martigues, 810-03, Lelièvre
6 Tulipan, 4453/1, Marvic
7 Camargue, 3808/1, Percheron (Laller)
8 Weaves, FWS01, Osborne & Little
9 Fleur de Lys, 15377 (Rouge), Percheron (Edmond Petit)
10 FM 1631/3, Turnell & Gigon

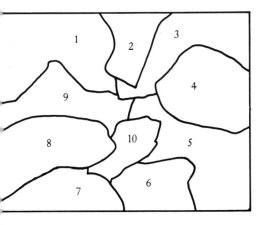

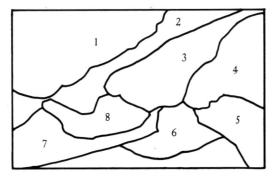

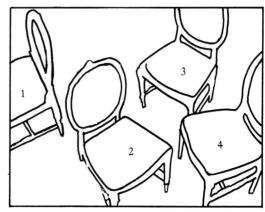

TRANSLUCENT p.106-7

1 Pimpernel, 68, Anna French
2 Terasson, 69033/1, Percheron (Rubelli)
3 Argentan, 69006/1, Percheron (Rubelli)
4 Fleurs, 69004/1, Percheron (Rubelli)
5 Polka Dot, BN 6076/1, Arthur Sanderson
6 Lormes, 60021, Percheron (Rubelli)
7 My Lady's Garden, C7071/12, Parketex
8 White Silky Muslin, Ian Mankin
9 Dentelle Guirlande, Beige, Percheron (Tassinari & Chatel)
10 Nancy, 62301/1, Percheron (Rubelli)

PRINTED OPENER p.122-123

1 Jeanne, CW/C, Alexander Beauchamp
2 Grata, F107/04, Designers Guild
3 Allegro, ST 1211, Pallu & Lake
4 Fresco, Neil Bottle
5 Brumes, FBR 319, Osborne & Little
6 Wild Orchid, RF 703/01, Muriel Short
7 Logetta Medici, K57/246 721 714, Laura Ashley
8 Mahal Co 17, John Stefanidis

TOILE p.130-131

1 Pillemont toile, 1662 bleu 1 (H A Percheron-Burger)
2 Toile La Batile, 2339 Vert 1 (H A Percheron-Burger)
3 QP 06512, Aqua (Alton Brooke – Edith de L'Isle design)
4 QP 06514, Green (Alton Brooke – Edith de L'Isle design)

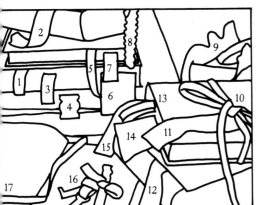

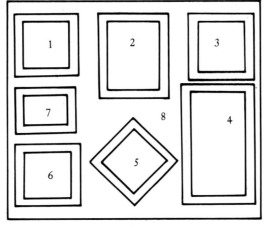

BRAIDS AND RIBBONS p.118-19

1 Silk Braid "B", Queen Caroline's Bed, Hampton Court Palace, Context Weavers
2 Jura Island Tabby Braid, Green/Red, Wendy Cushing
3 Gingham Braid, Dark Green, Wendy Cushing
4 Dauphine, 32420/9783, Houles
5 Silk Braid, Hampton Court Palace, Context Weavers
6 Tabby Braid, Pink/Light Blue, Wendy Cushing
7 Small Picot Braid, 04, Osborne & Little
8 Stewart Tartan, 2" Border Braid, Wendy Cushing
9 Bragance Giselle, France, 33056/9536, Houles
10 Charcoal Cord Braid, Wendy Cushing
11 Tartan Ribbon, 48 (Cameron), H.A. Caldicott
12 Small Picot Braid, Dark Blue, Colefax & Fowler
13 Perhyn Silk and Cotton Braid, Context Weavers
14 Large Picot Braid, Dark Blue, Colefax & Fowler
15 Kenwood Silk Braid, Context Weavers
16 Silk Ribbon, Hampton Court Palace, Context Weavers

PICTORIAL GROUP (in frames) p.134-135

1 Toile Ballon de gonesse, 1348 Percheron, Burger
2 Michele Geslin les Quatre Saisons, ST 3132, Pallu & Lake
3 Phoebus et borée, TF 18, Timney Fowler
4 Le Serment d'aimer, 9447.69, Nobilis et Fontan
5 Harvest blue, Design Archives
6 Sous le Signe de Neptune, Nobilis et Fontan
7 Chasse aux étangs, 1723/3 (Noir), David Ison Braquerie
8 Los Angles/historistamus TF 34, Timney Fowler

TOILE p.132-133

1 Toile Fragonnard, 1471/4 (H A Percheron-Burger)
2 Amadeus, Red (Design Archives)
3 Fete Champetre (Prelle)
4 Zinnia, 10982 (Burger)
5 Le Temps et L'amour, 1778/1 (Braquenie)
6 Villageoire, 1731-4 (Braquenie)
7 Pillemont Toile, 1662-2 (H A Percheron-Burger)
8 Toile les Pecheurs, 1589/1 (H A Percheron-Burger)
9 Toile Fete Navale, 1414/1 9H A Percheron-Burger)
10 La Chasse, 5550/112 (Marvic)
11 Toile Fragonnard, 1471/4 (H A Percheron-Burger)
12 Les Attributs, 1732/3 (Braquenie)

fabric directory

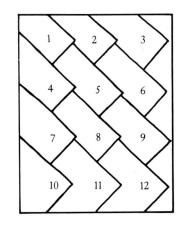

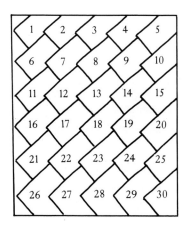

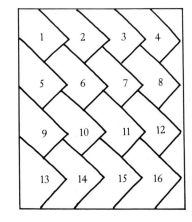

MODERN PICTORIAL p.134
1 Flower and Twig, Reputation
2 Party Print, Reputation
3 Crown Jewels, Reputation
4 Fruit and Veg, Reputation
5 Diddle-Dee-Dum, Reputation
6 Dressing Table, Janet Milner
7 Ablution, Janet Milner
8 Statues, TF38, Janet Milner
9 Mexico, Janet Milner
10 Deckchairs, Reputation
11 Small Roman Heads, TF276, Timney Fowler
12 Big Chief, Janet Milner

FLORAL p.136-137
1 Casa Del Campo, 7011/1, Percheron (Rubelli)
2 Le Grand Corail, 1080A/2, David Ison (Braquenie)
3 Clarissa (Mauve/Green), 1044/03, Colefax & Fowler
4 Ribbon Flower, Hodsoll McKenzie
5 Percale Persane, 2315/5, Percheron (Burger)
6 California at Night, White on red, Celia Birtwell
7 Passion Flower, Blue, Lewis & Franco
8 Picardy, R1203/004, Baker
9 Tits and Cherries, George Smith
10 Madura Tree, Blue/Green, Habitat

CHINTZ p.143
1 Tulipan Pink, 445853, Osborne & Little (Nina Campbell)
2 Anemone Stripe, 85/01, Designers Guild
3 Ashill, 1202/06 (Apricot), Colefax & Fowler
4 Dog Rose, 777531, Cole
5 Dog Rose, 77754, Cole
6 Canterbury (Crushed Strawberry/Sand), 217 307 109, Laura Ashley
7 Les Tableaux Chinois, 320 10/2, Tissunique (Clarence House)
8 Dianthus, M722 (Blue), Jean Monro
9 Mansfield Park, 20300/002 (Blue), Design Archives
10 Hydrangea and Rose, M768 (Green/Pink), Jean Monro
11 Sweet Pea, 217 306 492 (Burgundy/Multi Sand), Laura Ashley
12 Manon, M776 (Blue), Jean Monro
13 Fuchsia, 1070/01, Colefax & Fowler
14 Chelsea Bouquet, 50400/002, Design Archives
15 Manon, M777 (Mellon), Jean Monro
16 Rose Cuttings, Guy Evans
17 Lily and Auricula, M520 (Blue), Jean Munro
18 Selwood, FR115, Today Interiors
19 Peony, 68343, Cole
20 Cranford, M786 (Burgundy), Jean Munro
21 Seaweed, 217 169 115 (Burgundy/Tobacco), Laura Ashley
22 Rose Fern, M781 (Cream/Pink), Jean Munro
23 Fontaine Bleau, F6440, Muriel Short
24 Charleston, 90060 A002 (Blue), Jean Munro
25 Grapevine, M732, Jean Munro
26 Jean, M 764 (Cream), Jean Munro
27 Lochryan, M 749 (Slate), Jean Munro
28 Roses and Leaves, E 8507, Ramm, Son & Crocker
29 Selwood, FR 117, Today Interiors
30 Rose Bouquet, 68322, Cole

ARTS AND CRAFTS p.148
1 Acorn, PR 7422/4, Arthur Sanderson
2 Acorn, PR 7422/3, Arthur Sanderson
3 Blackberry, PR 7425/3, Arthur Sanderson
4 Madura Tree, Gray and Green, Habitat
5 African Marigold, 1066012/G, Liberty
6 Trent, 1066010/J, Liberty
7 Madura Leaf, Claret and Navy, Habitat
8 Rosy Buds, Alexander Beauchamp
9 Foliage, 7424/3, A. Sanderson
10 Honeysuckle, 1067033/E, Liberty
11 Willow, 1067030/A, Liberty
12 Sweet Briar, PR 7421/1, Arthur Sanderson
13 Ianthe, 1069604, Liberty
14 Foliage, PR 7424/2, Arthur Sanderson
15 Lodden, 110 8119, Liberty
16 Sweet Briar, PR 7421/2, Arthur Sanderson

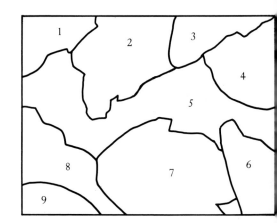

BIRDS AND ANIMALS p.150-151
1 Elephant, TF77, Timney Fowler
2 Les Papillons, 1862, Pierre Frey
3 Animal Solo, Red on white, Celia Birtwell
4 Night Bird, ST1307, Pallu & Lake
5 Little Animals, White on blue, Celia Birtwell
6 Pekin, S1090/05, Baker
7 Leaf and Bird, LB1, Hill & Knowles
8 Perdrix, 1785/1, David Ison (Braquenie)
9 Thomas, A1173/02, Baker

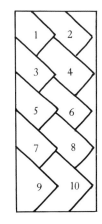

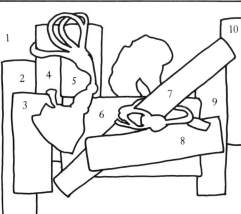

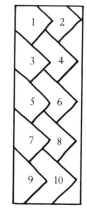

ANIMALS AND BIRDS MODERN p.152

1 Leopard Print, Reputation
2 Cockerels, Reputation
3 Cats, Celia Birtwell
4 Tahiti, 07464, Sahco Hesslein
5 Foxes, TF78, Timney Fowler
6 Little Animals, Red on white, Celia Birtwell
7 Animals, Blue, Reputation
8 Babar, 6839 col. 1, Percheron
9 Small Animal Trellis, Black and red on white, Celia Birtwell
10 Birds and Berries, col. 1, Schemes

PRINTED MOTIFS p.154-155

1 Leaf, 464 A595, Hodsoll McKenzie
2 Jaisal Mir, 13, John Stefanidis
3 Lincoln, PF 570, Today Interior
4 Clover, F293/01, Osborne & Little
5 Periwinkle, F292/03, Osborne & Little
6 Coup de Pied de la Lune, 9854/89, Nobilis Fontan
7 Lincoln, JA11F/01, Jane Churchill
8 Pembroke, PF558, Today Interior
9 Grotto, F295/01, Osborne & Little
10 Pelham, FR106, Today Interior

PAISLEY p.164

1 Paisley Ribbons, C5336531 (Jade/Aqua/Navy), Warner
2 Cadiz, CF808, Today Interiors
3 Surat, col. 4, Titley & Marr
4 Kalif, Brooke Fairbairn (Boussac)
5 Provençale, 0190-12, Today Interiors
6 Provençale, 0280-12TT, Today Interiors
7 Jodhpur, 20017/4, Pierre Frey
8 Katmandou, 6210/4, Percheron (Rubelli)
9 Shabanou, 3790/1, Percheron (Rubelli)
10 Facsimile, F180181, Brian Yates

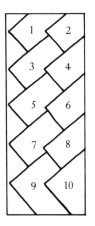

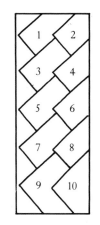

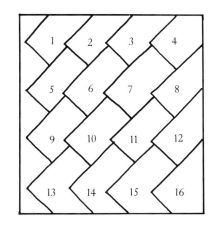

ANIMALS AND BIRDS TRADITIONAL p.153

1 Morelo, Rust/Beige, Habitat
2 Ornis, 7748/559, Clifton Textiles (Zimmer Rohde)
3 Les Enfants, 5440/002, Marvic
4 Calico Bird, 70P972 (Red, white & blue), Elizabeth Eaton
5 Tits and Cherries, George Smith
6 Bird Arcade, F 10721, Elizabeth Eaton
7 Amadeus, 70200/003 (Green), Design Archives
8 Bestiaire des Indes, 9947/01, Guy Evans (Prelle)
9 Buckingham Toile, LJ 8761/1, Pallu & Lake
10 Ascari, 224/02, Elizabeth Eaton (Diament)

PROVENÇAL p.159

1 La Fleur de Maussane, 1220/04, Souleiado
2 Embarras, QQ0060/044, Les Olivades
3 Troubadour, QQ0115/117, Les Olivades
4 Petite Perse, 1978/03, Souleiado
5 Bonis, QQ078/41, Les Olivades
6 Le Trastevere, 1779/08, Souleiado
7 Maillanenco, QQ0010/004, Les Olivades
8 Pietá, QQ0124/004, Les Olivades
9 Campano, QQ0029/005, Les Olivades
10 Le 14 Juillet, 1759/01, Souleiado

MODERN PRINTED MOTIFS p.167

1 Caliph, 2, Textra
2 Provence, PR7532/22, Arthur Sanderson
3 Papageno, MU172, Baumann
4 Barberini, F231B, Osborne & Little
5 Papageno, MU199, Baumann
6 Papageno, MU188, Baumann
7 Ornato, 21, Baumann
8 Empreinte, F6026, Designers Guild (Jacques Grange)
9 Ruskin, T250/09, Brian Yates
10 Montana, TT6341, Tissunique (Tissart)
11 Chelmsford, 02, Brian Yates (Dovedale)
12 Ashpy, 2, Textra
13 Minium, 32, Textra
14 William, T240/07, Brian Yates
15 Foliat, 590/6, Tekko & Sallubra (Fuggerhaus)
16 Montana, TT6341, Tissunique (Tissart)

fabric directory

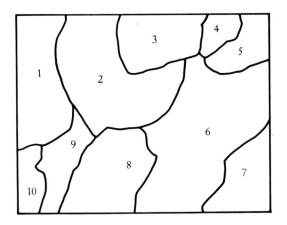

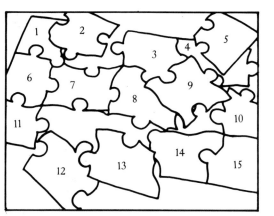

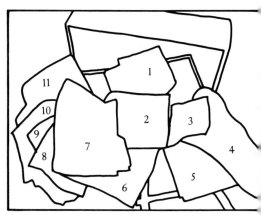

STRIPES AND GEOMETRICS p.168-169
1 Perugia, F233C, Osborne & Little
2 Design Stripe, TF57, Timney Fowler
3 Park Avenue, Mediterranean, ST1760, Pallu & Lake
4 Tiger Stripe, PR7304/21, Arthur Sanderson
5 Scritch Scratch, 17, John Stefanidis
6 Volterra, F232B, Osborne & Little
7 Medium Stripe, TF102, Timney Fowler
8 Kim, 04, Osborne & Little
9 Art Nègre, 17, John Stefanidis
10 Caterina, F875/05, Designers Guild (I. De Borchrave)

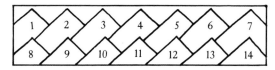

PRINTED STRIPES & GEOMETRICS p.172-173
1 Darby, 600A, Elizabeth Eaton (Alan Campbell)
2 Harmony, 5570/01, Marvic
3 Messare Stripe, 11, Osborne & Little
4 Clifton, 604A, Elizabeth Eaton (Alan Campbell)
5 Memrie Stripe, Elizabeth Eaton (Alan Campbell)
6 Moorea, 03, St. Leger
7 Zig, Perle, Elizabeth Eaton (Regis Dhellemes)
8 Fez, Verone, St Leger
9 Kew FR, 202, Textra
10 Plaid, F137/04, Designers Guild
11 Lincoln Stripe, X12F, Hill & Knowles
12 Quadro, 11-6063-155, Mary Fox Linton
13 Tiger Stripe, PR7304/3, Arther Sanderson
14 Elveden Stripe, Blue, 2012/01, Colefax & Fowler

ABSTRACT p.174-175
1 Ruffles, 214c, Osborne & Little (Zandra Rhodes)
2 Duero, 543/15, Kendix
3 Clay Pots and Shelves, Reputation
4 Kreppa, 7812-335, Clifton Textiles
5 Pyrit, 6220/2, Baumann
6 Kasbah, 15825/16, Collier Campbell
7 Still Life, 15944/419, C.Fishbacher
8 Srinagar, F210A, Osborne & Little (Zandra Rhodes)
9 Graffiti, 15945/511, C.Fishbacher
10 Alina, 7874/905, Clifton Textiles (Zimmer Rohde)
11 August, 12, Collier Campbell
12 Foxtrot, 15917/3, Collier Campbell
13 Waterstone, F33, Designers Guild
14 Chianti Wine and Smelly Cheese, Reputation
15 Punchinella, B4, Celia Birtwell

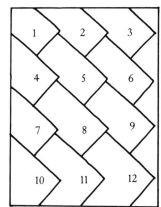

ABSTRACT p.176
1 Our Garden, 5086, Collier Campbell
2 Olivia, Holland, 550/75, Kendix
3 Calypso, Germany, 1196, Tissunique (Volland)
4 Bedouin Stripe, 5014, Collier Campbell
5 Tintura, Holland, 558/69, Kendix
6 Willow Weave, 5048, Collier Campbell
7 Lima, Holland, 532/78, Kendix
8 Guitar Stripe, 5144, Collier Campbell
9 Park Stripe, Col.1., Schemes
10 Maya, TU329053, Germany, Tissunique (Tulipan)
11 Blaise, 5077, Collier Campbell
12 Havana, 5061, Collier Campbell

ETHNIC PRINTS p.180-181
1 Kokors, Keturah
2 Onipa Nni Aye, Fabric from Sierra Leone
3 Wisa, Keturah
4 Oboba, Keturah
5 Tie-dyed cloth from Nigeria, 7234, Joss Graham
6 Batik from Indonesia with Animals
7 Afi, Keturah
8 Waves, Keturah
9 Okyeyami, Keturah
10 Kotere, Keturah
11 Adere Cloth from Nigeria, Joss Graham

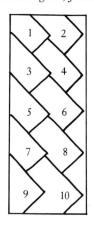

MODERN ETHNIC PRINTS p.182
1 Batik, 1066/00, Elizabeth Eaton
2 India XVIII Terracotta – Blue, 33537/07, Colefax & Fowler (Gaston y Daniela)
3 Maruk, 7654/315, Zimmer Rohde
4 Batik, 1319/06, Elizabeth Eaton
5 Bukhara, USA, 2157/03, Clifton Textiles, Jack Lenor Larsen
6 Batik, 80013, Elizabeth Eaton
7 Batik, 1391/23, Elizabeth Eaton
8 Kermanshah, red, 30400A012, Design Archives
9 Isoro Ne Asase, Keturah
10 Fathia, Keturah

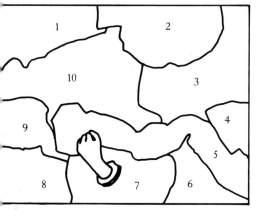

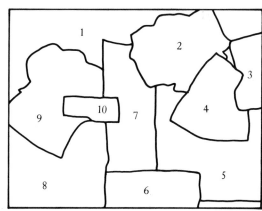

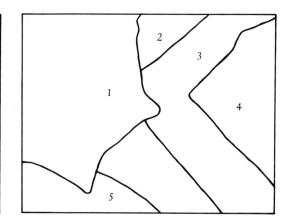

HAND PRINTED p.186-187
1 Original Printed Fabric, Jane Wildgoose
2 Tassel Print, Ian Morris
3 Pottery, Ian Morris
4 Warp Printed Silk (blue/white), Kab
5 Warp Printed Silk, (yellow/red), Kab
6 Original printed fabric, Jane Wildgoose
7 Yellow Garden, DO52, Bentley & Spens
8 Hand Printed Scarf, Sian Tucker
9 Hand Printed on Red Silk, Neil Bottle
0 Hand Printed Wall Hanging, Jasia Szerszynska

EMBROIDERY p.196-197
1 Beadwork, Guinevere Antiques
2 Green Embroidery on White Linen, Guinevere Antiques
3 Jacobean Crewelwork, Nice Irma's
4 Green Silk with Bunches Embroidered in Gold Threads, Guinevere Antiques
5 Embroidered Felt Lambrequin, McKinney Kidston
6 Panel of Crewelwork c.1742, Antique Textile Co
7 Embroidery Sample, Sarah King
8 Eskimo Art Collection Embroidery Sample, Loughborough College of Art (Dona Martin)
9 18th century Italian Linen Panel, Antique Textile Co
10 Machine Embroidery and Quilt Sample, Sarah King

FELT p.214-215
1 Felt Tent Hanging from Afghanistan, Joss Graham
2 Felt Wall Hanging, Victoria Brown
3 Felt Wall Hanging, Victoria Brown
4 Felt Tent Hanging from Afghanistan, Joss Graham
5 Yellow Felt, Brown

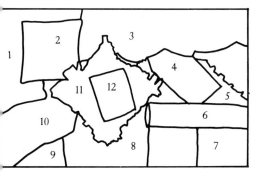

APPLIED OPENER p.192-193
1 Needlepoint Carpet, Guinevere Antiques
2 Petit Point Pillow, Kaffe Fassett
3 Antique Applied Valance, McKinney Kidston
4 Sample of Appliqué and Embroidery, Loughborough College of Art (Michelle Emsley)
5 Felt Wall Hangings, Victoria Brown
6 Felt Wall Hangings, Victoria Brown
7 Sample of Appliqué and Embroidery, Lorna Moffat
8 Appliqué Pillow from Egypt, Joss Graham
9 Sealife Collection Sample of Appliqué, Loughborough College of Art (Dona Martin)
0 Pillow with Patchwork Appliqué on Ticking, Sarah King
1 Jacobine, 4182 qui78, Manuel Canovas
2 Black Felt, Brown

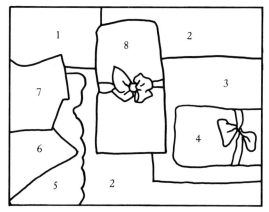

QUILTS p.208-209
1 Appliqué Pillow from Egypt, Joss Graham
2 Kansas Lily Quilt, American, c.1860, Antique Textile Co
3 20th century Rosy Quilt, McKinney Kidston
4 19th century Blue Patchwork Quilt, Antique Textile Co.
5 Appliqué piece, Guinevere
6 Black and White Quilted and Printed Pillow, Sarah King
7 Quilted Silk Sample, White and Blue, Sarah King
8 Cream Quilted Bedcover, Pillow and Covers

Set Details

Sets designed by
JACQUI SMALL

Fabrics supplied and
styled by
MELANIE PAINE

Made up by
PAINE & CO.,
49-51 Barnsbury Street,
Islington,
London N1 1TP.
(071) 607 1176

Sets propped by
KARINNA
GARRICK,
23 Guinness Trust
Buildings,
Kennington Park Road,
London SE11 4JG.
(071) 582 4999

Sets painted by
MATTHEW
USMAR LAUDER,
13 Marrell House,
Elmington Estate,
London SE5 7JD.
(071) 701 0575

Sets built by
HARRY
METCALFE,
71 Leonard Street,
London EC2.
(071) 739 2530

Flowers supplied by
PAULA PRYKE,
20 Penton Street,
Islington,
London N1.
(071) 837 7336

Window backdrops
painted by
PHILIPPA
DANIELS,
19A Gibson Square,
London N1
(071) 704 9168

All textile suppliers and
manufacturers'
addresses can be found
on pages 230-5.

TITLE PAGE
pages 2/3

Armoire from:
GUINEVERE
ANTIQUES,
578 King's Road,
London SW6
Tel (071) 736 2917

MODERN PRINTED
page 4

Fabric on chair:
ENGLISH
ECCENTRICS,
'Gaudi' slub silk
Pleated fabric:
METAPHORES,
'Venise'
Chair by:
ANDRE DUBREUIL
from:
UNEASY,
12 Porters Walk,
Tobacco Dock,
London E1.
Tel (071) 488 4563
Hand by:
SCOT
CUNNINGHAM
from:
THE STUDY,
55 Endell Street,
London WC2.
Tel (071) 240 5844

ANTIQUE SILKS
pages 12/13

Articulated hands from:
CORNELISSEN &
SON LTD,
105 Great Russell
Street,
London WC1.
Tel (071) 636 1045

**WOOLLEN AND SILK
DAMASKS**
pages 14/15

Fabrics:
all by STUART
INTERIORS
Background (on wall):
"Norwich" SRT-LA-
4005-B
on chair: "Rose, Pansy"
SRT-LAST-4047-A
over chair: "Hunting
Park" SRT-LA-3583-B
over table (top):
"Abbeville" SRT-
LALI-4011-B
over table (bottom):
"Heraldic Beasts" SRT-
LALI-4211-B
Table and wooden
accessories from:
STUART
INTERIORS
Barrington Court,
Barrington,
Somerset.
Tel (0460) 40349
Pewter accessories from:
JACK CASIMIR LTD
23 Pembridge Road,
London W11.
Tel (071) 727 8643

TICKING
pages 16/17

Fabric details:
on picture frame
IAN MANKIN: black/
white ticking
on chair
F. R. STREET: navy/
white mattress ticking
cushion:
OSBORNE &
LITTLE: "Chemise"
5864 Coal 29
blind:
ELIZABETH
EATON: "Berber" noir
tablecloth:

top cloth: IAN
SANDERSON
"Ticking Grey" 01
undercloth:
DESIGNER'S GUILD
"lapalone" F185/05
Paintings by:
W. SUMMERS,
15 Morley Road,
East Twickenham,
Middlesex.
Tel (081) 892 6810
Glassware from:
COLLIER
CAMPBELL

**WOVEN AND
PRINTED OPENERS**
pages 20/21 and
122/123

Tiles from:
LASSCO,
Mark Street,
London EC2.
Tel (071) 739 0448

CALICO
pages 30/31 and 32/33

Twig four poster bed:
PINEAPPLE,
Cleveland Cottages,
London Street,
Bath,
Avon BA1 5DD.
Tel (0225) 446181
Chair by:
RUTH HARJULA,
The Coach House,
Westmill Lane,
Hitchin, Herts,
SG5 3RP.
Tel (0462) 422118
Rope pot by:
KARINNA
GARRICK,
23 Guinness Trust
Buildings,
Kennington Park Road,
London SE11 4JG.
Tel (071) 582 4999

Calico from:
F. R. STREET
(trade only)
Canvas & cord from:
RUSSELL &
CHAPPLE LTD
and on the bed:
GERRIETS
Rosettes by:
HUNTER AND
HYLAND LTD
(trade only)
Chair and tabard by:
SOHO DESIGNS,
263 King's Road,
London SW3.
Tel (071) 376 5855

RICH SILK
pages 40/41

Antique lead urns from:
LASSCO,
Mark Street,
Off Paul Street,
London EC2.
Tel (071) 739 0448

SILKS
pages 44/45

Plain silk taffeta by:
PONGEES LTD
Striped silk (on wall):
OSBORNE &
LITTLE
"Carmen" col 01
Purple cushion:
SAHCO HESSLEIN
Napoleonic "Bee" pattern
silk fabric, also antique
Empire bed, chest and
candelabra
from:
RUPERT
CAVENDISH,
610 King's Road,
London SW6.
Tel (071) 731 7041
Coronet by:
McKINNEY
KIDSTON

DAMASK pages 50/51

Fabrics details:
THE ANTIQUE
TEXTILE
COMPANY (left hand,
on sofa)
and
McKINNEY
KIDSTON (right hand,
on sofa)
Cushions from:
CHRISTOPHE
GOLLUT
Curtain from:
McKINNEY
KIDSTON
Tassels from:
G. J. TURNER
Pole from:
McKINNEY
KIDSTON
Wallpaper:
WATTS & CO
Georgian sofa from:
ANTHONY
OUDRED,
533 Furniture Cave,
Kings Road,
London SW10.
Tel (071) 352 8840
Antique Aubusson carpet
from:
THE VIGO CARPET
GALLERY
6a Vigo Street,
London W1.
Tel (071) 439 6971

**MODERN
TAPESTRY**
pages 58/59

Fabric on sofa, shelf unit
and curtain:
BRUNSCHWIG &
FILS "Warwick
Tapestry"
Other chair:
OSBORNE &
LITTLE Tapestry Stria
F312-03

Sofa and armchair from:
SIMON TRACY,
18 Church Street,
London NW8.
Tel (071) 724 5890
*Blue and white patterned
china from:*
THE REJECT
SHOP,
245 Brompton Road,
London SW3.
Tel (071) 584 7611

KILIM
pages 68/69

*Kilim upholstered
furniture from:*
GEORGE SMITH,
587-589 King's Road,
London SW6.
Tel (071) 384 1004
Large Orary from:
FIVE FIVE SIX
ANTIQUES,
556 Kings Road,
London SW6.
Tel (071) 731 2016 /
071) 624 5173
*Paintings, lamps and
accessories from:*
CHRISTOPHER
HODSALL,
91 Pimlico Road,
London SW1.
Tel (071) 730 3370 /
2320 / 8076

WOVEN ETHNIC
pages 76/77 and 218

Fabric details:
*100% cotton ikat
from:*
THE CONRAN
SHOP,
*Bed, antique Indian
wooden canopy (over bed)
also dhurry, blue
and white cushions,
bedcover, side tables
and vases
all from:*
THE CONRAN
SHOP,
Michelin House,
81 Fulham Road,
London SW3.
Tel (071) 589 7401
*Antique wallhangings and
cloths from:*
JOSS GRAHAM,
10 Eccleston Street,
Pimlico,
London SW1.
Tel (071) 730 4370

Linen carpet on bed by:
ANGUS WILLIAMS,
10 Worthington Road,
Surbiton, Surrey,
KT6 7RX.
Tel (081) 399 8563
Cushions by:
JOHANNA
HOLDEN,
Unit C18 Metropolitan
Workshops,
Enfield Road,
London N1 5AZ.
Tel (071) 254 6843

MADRAS
page 78

Fabric details:
bed: IAN MANKIN
and cushions:
LIBERTY,

TARTAN
pages 82/83

Fabric details:
Swag:
"Campbell tartan" NCF
202/05
OSBORNE &
LITTLE
Nina Campbell design
Curtains:
ANTA (blue)
Design no 25 2106
Twill
ANTA (yellow)
Design no 27 2106
Twill
Bench squab:
ANTA Design no 33
236 NC2 Twill
Stools/books:
as curtains or bench
squab
Throws:
ANTA (over stool)
Design no 46 236 NC2
Twill
(over bench – red)
ANTA Design no 92
TWDC Worsted
(over bench – green)
ANTA Design no 30
TWDC Worsted
Floor:
ANTA 316 Carpet
and ropes:
TURNER & CO LTD
Plaster thistles from:
LONDON FINE ART
PLASTER
79 Audrey Street,
London E2.
Tel (071) 739 3594

Lead urn from:
ST. BRELADES
GALLERY
1st Floor,
Furniture Cave,
533 King's Road,
London SW3.
Tel (071) 351 1204

GINGHAM
pages 92/93

Fabric details:
Cushions:
PALLU & LAKE:
"Nantucket Navy"
ST3492 (blue/cream
tiny check)
MANUEL
CANOVAS: "Vitry"
4262/43 (green/cream
plaid)
"Passy" 4261/58 (blue/
cream)
"Passy" 4261/41 (green/
cream)
Squab:
"Pagan" 4270/08
Curtains:
TURNELL &
GRIGON 1530/04
Tabs on curtains:
ELIZABETH
EATON "Edinburgh
Check" 83174
Throw:
DESIGNER'S
GUILD "Mirepoix"
F183/02
Spanish sofa from:
LENA NORDMARK
F8184 Alfies Antique
Market
1325 Church Street,
Marylebone,
London NW8.
Tel (071) 723 0429
*Tables, plate rack, old
spoons and patterned
china from:*
CHALON
ANTIQUES,
The Plaza,
535 King's Road,
London SW10.
Tel (071) 351 0008
Blue pottery from:
THE CONRAN
SHOP,
Michelin House,
81 Fulham Road,
London SW3.
Tel (071) 589 7401
Pole from:
McKINNEY
KIDSTON

WOVEN STRIPES
pages 94/95

*Table, chairs and wall
lights from:*
SOHO DESIGN,
263 King's Road,
London SW3.
Tel (071) 376 5855
Tableware from:
THE CONRAN
SHOP,
Michelin House,
81 Fulham Road,
London SW3.
Tel (071) 589 7401
Tableware also from:
THOMAS GOODE
& CO,
19 South Audley Street,
London W1.
Tel (071) 499 2823
Fabric details:
On walls & tablecloth:
F. R. STREET
coloured mattress
tickings
squab cushions & blind:
WARNER & SONS
LTD
"Highfield" GWC
89803 (Emerald/beige)
"Highfield" GWC
89802 (navy/white)
"Casual Colours" GWC
89760 (Indigo)
(piping)
"Casual Colours" GWC
89758 (red)

**SOPHISTICATED
STRIPES**
pages 101/102

Fabric details:
Curtain:
PERCHERON
"Carlos" 7002/1
Drapes:
PIERRE FREY "Faille
Padque" 1826 Acajon 6
"Faille Padque" 1826
Montarde 3
Chair:
PARKERTEX Paul
Stripe ST3311
"Citrine"
*Furniture and
candlestick by:*
MARK
BRAZIER JONES,
Hay Farm House,
Police Row,
Therfield,
Hertfordshire.
Tel (07638) 7550

Painting by:
W. SUMMERS,
15 Morely Road,
East Twickenham,
Middlesex,
London.
Tel (081) 892 6810

WOVEN MOTIFS
page 105

Fabric details:
Squab:
MARVIC "Pine Tree"
515-4 Bronze
Cushions lent by:
from left to right
OSBORNE &
LITTLE F512/05
MARVIC "Clover"
dark red ground gold/
fine motif)
616-1 Flame
MARVIC "Seqoria'
6008/3
COLEFAX "Star
Weave" 3051/02 - dark
red ground (with star
motif)
CHRISTOPHER
HODSOLL 991/32
Antique sofa from:
LENA NORDMARK,
F81-84 Alfies Antique
Market,
13-25 Church Street,
London NW8.
Tel (071) 723 0429
Sisal matting from:
CRUCIAL
TRADING,
Unit 4,
Long Lane Trading
Estate,
Craven Arms,
Shropshire
Tel (05887) 666

LACE
page 113

*Lace curtains and panels
from:*
SUE MADDEN,
Strand 128,
Grays Antique Market,
58 Davies Street,
London W1.
Tel (071) 493 1307
White P.V.C. from:
B. BROWN
(HOLBORN) LTD,
Warriner House,
3233 Greville Street,
London EC1.
Tel (071) 405 5671

Glass furniture objects by:
DANNY LANE,
Units 55-60,
Metropolitan Works,
Enfield Road,
London N1.
Tel (071) 923 3345
Lent by:
THEMES AND
VARIATIONS,
231 Westbourne Grove,
London W11.
Tel (071) 727 5531
Glass bricks from:
LUXCRETE,
Disraeli Road,
London NW10.
Tel (081) 965 7292
Glass bowls by:
ALICE RAYMENT,
Unit B7,
Metropolitan Works,
Enfield Road,
London N1.
Tel (071) 923 3345

MUSLIN
pages 115 and 116/117

Muslin from:
IAN MANKIN
Bed and mattress from:
THE FUTON
COMPANY,
654 Fulham Road,
London SW6.
Tel (071) 736 9190
Large ribbed pot from:
THE CONRAN
SHOP,
81 Fulham Road,
London SW3.
Tel (071) 589 7401

BRAIDS & RIBBONS
pages 118/119

Antique books from:
CHRISTOPHER
HODSALL,
91 Pimlico Road,
London SW1.
Tel (071) 730 3370

FLORAL PRINTED
pages 136/137

Plants and pots from:
CLIFTON
NURSERIES,
Clifton Villas,
Warwick Avenue,
London W9.
Tel (071) 289 6851
*see page 224 for fabric
details*

CHINTZ
page 144

Fabric details:
Back wall:
CHARLES
HAMMOND
(supplied by Pallu &
Lake) "Gladstone"
C2371
curtain: COLEFAX
"Fox Glove" 1067/01
Top box (left hand pile):
MURIEL SHORT
"Wisley Park" Summer
W6010
Base box:
CHARLES
HAMMOND
(PALLU & LAKE)
"Gaiety" C2240
Tiny box (on one above):
DESIGN ARCHIVES
"Palais Royal" - beige
top box (yellow):
DESIGN ARCHIVES
"Palais Royal" - yellow
next one:
CHARLES
HAMMOND
"Samson" C2353
main one:
DESIGN ARCHIVES
"Garden Party"
50200-002
small one (in front):
MURIEL SHORT
"Wild Orchid"
RF703/01
Pot holding plant:
RAMM SON &
CROCKER "Roses &
Leaves" E7574
Furniture from:
CHALON
ANTIQUES,
The Plaza,
535 King's Road,
London SW10.
Tel (071) 351 0008
Mens shirts from:
HACKETT,
1 Broxholme House,
London SW6.
Tel (071) 731 2790

FLORAL
page 145

Fabric details:
BENNISON,
16 Holbein Place,
London SW1.
Tel (071) 730 8076
Curtain:
India All-over

Cloth & Cushions:
English Oakleaf
Wall:
"All-over floral" (pink)
Armchair:
"All-over floral" (pink)
Sofa:
"Regular Rosevine"
(purple)
Sofa and armchair from:
GEORGE SMITH,
587-589 King's Road,
London SW6.
Tel (071) 384 1004
*Framed flower prints
from:*
O'SHEA GALLERY,
89 Lower Sloane Street,
London SW1.
Tel (071) 730 0081/2
Aubusson carpet from:
THE VIGO CARPET
GALLERY,
6a Vigo Street,
London W1.
Tel (071) 439 6971
Glassware and china:
THE CONRAN
SHOP,
Michelin House,
81 Fulham Road,
London SW3.
Tel (071) 589 7401

PROVENÇAL
pages 160/161

Fabric details:
SOULEAIDO
1061-01; 1061-02;
1061-03; 1220-01;
03 & 04
Chair and cushions from:
SOULEAIDO
Chest from:
CHALON
ANTIQUES,
The Plaza,
535 King's Road,
London SW10.
Tel (071) 351 0008
Large pots from:
JEAN BROWN
ANTIQUES,
The Furniture Cave,
533 King's Road,
London SW10.
Tel (071) 352 1575
*Provençal pots by Solano
from:*
CLIFTON
NURSERIES,
Clifton Villas,
Nr. Warwick Avenue,
London W9.
Tel (071) 289 6851

Tableware from:
THOMAS GOODE
& CO,
19 South Audley Street,
London W1.
Tel (071) 499 2823

PAISLEY
pages 164/165

Fabric details:
Napkin & drape:
PIERRE FREY
"Shrinagar" 1776/1
Squabs:
PALLU & LAKE
MN701-01
Curtains:
PALLU "Chandapur"
ST1591 *(left)*
TITLEY & MARR
"Sinat" *(right)*
Tablecloth:
SALANDRE 2211,
Metaphors,
55% acrylic 45% rayon
*Chairs, chandelier, shelf
unit and wall lights
all by:*
MONICA PITMAN,
1 Elystan Place,
London SW3.
Tel (071) 581 1404
Pewter tableware from:
THE PEWTER
SHOP,
16 Burlington Arcade,
Piccadilly,
London W1.
Tel (071) 493 1730
Antique glassware from:
MARK J. WEST,
Cobb Antiques,
39B High Street,
Wimbledon Village,
London SW19.
Tel (081) 946 2811

**PRINTED
ETHNIC**
pages 180/181 and 183

Suitcases from:
THE CONRAN
SHOP,
Michelin House,
81 Fulham Road,
London SW3.
Tel (071) 589 7401
Chair from:
PAINE & CO,
49 Barnsbury Street,
London N1 1TP.
Tel (071) 607 1176
Fabric details:
JAVA COTTON CO

Quilt from:
COLLIER
CAMPBELL,
45 Conduit Street,
London W1.
Tel (071) 287 2277
*All furniture, fabrics and
accessories from:*
COLLIER
CAMPBELL
and
HINCHCLIFFE
AND BARBER

HAND PRINTED
pages 186/87

Fabric printed by:
JANET MILNER
*Sofa and black shelf units
from:*
SOHO DESIGN,
263 King's Road,
London SW3.
Tel (071) 376 5855
*Indian and African pots,
figures, child's chair, rug
and fabric strip (pelmet)
from:*
JOSS GRAHAM,
10 Eccleston Street,
Pimlico,
London SW1.
Tel (071) 730 4370
Glass bricks from:
LUXCRETE,
Disraeli Road,
London NW10.
Tel (081) 965 7292
Sisal matting from:
CRUCIAL
TRADING,
Unit 4,
Long Lane Industrial
Estate,
Craven Arms,
Shropshire,
Tel (05887) 666
London showroom:
77 Westbourne Park
Road,
London W11.
Tel (071) 221 9000

HANDPAINTED
pages 188/189

Easels kindly lent by:
THE
FOUNDATION
DEPARTMENT,
ST MARTINS
SCHOOL
OF ART,
Charing Cross Road,
London W1.

top left and right:
SARANATA,
3/137 Childers Street,
North Adelaide,
S.A. 5006,
Australia.
Tel (071) 382 4999
ALTHEA WILSON,
"Atire" (bottom right)
43 Burnaby Street,
Lots Road,
London SW10.
Tel (071) 352 9394
Centre:
ANNABEL GREY,
102 Reform Street,
Battersea,
London SW11.
Tel (071) 223 0919
bottom left:
THE HOUSE OF
BEAUTY AND
CULTURE

HANDPAINTED
pages 190/191

*Fabric, table, chairs and
accessories all by:*
CAROLYN
QUARTERMAINE,
72 Philbeach Gardens,
London SW7.
Tel (071) 373 4492

CREWEL
pages 202/203

Fabric details:
Curtains:
NICE IRMA'S
"White on white crewel
floral"
tablecloth (base):
"white on white crewel
birds"
Chaise from:
PAINE & CO,
49 Barnsbury Street,
London N1 1TP.
Tel (071) 607 1176
Pole from:
COPE AND
TIMMINS
All other fabrics:
SHYAM AHUJA
via Alton Brooke
Unit 5 Sleaford Street,
London SW8 5AB.
Tel (071) 622 9372
Bust from:
RUPERT
CAVENDISH,
610 King's Road,
London SW6.
Tel (071) 731 7041

Mirror by:
CAS STANNIER,
5 Craster Road,
Brixton Hill,
London SW2.
Tel (071) 671 4045
Candle lights by:
EDWARD RUSSELL
DECORATIVE
ACCESSORIES,
18-20 Scrutton Street,
London EC2.
Tel (071) 377 6946

NEEDLEPOINT
pages 206/207

*Furniture, carpet,
cushions and panels all
from:*
LINDA GUMB,
9 Camden Passage,
London N1.
Tel (071) 354 1184

FELT
pages 217/218

*Felt wallhangings and
rug by:*
ANNIE
SHERBOURNE,
Waterside Workshops,
99 Rotherhithe Street,
London SE16.
Twist table by:
TIM SHERBOURNE,
South Bank Craft
Centre,
164-167 Hungerford
Arches,
Royal Festival Hall,
South Bank,
London SE1.
Tel (071) 928 1964
Lent by:
THE IKON
CORPORATION,
B5L Metropolitan
Wharf,
Wapping Wall,
London E1.
Tel (071) 702 4826
*Display felt (on walls
and floor) supplied by:*
D. BROWN
(HOLBORN) LTD,
Warriner House,
32-33 Greville Street,
London EC1.
Tel (071) 405 5671

Fabric Suppliers

ANTA
46 Crispin Street
London E1 6HQ
England
071-247 1634
samples and orders:
FEARN, by Tain
Rosshire
Scotland IV20 1TL
(0862) 832477

**THE ANTIQUE
TEXTILE COMPANY**
100 Portland Road
London W11
England
071-221 7730

LAURA ASHLEY
150 Bath Road
Maidenhead
Berks SL6 4YS
England
0628-773 909
American supplier:
BILL HAYES
1300 MacArthur
Boulevard
Mahwah, NJ
07430

ARDECORA
Postfach 100126
8000 Munich
Germany
British supplier:
TISSUNIQUE
58-60 Berners Street,
London W1P 3AE
071-491 3386

BAKER/PARKERTEX
18 Berners Street
London W1P 4JA
England
071-636 8412
American supplier:
LEE JOFA
800 Central Boulevard
Carlftodt, NJ
07072
(201) 434-8444

BAILEY & GRIFFIN
1406 East Mermaid
Lane
Philadelphia, PA
19118
**BRUNSCHWIG &
FILS**
979 Third Avenue
New York, NY
10022-1234
(212) 838-7878

BAUMANN
4901 Langenthal
Switzerland
063-226262
British supplier:
**BAUMANN-
KENDIX**
41/42 Berners Street
London W1P 3AA
071-637 0253
American supplier:
CARNEGIE
110 North Center
Avenue
Rockville Center, NY
11570
(516) 678-6770

**ALEXANDER
BEAUCHAMP**
Griffin Mill
Thrupp
Stroud
Glos GL5 2AZ
England
0453-884537
American supplier:
**CHRISTOPHER
HYLAND**
979 Third Avenue
Suite 1714
New York, NY
10022
(212) 688-6121

BENNISON
16 Holbein Place
London SW1W 8NL
England
071-730 8076

in America:
BENNISON
73 Spring Street
New York, NY
10012
(212) 226-4747

BENTLEY & SPENS
Studio 25
90 Lots Road
London
SW10 0QD
England
071-352 5685
American supplier:
**CHRISTOPHER
HYLAND**
979 Third Avenue
Suite 1714
New York, NY
10022
(212) 688-6121

CELIA BIRTWELL
71 Westbourne Park
Road
London
W2 5QH
England
071-221 0877
American supplier:
**CHRISTOPHER
HYLAND**
979 Third Avenue
Suite 1714
New York, NY
10022
(212) 688-6121

BISES NOVITA
55 Via Fleming
00191
Roma
Italy
3332435
British supplier:
**ALTON
BROOKE**
5 Sleaford Street
London
SW8 5AB
071-622 9372

American suppliers:
**BRUNSCHWIG &
FILS**
979 Third Avenue
New York, NY
10022-1234
(212) 838-7878

**ISABELLE DE
BORCHGRAVE**
Rue Gachard, 52
1050 Brussels
Belgium
2-648 5350
British supplier:
**DESIGNER'S
GUILD**
271 and 277 King's
Road
London SW3 5EN
071-581 5775
American suppliers:
**BOUSSAC OF
FRANCE**
979 Third Avenue
New York, NY 10022
(212) 482-7866
CLARENCE HOUSE
211 58th Street
New York, NY
10022
(212) 752-2890

NEIL BOTTLE
3 Coopersale Road
London E9 6AU
England
081-533 6213

BRAQUENIE
111 boulevard
Beaumarchais
75003 Paris
France
1-48 04 30 03
British supplier:
DAVID ISON
14 Percy Street
London
W1P 9FD
071-255 3440

American supplier:
**BRUNSCHWIG &
FILS**
979 Third Avenue
New York, NY
10022-1234
(212) 838-7878

VICTORIA BROWN
The South Bank Craft
Centre
London SE1 8XX
England
071-401 3128

BRUNSCHWIG & FILS
979 Third Avenue
New York, NY
10022-1234
U.S.A.
(212) 838-7878
British supplier:
**BRUNSCHWIG &
FILS**
Chelsea Harbour Drive
London SW10 0XF
071-351 5797

BURGER
39 rue des Petits
Champs
75001 Paris
France
1-42 97 46 19
British supplier:
PERCHERON
97-99 Cleveland Street
London
W1P 5PN
071-580 5156
American suppliers:
LEE JOFA
800 Central Boulevard
Carlftodt, NJ
07072
(201) 438-8444
CLARENCE HOUSE
211 58th Street
New York, NY
10022
(212) 752-2890

**BRUNSCHWIG &
FILS**
979 Third Avenue
New York, NY
10022-1234
(212) 838-7878
COWTAN & TOUT
979 Third Avenue
New York, NY
10022
(212) 753-4488

ALAN CAMPBELL
British supplier:
**ELIZABETH
EATON**
25a Basil Street
London
SW3 1BB
071-589 0118

CASAL
40 rue des Saints Pères
75007 Paris
France
1-45 44 78 70
British supplier:
PALLU & LAKE
Unit M27
Chelsea Garden Market
Chelsea Harbour
Lots Road
London SW10 0XE
081-746 1199

MANUEL CANOVAS
7 place Furstemberg
75006 Paris
France
1-43 25 75 98
in Britain:
CANOVAS
2 North Terrace
Brompton Road
London SW3 2BA
071-225 2298
in America:
CANOVAS
979 Third Avenue
New York, NY
(212) 752-9588

fabric suppliers

MANUEL
CANOVAS
P.D.C. 8687 Melrose
Avenue
West Hollywood, CA
90060
(213) 657-0587

JANE CHURCHILL
137 Sloane Street
London
SW1X 9BZ
England
071-824 8484
American supplier:
COWTAN & TOUT
979 Third Avenue
New York, NY
10022
(212) 753-4488

CHANEE-DUCROCQ
25 rue de Clery
75012 Paris
France
1-42 36 27 81
In Britain:
CHANEE-
DUCROCQ
168 New Cavendish
Street
London
W1M 7FL
071-631 5223
American supplier:
ETOFFE
D&D Building
979 Third Avenue
New York, NY
10022
(212) 888-3410

CHOTARD
5 rue du Mail
75002 Paris
France
1-42 61 54 94
British supplier:
PERCHERON
97-99 Cleveland Street
London
W1P 5PN
071-580 5156

CLARENCE HOUSE
211 East 58th Street
New York, NY
10022
(212) 752-2890
U.S.A.
British suppliers:
ELIZABETH
EATON
25a Basil Street
London SW3 1BB
071-589 0118

TISSUNIQUE
58-60 Berners Street
London W1P 3AE
071-491 3386

COLE & SON
18 Mortimer Street
London W1A 4BU
England
071-580 1066
American supplier:
CLARENCE HOUSE
211 58th Street
New York, NY
10022
(212) 752-2890

COLEFAX & FOWLER
39 Brook Street
London W1Y 2JE
England
071-493 2231
American supplier:
COWTAN & TOUT
979 Third Avenue
New York, NY
10022
(212) 753-4488

COLLIER CAMPBELL
45 Conduit Street
London W1R 9FB
England
071-287 2277
American supplier:
ROGER
ARLINGTON
979 Third Avenue
New York, NY
10022

CONRAN
Michelin House
81 Fulham Rd
London SW3 6RD
England
071-589 7401

CONTEXT WEAVERS
Park Mill
Holcombe Road
Helmshore, Rossendale
Lancs, England
0706-229341

BELINDA COOTE
29 Holland Street
London W8 4NA
England
071-937 3924

**CREATIONS
METAPHORES**
8 rue de Furstemberg
75006 Paris, France
1-46 33 03 20

British supplier:
PIERRE FREY
253 Fulham Road
London SW3 6HY
071-376 5599
American supplier:
METAPHORES
979 Third Avenue
New York, NY
(212) 758-5281

**JEAN
DESCHEMAKER**
22 rue du Mail
75002 Paris
France
1-42 33 35 80
British supplier:
MARVIC
12-14 Mortimer Street
London W1N 7RD
071-580 7951
in America:
JEAN
DESCHEMAKER
D&D Building
979 Third Avenue
New York, NY
10022
(212) 319-5730

DESIGN ARCHIVES
79 Walton Street
London SW3 2HP
England
071-581 3968
American suppliers:
COWTAN & TOUT
979 Third Avenue
New York, NY
10022
(212) 753-4488
BAKER
FURNITURE
2219 Chose Drive
High Point, NC
27263
(919) 431-9115
CLARENCE HOUSE
211 58th Street
New York, NY
10022
(212) 752-2890
RANDOLPH &
HEIN
1 Arkansas Street
San Francisco, CA
94107
(415) 864-3371

DESIGNER'S GUILD
271 and 277 King's
Road
London SW3 5EN
England
071-351 5775

American supplier:
OSBORNE &
LITTLE
979 Third Avenue
New York, NY
10022
(212) 751-3333

REGIS DHELLEMMES
28 rue de Buci
75006 Paris
France
British supplier:
ELIZABETH
EATON
25a Basil Street
London SW3 1BB
071-589 0118

DIAMENT
British supplier:
ELIZABETH
EATON
25a Basil Street
London SW3 1BB
071-589 0118

ELIZABETH EATON
25a Basil Street
London SW3 1BB
England
071-589 0118

**ENGLISH
ECCENTRICS**
9/10 Charlotte Street
London EC2
England
071-729 6233

ETAMINE
2 rue Furstemberg
75006 Paris
France
1-47 28 36 90
British supplier:
DESIGNER'S
GUILD
271 and 277 King's
Road
London SW3 5EN
(071) 351-5775

GUY EVANS
51a Cleveland Street
London W1P 5PQ
England
071-436 7914
American supplier:
CLASSIC REVIVALS
1 Design Center Place
6th Floor
Suite 545
Boston, MA
02210
(617) 574-9030

FARDIS
British supplier:
OSBORNE &
LITTLE
304 King's Road
London SW3 5UH
071-352 1456

KAFFE FASSETT
62 Fordwich Road
London NW2 3TH
England
081-452 3786
American supplier:
EHRMAN
5 Northern Boulevard
Amherst, NH
03031
(800) 433-7899

PIERRE FREY
47 rue des Petits
Champs
75001 Paris
France
1-42 97 44 00
In Britain:
PIERRE FREY
253 Fulham Road
London
SW3 6HY
071-376 5599
American suppliers:
BRUNSCHWIG &
FILS
979 Third Avenue
New York, NY
10022-1234
(212) 838-7878
CLARENCE HOUSE
211 East 58th Street
New York, NY
10022
(212) 752-2890

ANNA FRENCH
343 King's Road
London SW3 6HY
England
071-351 1126
American suppliers:
CLASSIC REVIVALS
1 Design Center Place
6th Floor, Suite 545
Boston, MA
02210
(617) 574-9030
LEE JOFA
979 Third Avenue
New York, NY
10022
LEE JOFA
800 Central Boulevard
Carlftodt, NJ
07072
(201) 438-8444

CHRISTIAN
FISHBACHER
913 Fulham Road
London
SW6 5HU
071-371 5388
American suppliers:
STROHEIM &
ROMANN
31-11 Thomson Avenue
Long Island City, NY
11101
ROGER
ARLINGTON
979 Third Avenue
New York, NY
10022

FUGGERHAUS
Zeuggasse 7
Postfach 10 1640
D-8900 Augsburg
Germany
0821-3205
British supplier:
TEKKO & SALUBRA
18 Newman Street
London
W1P 4AB
071-631 4811
American suppliers:
JACK HURWITZ
1201 Sevenlocks Road
Rockville, MD
20854
PEACOCK
CHAPMAN
200 Camsas Street
Suite 25
San Francisco, CA
(415) 255-6011

**GAINSBOROUGH
SILK WEAVING CO**
Alexandra Road
Chilton
Sudbury, Suffolk
England
0787-72081
American suppliers:
COWTAN & TOUT
979 Third Avenue
New York, NY
10022-1234
(212) 753-4488
LEE JOFA
800 Central Boulevard
Carlftodt, NJ
07072
(201) 438-8444

GASTON Y DANIELA
Hermosilla 26
28001 Madrid
Spain
435 2740

British supplier:
COLEFAX &
FOWLER
39 Brook Street
London W1Y 2JE
071-493 2231

GERRIETS
Unit 18
Tower Workshops
Riley Road
London SE1 3DG
071-232 2262

MOSS GRAHAM
10 Eccleston Street
London SW1W 9LT
England
071-730 4370

DAPHNE GRAHAM
1 Elystan Street
London SW3 3NT
England
071-584 8724

SALLY GREAVES-
LORD
55 Charlotte Road
London EC2 3QT
England
071-739 9109

GUINEVERE
ANTIQUES
578 King's Road
London SW6 2DY
England
071-736 2917

HABITAT
22 Torrington Place
London WC1
England
071-631 3464

CHARLES HAMMOND
at PALLU & LAKE
Unit M27, Chelsea
Garden Market, Chelsea
Harbour, Lots Road
London SW10 0XE
England

DAVID HICKS
4a Barley Mow Passage
Chiswick
London W4 4PH
England
071-994 9222

HILL & KNOWLES
133 Kew Road
Richmond
Surrey TW9 2PN
081-891 4304

American suppliers:
CLARENCE HOUSE
211 East 58th Street
New York, NY
10022
(212) 752-2890
CLASSIC REVIVALS
1 Design Center Place
6th Floor, Suite 545
Boston, MA
02210
(617) 574-9030

HINCHCLIFFE &
BARBER
5 Town Farm Workshops
Dean Lane, Sixpenny
Handley
Salisbury SP5 5PA
0725-52549

HODSOLL McKENZIE
CLOTHS
52 Pimlico Road
London SW1W 8LP
071-730 2877
American suppliers:
CLARENCE HOUSE
211 East 58th Street
New York, NY
10022
(212) 752-2890

JOHANNA HOLDEN
Unit C
Metropolitan
Workshops
Enfield Road
London N1 5AZ
England
071-254 6843

LES IMPRESSIONS
British supplier:
DESIGNERS GUILD
271 and 277 King's
Road
London
SW3 5EN
071-351 5775

INTAIR
Stresemannallee 90
2000 Hamburg 54
Germany
British supplier:
MARY FOX
LINTON
249 Fulham Road
London SW3 6HY
071-351 0273
American supplier:
INTAIR
4100 NE 2nd Ave
Miami, FL
(305) 573-8956

INTERIOR
SELECTION
Unit M27
Chelsea Garden Market
Chelsea Harbour
Lots Road
London SW10 0XE
England

JAB
Potsdamer Strasse 160
D-4800 Bielefield 17
Germany
0521-2093-0
In Britain:
JAB
15-19 Cavendish Place
London W1M 9DL
071-636 1343
American supplier:
STROHEIM &
ROMANN
155 East 56th Street
New York, NY
10022
(212) 691-0700

JAMASQUE
The Glasshouse
11-12 Lettice Street
London SW6 4EH
England
071-736 3812
American supplier:
KIRK BRUMMEL
826 Broadway
New York, NY
10003
(212) 477-8590

JAVA COTTON
COMPANY
52 Lonsdale Road
London W11
01-229 3022

K.A.B.
Whitchurch Silk Mill
28 Winchester Street
Whitchurch
Hampshire RG28 7AL
England
0256-892030

KENDIX
5580CA Waalra
Postbus 2023
Holland
04904-14434
In Britain:
BAUMANN-
KENDIX
41-42 Berners Street
London
W1P 3AA
071-637 0253

In America:
KENDIX
56-208 37th Avenue
P.O. Box 7708
Woodside, NY
11377
(718) 335-9000

KETURAH
General Store
Covent Garden
London W1
England

SARAH KING
39 High Oaks Road
Welwyn Garden City
England
0707-326 457

CHRISTIAN LANZANI
LA FILANDIERE
80 Avenue Ledru-rollin
75012 Paris
France
1-43 41 01 01
British supplier:
CHANEE-
DUCROCQ
168 New Cavendish
Street
London W1M 7FJ
071-631 5223
American suppliers:
All 979 Third Avenue
New York, NY
BRUNSCHWIG &
FILS
(212) 838-7878
ROGER
ARLINGTON
(212) 752-5288
TOUT PARIS
(212) 288-9730
KIRK BURMMEL
826 Broadway
New York, NY
10003
(212) 477-8590
PIERRE DEUX
870 Madison Avenue
New York, NY
10014
(212) 570-9343

JACK LENOR LARSEN
41 East 11th Street
New York, NY
10003
U.S.A.
(212) 674-3993
British supplier:
ZR CLIFTON
TEXTILES
103 Cleveland Street
London W1P 5PL
071-323 1526

LAUER
5 avenue de l'Opéra
75001 Paris
France
1-42 61 63 52
British supplier:
PERCHERON
97-99 Cleveland Street
London W1P 5PN
071-580 5156

LEE JOFA
979 Third Avenue
New York, NY
10022
U.S.A.
British supplier:
PALLU & LAKE
Unit M27
Chelsea Garden Market
Lots Road
London SW10 0XE
071-351 7281

LELIEVRE
13 rue du Mail
75002 Paris, France
1-42 61 53 03
In Britain:
LELIEVRE
16 Berners Street
London W1P 3DD
071-636 3461
American suppliers:
ANDRE BON
979 Third Avenue
New York, NY 10022
(212) 355-4012

LEWIS & FRANCO
Pall Mall Depositories
124-128 Barlby Road
London W10 6BL
England
081-960 5444
American suppliers:
BAILEY & GRIFFIN
1406 E. Mermaid Lane
Philadelphia, PA
(215) 836-4350
SAMARKAND
SELECTION
P.O. Box 2198
1931 West Green Drive
High Point, NC 27261
(919) 841-8777

LIBERTY
Regent Street
London W1, England
071-734 1234
In America:
LIBERTY
Rockefeller Center
5th Avenue
New York, NY
(212) 459-0080

LOUGHBOROUGH
COLLEGE OF ART
AND DESIGN
Radmoor
Loughborough
Leicestershire
LE11 3BT, England
0509-261515

McCULLOCH &
WALLIS
25-26 Dering Street
London W1R 0BH
England
071-629 0311

IAN MANKIN
109 Regent's Park Road
London NW1
England
071-722 0997
American supplier:
AGNES BOURNE
550 15th Street
San Francisco, CA
94103
(415) 626-6883

LUCIANO MARCATO
Cinisello Balsamo
Via Pacinotti 30
Milano, Italy
02-612 7021
British supplier:
ALTON-BROOKE
5 Sleaford Street
London SW8 5AB
071-622 9372
American suppliers:
QUADRILLE
979 Third Avenue
New York, NY
10021
BRUNSCHWIG &
FILS
979 Third Avenue
New York, NY
10022-1234
(212) 838-7878
LEE JOFA
800 Central Boulevard
Carlftodt, NJ
07072
(201) 438-8444

MARVIC
12-14 Mortimer Street
London W1, England
071-580 7951
American suppliers:
BRUNSCHWIG &
FILS
979 Third Avenue
New York, NY
10022-1234
(212) 838-7878

fabric suppliers

CLARENCE HOUSE
211 East 58th Street
New York, NY
10022
(212) 752-2890

METAPHORES
8 rue de Furstemberg
75006 Paris
France
1-46 33 03 20
British supplier:
PIERRE FREY
253 Fulham Road
London SW3
071-376 5599

JANET MILNER
A1 Landside
Metropolitan Wharf
Wapping Wall
London E1 9SS
England
071-481 3273
fax 071-278 5719

LORNA MOFFAT
2 Cranbrooks
Blind Lane
Mersham, Ashford
Kent TN25 7HB
England
0233-720650

Mrs MONRO
16 Motcomb Street
London SW1, England
071-235 0326

IAN MORRIS
21a Topsfield Parade
London N8, England

BEN NEVIS KILTS
150 Southampton Row
London WC1B 5AL
England
071-837 6743

NICE IRMA'S
46 Goodge Street
London W1P 1FJ
England
071-580 6921

NOBILIS-FONTAN
29 rue Bonaparte
75006 Paris
France
1-43 29 21 50
In Britain:
NOBILIS-FONTAN
1-2 Cedar Studios
45 Glebe Place
London SW3 5JE
071-351 7878

In America:
NOBILIS-FONTAN
1823 Springfield
Avenue
New Providence, NJ
07974
(201) 464-1177

LES OLIVADES
Avenue Barberin
13150
St Etienne-du-Gres
France
33-90 49 16 68
In Britain:
LES OLIVADES
16 Filmer Road
Fulham
London
SW6 7BW
071-386 9661

OSBORNE & LITTLE
304-308 King's Road
London
SW3 5UH
England
071-352 1456
In America:
979 Third Avenue
New York, NY
10022
USA
(212) 751-3333

NINA CAMPBELL
at OSBORNE & LITTLE

PALLU & LAKE
Unit M27
Chelsea Garden Market
Chelsea Harbour
Lots Road
London SW10 0XE
England
081-746 1199

PANSU
42 rue du Faubourg
Poissonière
75010 Paris
France
1-42 46 72 45
British supplier:
HENRY NEWBERY
18 Newman Street
London
W1P 43AB
071-636 5970

PARKERTEX
PO Box 30
West End Road
High Wycombe
Bucks HP11 2QD
0494-471155

PAYNE
3500 Kettering Blvd
P.O. Box 983
Dayton, OH
45401
USA
(513) 243-4121
British supplier:
DAVID ISON
14 Percy Street
London
W1P 9FD
071-255 3440

PEPE PENALVER
Valdegovia
Madrid
Spain
341-729 3357
British suppliers:
BRIAN YATES
3 Riverside Park
Caton Road
Lancaster
0524-35035
BRIAN YATES
4 Berners Street
London
W1P 3AG

H. A. PERCHERON
97-99 Cleveland Street
London
W1P 5PN
071-580 5156

EDMOND PETIT
23 rue du Mail
75002 Paris
France
1-42 33 48 56
British supplier:
PERCHERON
97-99 Cleveland Street
London
W1P 5PN
071-580 5156
American supplier:
ANDRE BON
979 Third Avenue
Room 606
New York, NY
10022

PONGEES
184-186 Old Street
London
EC1V 9BP
England
071-253 0428

PRELLE
5 place des Victoires
75001 Paris
France
1-42 36 67 21

British supplier:
GUY EVANS
51a Cleveland Street
London W1P 5PQ
071-436 7914
American supplier:
CLASSIC REVIVALS
1 Design Center Place
Suite 545
Boston, MA
02210
(617) 574-9030

SHEILA RABBITS
112 Mill Lane
Hurst Green
Oxted
Surrey RH8 9DD
England
0883-716238

**RAMM SON &
CROCKER**
13-14 Treadaway
Technical Centre
Treadaway Hill
Loudwater
High Wycombe
HP10 9PE
England
0628-850 777
American supplier:
BRUNSCHWIG &
FILS
979 Third Avenue
New York, NY
10022 1234
(212) 838-7878

REPUTATION TWO
2 Harris Arcade
Reading
Berkshire RG1 1DN
England
0734-507200

ROMO FABRICS
Lowmoor Road
Kirkby-in-Ashfield
Notts, NG17 7DE
England
0623-750005
American supplier:
TOWN &
COUNTRY
LINEN CORP.
295 5th Avenue
New York, NY
10016
(212) 889 7911

LORENZO RUBELLI
Palazzo Corner Spinelli
San Marco 3877
30124 Venice
Italy

British supplier:
PERCHERON
97-99 Cleveland Street
London W1P 5PN
071-580 5156
American supplier:
BRETEUIL
221 East 48th Street
New York, NY
10019

**RUSSELL & CHAPPLE
LTD**
23 Monmouth Street
London WC2H 9DE
071-836 7521

SAHCO HESSLEIN
Kreuzburger Str.19
D-8500 Nurnberg 51
West Germany
09 11-83 32-0
In Britain:
SAHCO-HESSLEIN
101 Cleveland Street
London W1P 5PN
071-636 3552
American supplier:
IAN WALL
979 Third Avenue
16th Floor
New York, NY
10022
(212) 758-5357

**ARTHUR
SANDERSON**
53 Berners Street
London W1, England
071-636 7800
In America:
ARTHUR
SANDERSON
979 Third Avenue
Suite 403
New York, NY
(212) 319-7220

IAN SANDERSON
5 Arnhem Road
Bone Lane
Newbury, Berks
England
American supplier:
BEAUDESERT
Village Green
Box 640
Bedford, NY
(914) 234-6017

SCHEMES
56 Princedale Road
London
W11 4NL
England
071-727 3775

American supplier:
CHRISTOPHER
HYLAND
979 Third Avenue
Suite 1714
New York, NY
10022
(212) 688-6121

SCHUMACHER
939 Third Avenue
New York, NY
10022
USA
(212) 415-3922
British supplier:
ELIZABETH
EATON
25a Basil Street
London SW3 1BB
071-589 0118

ANNIE SHERBURNE
Waterside Workshops
99 Rotherhithe Street
London SE16 4NF
England
071-237 5630

MURIEL SHORT
Hewitts Estate
Elmbridge Road
Cranleigh
Surrey
England

SHYAM AHUJA
32 Dr A.B. Road
Worli
Bombay 400018
India
4938030/31/32
British supplier:
ALTON-BROOKE
5 Sleaford Street
London SW8 5AB
071-622 9372
In America:
SHYAM AHUJA
201 East 56th Street
Third Avenue
New York, NY
(212) 644-5910

GEORGE SMITH
587-589 King's Road
London
SW6 2EH
England
071-384 1004
In America:
GEORGE SMITH
67-73 Spring Street
New York, NY
10012
(212) 226-4747

OULEIADO
9 rue Proudhon
B.P.21
13151 Tarascon Cedex
France
90 91 08 80
In Britain:
SOULEIADO
171 Fulham Road
London SW3
071-589 6180
American supplier:
PIERRE DEUX
870 Madison Avenue
New York, NY
(212) 570-9343

JOHN STEFANIDIS
261 Fulham Road
London SW3 6HY
England
071-376 3999

F. R. STREET
(trade only)
Frederick House
Hurricane Way
Wickford Business Park
Wickford
Essex SS11 8YB
0268-766677

STUART INTERIORS
Barrington Court
Barrington, Ilminster
Somerset TA19 ONQ
England
0460-40349
American supplier:
CLASSIC REVIVALS
1 Design Center Place
5th Floor, Suite 545
Boston, MA
02210
(617) 574-9030

ASIA SZERSZYNSKA
144 Haberdasher Street
London N1 6EJ
England
071-608 0647

TASSINARI &
CHATEL
26 rue Danielle
Casanova
75002 Paris
France
1-42 61 74 04
British supplier:
PERCHERON
97-99 Cleveland Street
London
W1P 5PN
England
071-580 5156

TEXTRA
16 Newman Street
London W1
England
071-637 5782
American suppliers:
IN HOUSE
DESIGNS
48 Forest Road
Asheville, NC
28803
(704) 274-7697

JIM THOMPSON
British suppliers:
MARY FOX
LINTON
249 Fulham Road
London SW3 6HY
071-351 0273
American suppliers:
RODOLPH
999 West Spain Street
P.O. Box 1249
Sonoma, CA
95476-1249

THORP
53 Chelsea Manor St
London SW3, England
071-352 5457
American suppliers:
JANE BANDER
1400 Turtle Creek
Suite 208
Dallas, TX
(214) 760-8388

TIMNEY FOWLER
388 King's Road
London SW3 5UZ
England
071-352 2264

TISSART/TULIPAN/
RODOLPH VOLLAND
Industre Strasse
5000 Köln
50 Rodenkirchen
Germany
British supplier:
TISSUNIQUE
58-60 Berners Street
London W1P 3AE
071-491 3386

TITLEY & MARR
141 Station Road, Liss
Hampshire GU33 7AJ
England
0730-89 4351
American suppliers:
CLARENCE HOUSE
211 East 58th Street
New York, NY
(212) 752-2890

COWTAN & TOUT
979 Third Avenue
New York, NY
10022
(212) 753-4488
PAYNE
3500 Kettering Blvd
P.O. Box 983
Dayton, OH
45401
(513) 293-4121
HINSON
27-35 Jackson Avenue
3rd Floor
Long Island City, NY
11101
(718) 482-1100

TODAY INTERIORS
122 Fulham Road
London SW3 6HU
England
071-244 6661
American suppliers:
PAYNE
3500 Kettering Blvd
P.O. Box 983
Dayton, OH
45401
(513) 293-4121

SIAN TUCKER
2-4 Rufus Street
London N1 6PE
England
071-729 6815

TURNELL & GIGON
Unit M20
Chelsea Garden Market
Chelsea Harbour
Lots Road
London
SW10 0XE
England
071-351 5142

SARAH TYSSEN
96 Slad Road
Stroud
Glos GL5 1QZ
England
0453-757930

WARNER
7-11 Noel Street
London
W1V 4AL
England
071-439 2411
American supplier:
GREEFF
150 Midland Avenue
Port Chester, NY
10573
(914) 939-6200

WATTS & CO
7 Tufton Street
London SW1P 3QE
England
071-222 2893
American supplier:
CHRISTOPHER
HYLAND
979 Third Avenue
Suite 1714
New York, NY
10022
(212) 688-6121

WESGATE
1000 Fountain Parkway
P.O. Box 534038
Grand Prairie, TX
75053
U.S.A.
(214)647-2323

ANGUS WILLIAMS
10 Worthington Road
Surbiton
Surrey KT6 7RX

AMERICAN
MUSEUM OF
QUILTS &
TEXTILES
766 South Second
Street
San Jose, CA
95112
(408) 971-0323

CARAMOOR
CENTER FOR
MUSIC & THE
ARTS, INC.
Girdle Ridge Drive
Katonah, NY
10536
(914) 232-5035

CRAFT & FOLK ART
MUSEUM
60677 Wilshire

England
081-399 8563

ALTHEA WILSON
43 Burnaby Street
London
SW10
England
071-352 9394

BRIAN YATES
4 Berners Street
London W1
England
American suppliers:
SCALAMANDRE
SILK SURPLUS
37-24 24th Street
Long Island City, NY
111011
(341) 729-3357
B. BERGER & CO
1608 East 24th Street
Cleveland, OH
44144
(216)241-5257

TEXTILE MUSEUMS

Boulevard
Los Angeles, CA
90036
(213) 934-3082

GASTON COUNTY
MUSEUM OF ART
AND HISTORY
131 West Main Street
Dallas, NC
28034
(704) 922-7681

GOLDSTEIN
GALLERY
University of Minnesota
250 McNeil Hall
1985 Buford Ave.
St. Paul, MN
55108
(612) 624-7434

ZIMMER + RHODE
Zimmersmuhlenweg
14-18
Postfach 1245
D-6370
Oberusel
4685
West Germany
In America:
Z + R
41 East 11th Street
New York, NY

ZOFFANY
63 South Audley Street
London W1Y 5BF
England
071-629 9262
American supplier:
CHRISTOPHER
HYLAND
979 Third Avenue
Suite 1714
New York, NY
10022
(212) 688-6121

MUSEUM OF
AMERICAN
TEXTILE
INDUSTRY
800 Massachusetts
Avenue
North Andover, MA
01845
(508) 686-0191

SCALAMANDRE
MUSEUM OF
TEXTILES
37-24 24th Street
Long Island City, NY
11101
(718) 361-8500

TEXTILE MUSEUM
2320 S St. N.W.
Washington, DC
20008
(202) 667-0441

CLEANING

The manufacturer's instructions should be consulted before cloths are cleaned. Furnishing items such as lined drapes or tablecloths should, in general, be dry-cleaned. Alternatively, there are cleaning specialists who can clean on site where appropriate. The cleaning of any antique textile should always be referred to an expert, as the piece could easily be destroyed if the correct cleaning procedure is not followed. For small stains a proprietary cleaning fluid could be used. However, you should test it first on a small, out-of-sight piece of the fabric.

FIRE REGULATIONS

Furnishing fabrics undergo strict testing for fire resistance, and different fire regulations apply to fabrics in different countries. Check with your supplier before you make your purchase, particularly where upholstery is concerned.

General Suppliers

BYRON & BYRON
4 Hanover Yard
off Noel Road
London N1 8BE
071-704 9290
*Poles, finials, brackets,
framed mirrors.*

H. V. CALDICOTT
16 Berners Street
London W1P 3DD
071-636 9212
Ribbons.

COPE & TIMMINS
Angel Road Works
Edmonton
London N18 3AY
081-803 3333
*Curtain poles and
window furnishings.*

WENDY A. CUSHING
14 Ingestre Place
London W1R 3LP
071-439 7620
Trimmings.

**CUSHIONS &
COVERS**
571 King's Road
London SW6 2EB
071-384 1808
Cushions & covers.

**DISTINCTIVE
TRIMMINGS**
17 Kensington Church
Street
London W8 4LF
071-937 6174
*A wide range of
trimmings.*

FIBRE SEAL (UK) LTD
Unit 4b
Wharfdale Road
Euroway Trading Estate
Bradford BD4 6SG
0274-651230
*Fire proofing,
Scotchguard treatment,
etc.*

**CHRISTOPHE
GOLLUT**
116 Fulham Road
London SW3
071-370 3025
Interior Designers.

HEREZ
25 Motcomb Street
London SW1X 8JU
071-245 9497

*Specialize in cushions
made from antique
textiles.*

WEMYSS HOULES
40 Newman Street
London W1P 3PA
071-255 3305
Trimmings.

HUNTER & HYLAND
201-205 Kingston Road
Leatherhead
Surrey KT22 7PB
Brass poles, etc.

KERSEN
87-95 Cleveland Street
London W1P 6JL
071-637 3591
Trimmings.

McKINNEY KIDSTON
1 Wandon Street
London SW6 2JF
071-384 1377
*Curtains, antique and
reproduction.*

MIRROR IMAGE
Unit 15, Sullivan
Business Centre
Sullivan Road
London SW6
071-736 5950
Poles, finials, brackets.

PILGRIM PAYNE LTD
Latimer Place
London W10 6QU
071-960 5656
*Cleaners of curtains,
tapestries, carpets.*

PORTER NICHOLSON
Portland House
Norlington Road
London E10 6JX
081-539 6106
Linings, interlinings, etc.

**THE SLOANE
COLLECTION**
57 East Hill
London SW18
081-877 9077
Decorative poles.

TEMPUS STET LTD
Trinity Business Centre
305-309 Rotherhithe St
London SE16 1EY
071-231 0955
*Finials, poles, decorative
items.*

Bibliography

'The Curtain Book' Caroline Clifton-Mogg and
Melanie Paine 1988   Mitchell Beazley

'Fabrics for Historic Buildings' Jane C. Nylander
1983   The Preservation Press (US)

'The National Trust Book of Furnishing Textiles'
Pamela Clabburn 1988   Penguin

'Living with Decorative Textiles' Nicholas Barnard
and James Merrell 1989   Thames and Hudson

'The Art of the Loom' Ann Hecht 1989   British
Museum Publications

'African Textiles' John Picton and John Mack
1979   British Museum Publications

'Labours of Love' Judith Reiter Weissman and Wendy
Lavitt 1987   Studio Vista

'Fabric Magic' Melanie Paine 1987   Frances
Lincoln/Windward

'Textiles of the Arts and Crafts Movement' Linda
Parry 1988   Thames and Hudson

'Colefax and Fowler – the best in Interior Decoration'
Chester Jones 1989   Barrie and Jenkins

'The Royal School of Needlework Book of Needlework
and Embroidery' General Editor Lanto Synge
1988   Collins

'From Fibres to Fabrics' Elizabeth Gale 1968   Mills
and Boon Ltd

'English and American Textiles' Mary Schoeser and
Celia Rufey 1989   Thames and Hudson

'Ornament' Stuart Durant 1986   Macdonald

'Baroque and Rococo Silks' Peter Thornton
1965   Faber

'Twentieth Century Decoration' Stephen Calloway
1988   Weidenfeld and Nicholson

'V & A Ikats' V & A Collection Introduction by Clare
Woodthorpe Browne 1989

'Classic Printed Textiles from France 1760-1843
Toiles de Jouy' Josette Bredif 1989   Thames and
Hudson

'Lace – History and Fashion' Anne Kraatz   Thames
and Hudson

'The Inspiration of the Past' John Cornforth
1985   Viking

'Authentic Decor, the Domestic Interior 1620-1920'
Peter Thornton 1984   Weidenfeld and Nicholson

'A History of Textile Art' Agnes Geijer
1979   Sotheby Parke Bernet

'The Official Illustrated History of the Paisley
Pattern' Valerie Reilly 1987   Richard Drew

'Felt' Sue Freeman 1988   David and Charles

Glossary

Batiste See muslin.

Brocade Today, a rich, heavy jacquard-woven fabric with patterns emphazised by contrasting surfaces and colors, not reversible. Previously, a hand-woven fabric with additional areas of colored threads laid in (brocaded) only where needed.

Brocatelle A fabric seldom made today, resembling damask in its patterns but with two warps, which causes the closely spaced (normally silk) warp to be pushed forward when on the surface, giving a repoussé effect; it has a cotton, linen or jute weft.

Calico Here used in the British sense to mean a coarse, tabby-woven cotton cloth and not, as in North America, a brightly printed cotton.

Damask A fabric with a pattern created by using a weave different from that of the background, usually satin, and reversible; normally with large or elaborate patterns. Woven on looms with a jacquard attachment.

Discharge printing A method of printing a dyed fabric with chlorine or other color-eliminating chemicals, leaving areas of white or colors, if a bleach-resistant dye is added to the bleaching paste.

Dobby An attachment to a loom that controls the harnesses and makes small, all-over patterns; also cloths with these types of woven patterns.

Doublecloth Two cloths, each with their own warp and weft, woven together by sharing some threads or by a separate binding warp or weft. One of the most variable of weave groups, producing reversible or entirely different face and back cloths.

Figured Patterned by the weave structure.

Gaufrage From the French *gaufrer* meaning to pattern fabric or velvet, the process of pressing with hot rollers to produce a design in relief.

Gauze A soft, sheer fabric with some warp threads twisted as in *leno*; also a tabby-woven limp sheer.

Genoa velvet Previously, a fine, thick, all-silk brocaded velvet, hand-woven on a satin ground. Today, meaning a machine-made imitation with a multicolored ground and cut and looped pile, most often made from a man-made fiber weft.

Kente cloth A type of cloth made in Africa by joining together 7-14 cm (3-6 in) strips woven on a native narrow loom.

Lampas A figured weave in which extra floating wefts are held by an extra binding warp, addding further pattern and color in addition to those formed by the main warp and weft.

Leno A strong, firm sheer fabric, made with two sets of warps which are paired and alternately twisted from left to right before each weft is inserted. Mock leno has similar diamond-shaped openings but has a distorted, not twisted, warp.

Matelasse From the French meaning padded or cushioned, a double or compound cloth with a quilted appearance that is created by puckering produced by using patterning threads that are either shrunk or overlarge.

Mercerization The soaking of cotton yarn or fabric under tension in a caustic soda solution, followed by neutralization in acid, causing the fibers to swell permanently, increasing their luster and enhancing their affinity for dyes.

Moiré A cloth, usually ribbed, finished with a rippling pattern obtained by pressing with engraved rollers; impermanent except on acetate.

Moquette A firm warp-pile fabric with looped or cut pile, or a combination of both; usually with a wool or mohair pile and a cotton ground.

Muslin A firm tabby-woven smooth cotton, made in a variety of weights up to sheeting but here used to indicate batiste, a sheer, combed, mercerized muslin.

Noil Short fibers combed out during yarn making; when spun with other yarns and woven the resulting cloth has the same name. Often said of silks.

Nottingham lace Today, a wide cotton machine-made lace typified by horizontal parallel lines, the pattern made by 'V'-shaped connections.

Offset printing Methods of printing in which the dye or mordant is applied in a predetermined pattern by means of another surface, whether wooden block, lino block, potato, calabash, wooden roller or engraved copper roller (the only among the latter to carry the color in the incised line, so making finer patterns).

Organdy A fine, sheer and very light fabric made with very fine cotton yarns and with a stiff, crisp, clear finish; now also in other fibers.

Organza A thin, transparent, tabby-woven acetate with a stiff finish; more wiry than organdy.

Ottoman A warp-faced horizontally ribbed tabby-woven fabric; firm and lustrous.

Passementerie A term applied to trimmings of all kinds, but especially the more elaborate looped, corded or beaded variety.

Pile fabrics Traditionally made by pulling a second, slack warp up over a wire, weaving these in with the main (backing) warp and weft and then cutting the wire away for cut pile, as velvet, or sliding it out for a looped pile. Today, most often made by slitting open face-to-face doublecloths or with a weft pile.

Resist printing Creating a pattern by placing a barrier between the fiber and the dye, as in tie-dye (using string on cloth), ikat (using string on yarn), or batik (wax on cloth).

Sateen Cotton satin; also, in damask weaving, the back of a satin weave.

Satin Warp-faced (unusually) or weft-faced fabric in which the surface appears to be made of closely laid fine yarns, originally silk, running in one direction, but actually woven in at intervals.

Set The number of threads per inch, especially, in the warp; also, in England, various methods to make such measures.

Swiss muslin A stiff, crisp cotton sheer made plain or with effects added by extra wefts, later cut away where not used; many are now patterned by applying flock. Also called DOTTED SWISS, SWISS MULL or SWISS CAMBRIC.

Taffeta Originally silk, now any tabby-woven, fine, smooth, crisp fabric, sometimes with a fine cross rib.

Tapestry When hand woven, the warp is completely covered by the weft, which builds up a reversible surface (excepting loose threads on the back) by use of individual areas of color woven only where needed and dovetailed, interlocked or separated (slit-woven) from the adjacent color. Once used to make Kashmiri shawls, kilims and European tapestries. Today, the latter are imitated by jacquard looms; these are not reversible.

Toile French for cloth, here meaning scenic prints as in *Toile de Jouy*.

Utrecht velvet Traditionally of mohair on a linen base, a fabric with a cut pile into which a pattern is pressed (see *gaufrage*) or printed; from 1840 also made with a pre-printed warp.

Warp-faced A fabric with a large proportion of vertical (warp, ends) threads on the surface.

Weft-faced A fabric with a large proportion of horizontal (weft, picks) threads on the surface.

Worsted A yarn made from combed wool which gives a smoother, shinier finish than carded wool. Also cloth made from worsted yarn, usually tightly woven and with a crisp hand, as in gabardine.

Index

*A*cknowledgments

Of all those who contributed to "The Textile Art", my thanks are especially due to Sophie Jolly, who deserves particular mention, for her patient assistance and fabric research. Also to Jacqui Small on hand, as ever, with encouragement and support, to Karinna Garrick whose work with props and sets was invaluable and to Bill Batten, who was great fun to work with and whose brilliant photographs are the visual inspiration of the book.   MELANIE PAINE

*C*redits

PHOTOGRAPHY CREDITS

Key: b bottom; c centre; l left; r right; t top.

All photographs by Bill Batten for Mitchell Beazley except for: 6tl Christie's; 6bl/r Spink & Son Ltd; 7l Spink & Son Ltd; 7tr Myron Miller; 7br G. P. & J. Baker Ltd; 8l Spink & Son Ltd; 8tr Christie's; 8cr Joss Graham; 8br Silver Studio Collection/ Middlesex Polytechnic; 9tl Watts & Co; 9cl Joss Graham; 9bl/r Spink & Son Ltd; 10tl/cl/bl Joss Graham; 10r Spink & Son Ltd; 11l Spink & Son Ltd; 11tr G. P. & J. Baker Ltd; 11cr Silver Studio Collection/Middlesex Polytechnic; 11br Joss Graham; 37 J. Gibson/ National Trust; 39bl Warner Fabrics Plc; 39tr/tl/bc/br Spink & Son Ltd; 47tl Antique Textile Company; 47tc Watts & Co.; 47tr Warner Fabrics Plc; 47cl John Bethell/ National Trust; 47cr Christie's; 47bl Spink & Son Ltd; 47bc/br Warner Fabrics Ltd; 52 Christie's; 53 Christie's; 54tl/bl Christie's; 54tr Warner Fabrics Plc; 54br Christie's; 55tl/tr/ br/bl Christie's; 60 Horst Kolo/National Trust; 61t/bl Spink & Son Ltd; 61bc John Bethell/National Trust; 61br Warner Fabrics Plc; 67tl/tr/cl/cr/bl/br Daphne Graham; 71t Paul Hughes; 71cl Antique Textile Company; 71cc/cr Joss Graham; 71bl/br Paul Hughes; 72 Joss Graham; 73l/r Joss Graham; 74 Joss Graham; 88 Antique Textile Company; 109 Antique Textile Company; 111tl/tr/bl/br Stephen Lunn of Lunn Antiques; 121tl Christie's; 121bl John Bethell/National Trust; 128 Christie's; 129tl/tr Christopher Moore; 129c/bl/bc Antique Textile Company; 129br Christie's; 139 Joss Graham; 141l/r Warner Fabrics Plc; 147tl/tr G. P. & J. Baker; 147cl Silver Studio Collection/ Middlesex Polytechnic; 147cr/bl/br G. P. & J. Baker; 152cr G. P. & J. Baker Ltd; 153cl Prelle; 157 Watts & Co.; 162 Paisley Museum & Art Galleries; 163 Paisley Museum & Art Galleries; 163tl Joss Graham; 163tr Antique Textile Co.; 171 G. P. & J. Baker Ltd; 198l/c/r Joss Graham; 199l Antique Textile Company; 199r Joss Graham; 200l Mr R. J. McCreery/Spink & Son Ltd; 200r Joss Graham; 201tl L & M Gayton/ National Trust; 201tc/tr John Bethell/National Trust; 208 John Bethell/ National Trust; 209t Spink & Son Ltd; 209bl Dr Mona Ackerman/ Spink & Son Ltd; 209br Spink & Son Ltd; 210 Myron Miller; 211tl/tc/tr/bl/br Myron Miller; 212l Antique Textile Company; 212r Joss Graham; 213tl/tr/bl/br Antique Textile Company.